Marketing Discour

T0353051

The marketing discipline has been dominated by managerial research that has never really been counterbalanced by a systematic critical analysis, which is problematic given the assumed legitimization of the managerialism that has ensued. This book is an attempt to redress the balance, articulating a social critique and evaluation of marketing.

The book offers a critical survey of the most important contributions to managerial marketing discourse from the earliest twentieth century onwards, covering traditions of research such as scientific selling, marketing management and service marketing and drawing from Michel Foucault's understanding of power and Ernesto Laclau and Chantal Mouffe's Discourse Theory. The analysis reveals that managerial marketing discourse has promoted a government of organizations that is centred around the customer and that the shifts and turning points in this rationality through time signify more fundamental shifts in emphasis in the type of power promoted by marketing discourse and the subject positions it ascribes to people.

In subjecting marketing discourse to a critical analysis, this book will be important reading for students and researchers engaged with critical marketing, the history of marketing and discourse analysis.

Per Skålén is Associate Professor of Business Administration at the Service Research Centre and Department of Business and Administration, Karlstad University, Sweden.

Martin Fougère is Assistant Professor in the Department of Management and Organization at the Swedish School of Economics and Business Administration, Helsinki, Finland.

Markus Fellesson is a Senior Lecturer in Marketing and Organization Studies at the Service Research Centre, Karlstad University, Sweden.

Routledge Interpretive Marketing Research
Edited by Stephen Brown and Barbara B. Stern
University of Ulster, Northern Ireland and Rutgers,
the State University of New Jersey, USA

Recent years have witnessed an 'interpretative turn' in marketing and consumer research. Methodologists from the humanities are taking their place alongside those drawn from the traditional social sciences.

Qualitative and literary modes of marketing discourse are growing in popularity. Art and aesthetics are increasingly firing the marketing imagination.

This series brings together the most innovative work in the burgeoning interpretative marketing research tradition. It ranges across the methodological spectrum from grounded theory to personal introspection, covers all aspects of the postmodern marketing 'mix', from advertising to product development, and embraces marketing's principal sub-disciplines.

Marketing Discourse

A critical perspective

Per Skålén, Martin Fougère and
Markus Fellesson

LONDON AND NEW YORK

First published 2008
by Routledge
2 Park Square, Milton Park, Abingdon, Oxon OX14 4RN

Simultaneously published in the USA and Canada
by Routledge
711 Third Avenue, New York, NY 10017

Routledge is an imprint of the Taylor & Francis Group, an informa business

First issued in paperback 2012

© 2008 Per Skålén, Martin Fougère and Markus Fellesson

Typeset in Times New Roman by
Keystroke, 28 High Street, Tettenhall, Wolverhampton

British Library Cataloguing in Publication Data
A catalogue record for this book is available from the British Library

Library of Congress Cataloging in Publication Data
Skålén, Per.
   Marketing discourse: a critical perspective/Per Skålén,
   Markus Fellesson and Martin Fougère.
        p. cm.
   Includes bibliographical references and index.
   1. Marketing.   I. Fellesson, Markus.   II. Fougère, Martin.   III. Title.
   HF5415.S539 2008
   658.8—dc22   2007027862

ISBN13: 978–0–415–41669–6 (hbk)
ISBN13: 978–0–415–54167-1 (pbk)
ISBN13: 978–0–203–93299–5 (ebk)

Contents

Preface

In this book we analyse the development of the managerialism of academic marketing discourse. But this does not mean that the book is addressed to readers who have a narrow interest in marketing only. Our point of departure is that marketing has had important implications for defining how organizations are managed today, how organizational members perceive themselves and what role the customer plays for contemporary organizations. Our goal has been to write a critical history of marketing and we believe that such an analysis should be founded on a position outside mainstream marketing itself, since the managerial research ethos fostered inside the boundaries of marketing offers very limited possibilities to accomplish this. Therefore our position is founded on the works of Foucault and his followers, and particularly on the notion of governmentality. The book thus offers a critical discourse analysis of marketing.

To us marketing is accordingly the object of study rather than our primary theoretical habitat. This position has implications for the branding of our research and how we perceive ourselves as researchers. We see marketing as one of several disciplines of management (accounting and general management are examples of other streams of management) and ourselves as management scholars. We are engaged in a broader project guided by a critical approach to management, usually referred to as Critical Management Studies, which has gained increasing importance within management studies in recent years.

The text has been developed and written by Per Skålén, Markus Fellesson (both the Service Research Centre, Karlstad University, Sweden) and Martin Fougère (the Swedish School of Economics and Business Administration, Helsinki, Finland). Although we have discussed the text at length jointly and continually, particular responsibility for writing has been divided as follows: Per Skålén has written the first, third, fourth, sixth, eighth, and most of the second chapter, Martin Fougère has written the fifth chapter, co-written the second chapter and worked on the language and integration of all chapters at the end of the writing process, and Markus Fellesson has written the seventh chapter.

We wish to point out that the book's structure and substance are inspired by and elaborate on an article which was written by the three of us and published in the *Scandinavian Journal of Management* as 'The governmentality of marketing discourse' (2006: 275–91). Parts of chapters seven and eight draw on another article written by two of us (Per and Martin), which was published in the *Journal of Organizational Change Management* as 'Be(com)ing and being normal – not excellent: service marketing, the gap-model and disciplinary power' (2007: 109–25).

We have benefited from the comments received by the reviewers of these papers and editors of these journals. Several other scholars have also read and commented on different versions of the manuscript. Christian Maravelias acted as opponent at a seminar devoted to the book held at the Service Research Centre on 1 March 2007. Mikael Holmqvist has provided extensive written feedback based on a reading of the seminar version of the manuscript. The comments given by Christian and Mikael have made us re-write and shorten the first four chapters as well as elaborate on our Foucauldian analysis in chapters five to seven. These editions, we believe, have strengthened the argument considerably. Johan Quist has read and commented on the first four chapters; he has convinced us that what was initially the second chapter really needed to be split into two chapters. In April and May, Gilles Marion, Hans Hasselbladh, Evert Gummesson, and Peter Svensson have read and commented on the manuscript. Gilles has guided us about the interpretation of his own important critical marketing work and suggested references in the field of business history which have strengthened our argument, particularly in the sixth chapter. Hans's reading has made us re-write the first chapter in a way that better corresponds to what we deliver in subsequent chapters and led to revisions in the fifth, sixth and seventh chapters. Peter has also suggested similar revisions within the same chapters, which has really convinced us that these changes had to be made. Evert has advised us on interpretations of service marketing which have particularly improved the seventh chapter. In addition, Mark Tadajewski has provided some comments on our projects and informed us about the connection between managerial marketing discourse and McCarthyism. Many thanks are due to all the above mentioned scholars for taking the time to comment on our work and enlighten us with their expertise. The errors of judgement that remain are our own.

We also would like to thank the Service Research Centre for supporting a two-month guest research period for Martin in Karlstad. This gave us the opportunity to focus on working on the book at a time when we needed it the most. Without the support from Bo Edvardsson and Patrik Larsson, Martin would not have been able to spend this time in Karlstad. Our editor at Routledge, Terry Clague, encouraged us to write this book. With a book proposal as the only safeguard, Terry believed in us, for which we are grateful.

Our families, friends and colleagues have supported our writing – probably more than they are aware of. Per wishes to thank his wife, Sofia, for her stimulating ability to think outside the black box and his two sons, Jaspar and Bruno, for their irresistible ability to get him out of the 'research box' and to focus on more important things than writing books, such as building Lego garages. Per and Markus would also like to thank their colleagues at the Service Research Centre, particularly Johan and Henrietta, for stimulating conversations about research in general and the present book in particular. Martin wishes to thank Per and his family, Markus, Henrietta and everyone from the Service Research Centre for their warm welcome during his two-month stay in Karlstad.

Karlstad and Helsinki
31 May 2007

1 Introduction

Academic marketing discourse can be approached from two basic perspectives. On the one hand, marketing can be perceived as focusing on issues of consumption and thus as preoccupied with understanding consumer choices on the market and how organizations might gain knowledge about and affect these choices. On the other hand, marketing can be perceived as a managerial discourse focused on prescribing a certain management of organizations that is 'marketing orientated'. Even though we acknowledge that managerialism and consumerism co-exist and are to some extent intertwined with each other in marketing discourse, it remains possible to make a distinction between them and to focus upon one of these two issues (Hunt 1976).

In this book we analyse the history of ideas of managerial marketing discourse. We focus upon analysing academic managerial marketing discourse from the time it was being established as an academic discipline in the early twentieth century to the present day. When managerial marketing discourse is approached from a historical and managerial perspective, it is quite evident that major changes have taken place in its articulation. In the early twentieth century the managerialism of marketing was only implicitly articulated within the perspectives that dominated academic marketing discourse. But there also existed explicit articulations of managerialism in marketing from around 1910 based on Frederick Taylor's scientific management (Taylor 1911). Taylorism influenced articulations of selling most, as exemplified by the work of Charles Hoyt.

> One of the most successful sales managers of my acquaintance has often said that in selling, method is 80 per cent, and men or salesmen only 20 per cent. He does not mean by this that one need not have good men. He means that the methods under which these men are employed and directed are the most important factors. He believes in making a sales plan, or in sales planning, and then in working that plan. He has the same idea as the exponents of scientific management, such as was developed by Frederick W. Taylor. These men believe that most of the responsibility is up to the management, and not up to the men.
>
> (Hoyt 1929[1912]: 11)

In the period 1930–60 the managerialism of marketing was developed and refined. The Academy of Marketing and its major journal, the *Journal of Marketing*, played a leading role in this re-articulation and elaboration. This trend reached a peak in the late 1950s with the launch of the marketing concept. Robert J. Keith (1960) summarized the managerial rationality of the marketing concept:

> No longer is the company at the center of the business universe. Today the customer is at the center. Our attention has shifted away from problems of production to problems of marketing, from the product we *can* make to the product the consumer *wants* us to make, from the company itself and the market place.
>
> (Keith 1960: 35, emphasis in original)

The marketing concept gained a hegemonic position in marketing discourse in the 1960s. However, in the 1970s a few marketing practitioners and academics argued that existing marketing practices were inapt for management and marketing in the rapidly growing service sector – it was claimed that existing practices were suited for organizations producing goods, not organizations that offered services (Grönroos 1978; Shostack 1977). A fundamental idea informing the re-articulation of managerial marketing discourse that followed within the emerging service marketing[1] field was that customers' evaluations of services are dependent not only on the substance of the offering (which was believed to be the case for products) but also on how it was delivered by the personnel (Grönroos 1982, 1984; Parasuraman et al. 1985). Therefore it was believed to be of vital importance to manage the personnel from a customer perspective, and this managerial rationality was soon broadened to include all organizations. The rationale behind this broadening was the belief that all organizations in some way or another offer services and thus have personal relationships with their customers. This led Christian Grönroos, one of the leading names in service marketing, to recently argue:

> To manage service quality a customer consciousness has to permeate all business functions. An interest in customers must be extended to everyone . . . who has a direct or indirect impact on the customer's perception of quality.
>
> (Grönroos 2006: 322)

A critical project

Since its emergence in the early twentieth century, managerial academic marketing discourse has thus been gradually rearticulated from focusing mostly on the management of salesmen in the early days to prescribing a rationality for managing every organizational function and type of employee within today's service marketing. Mainstream marketing scholars generally perceive this evolution in terms of progress. Accordingly, the 'success story' of managerial marketing, the reasons for it and the discipline's future direction are frequently reported and discussed in mainstream marketing textbooks (Brassington and Pettitt 2000; Jobber 2004; Kotler and Keller 2006), scholarly books (Hunt 1991; Webster 2002) and academic articles (Grönroos 1994; Keith 1960; Kotler and Zaltman 1971; Levitt 1960; Vargo and Lusch 2004; Webster 1992). Mainstream academic marketing discourse, which is a modernistic discourse dominated by positivism, functionalism and essentialism (Anderson 1983; Arndt 1983; Brown 1995; Hunt 1976, 1983, 1994), constantly reproduces rather than questions the managerialism of marketing (Brown 1995; Hackley 2003; Marion 1993, 2006; Morgan 2003). The modernistic and managerial understanding of the history of marketing has never really been counterbalanced by a more systematic critical analysis. In fact, not even those schools of marketing that portray themselves as 'reflexive', such as 'marketing history' or 'macro-marketing', have articulated a definitive social critique of managerial marketing (Morgan 2003).

In our view this lack of critique is problematic. It is problematic because marketing has not only turned into a general managerial discourse but its managerialism is also invested with power based on truth claims that are legitimated by its position as an academic discipline and expertise (Hackley 2003; Marion 2006). This has turned marketing into an important source of power for legitimizing, producing and reproducing not only consumerism but also the managerialism that characterizes contemporary society and its organizations (Brownlie et al. 1999; du Gay 1996). Through its undisputed place in business schools and executive training, its permeation of management guru literature (Furusten 1999) and its never-ending presence in our (post)modern environment (Brown 1995), marketing discourse has a huge impact on the management of private (du Gay and Salaman 1992; Hochschild 1983) and public organizations (Clarke and Newman 1997; Fairclough 1993). Discourses invested with such power must be fundamentally evaluated, critically analysed and reflected upon if we are to understand what they do or may do to societies and human beings. In order to articulate such a *social critique* of marketing discourse – which is one of the main aims of the present book – marketing needs to be perceived as political discourse invested with power rather than as a positive science.

Since mainstream marketing scholars have been unable to articulate a critical self-reflexive discourse (Alvesson 1994; Alvesson and Willmott 1996; Burton 2001; Morgan 2003) our point of departure is taken outside the boundaries of academic marketing. Within the framework of the established tradition of Critical Management Studies (CMS) we have been inspired by the work of Michel Foucault and particularly his notion of governmentality. Foucault's work has been much drawn upon to analyse managerial discourse within CMS (for overviews see Alvesson and Willmott 1996, 2003; Grey and Willmott 2005). For example, Foucault's conceptualization of power as embedded in knowledge has been used to understand how managerial discourse produces subjectivities and/or attributes certain subjectivities to people (Covaleski et al. 1998; Townley 1993, 1994) and his notion of resistance has been used to understand how workers formulate counter-discourses to these managerialistic initiatives (Covaleski et al. 1998; Kelemen 2000; Knights and McCabe 1999). From a CMS perspective, the main alternative to a Foucauldian approach would be a critical theory (CT) analysis.[2] Both Foucauldian and CT forms of analysis are rooted in Marxian analyses and are thus preoccupied with uncovering hidden power structures and aiming at emancipation. The main difference between them is that CT approaches propose emancipation through promoting a certain worldview (Alvesson and Willmott 1992, 1996), unlike Foucauldian approaches. With Foucault we believe that promoting a particular normativity is not necessarily desirable, not least because of the risk of being unable to see the potentially perverse power effects of this new normativity.

Governmentality and critique

In order to introduce the notion of governmentality it might be a good idea to take the point of departure in Foucault's notion of power since we see the former as contingent on the latter (Foucault 1977, 1981a, 2000a). To Foucault, power is not something that someone has and he accordingly rejects agency-orientated definitions of power (Clegg et al. 2006; Lukes 1974). Rather, in Foucault's view, power is embedded in discourse and the same goes for knowledge and, consequently, truth. Knowledge is thus intrinsic to power and vice versa. Immanent to regimes of 'power/knowledge' are particular subject positions that attribute identities to people that they eventually might make a part of themselves (Foucault 1977, 1985a; Knights and Willmott 1989).

We see governmentality analysis as a form of power/knowledge analysis but the notion of governmentality emphasizes that discourses invested with power/knowledge, such as marketing, foster government of people through ascribing certain mentalities to them and through advising them how to make these mentalities a part of themselves. With Dean (1999), we can see governmentality as derived from the terms 'government' and 'mentality'. But it is also possible to argue, as Townley (1994: 6) does, that Foucault introduced the term governmentality as 'a neologism derived from a combination of "government" and "rationality"'. Government is understood as any more or less calculated direction of human conduct based on certain rationalities (ways of knowing) furthering certain mentalities (ways of thinking) (Foucault 1981a, 1985a, 2000a, 2000c) embedded in discourses such as marketing. People govern themselves and others towards what they believe to be the truth and the right way to be, that is, towards a particular subjectivity. A central quest for the analysis of government is to explicate these subject positions and the subjectivity-producing governmental rationality embedded but often hidden in discourse. Discourse does not, however, determine a 'real' subjectivity. Consequently, an analysis of discourse from the standpoint of governmentality explicates what identities a particular discourse elicits, not what the eventual identities of people end up being (Dean 1999). Emphasis is put on what possibilities a particular discourse gives to people in constructing themselves when they choose ways of conducting themselves. Accordingly, a governmentality perspective also focuses on subjection, understood as working 'through the promotion and calculated regulation of spaces in which choice is to be exercised' (Dean 1995: 562), which is often facilitated by producing knowledge that suits particular ends. Government, hence, is not seen as coupled to the state but rather as dispersed in society and discourse – it does not have a clear centre.

Compared to mainstream academic marketing research,[3] the governmentality approach suggests a totally different form of analysis. Rather than producing or reproducing knowledge, a governmentality analysis is preoccupied with what knowledge produces – the subjectivities it fosters and the subjection it prescribes – and how it produces these effects – the managerial practices and technologies suggested. Thus, rather than prescribing new ways of managing organizations, as is usual in mainstream managerial marketing research, a governmentality analysis focuses on what type of management the prescriptions embedded in marketing discourse suggest. And rather than being the goal and the end point of the analysis, marketing discourse, its practices and associated technologies are turned into the very object of analysis.

A governmentality analysis is also much distanced from the notion of critique within positivistic and functionalistic marketing discourse. Positivism prescribes that research should start by problematizing and articulating a 'critique' towards existing knowledge, and based on this 'critique' create hypotheses, empirically test them and develop new theory with 'better' explanation power with the aim of ensuring cumulativity. Accordingly, such an approach to research never really questions the foundations of marketing and is unable to articulate a self-reflexive social critique. A governmentality analysis, on the other hand, is well suited to accomplish this latter type of critique. In developing his notion of critique, Foucault took his point of departure in the increasing governmentalization of society from the fifteenth century onwards (Foucault 1997; Townley 1994), manifested by the de-coupling of governmental discourse from the religious centres (secularization) and by the diffusion of 'the art of governing' within and across discursive and societal domains. As a counter-movement to this governmentalization and in tandem with it, Foucault argued that a political and moral attitude was born in Europe, which constitutes the central meaning of the concept and activity of critique; namely, 'the art of not being governed quite so much' (Foucault 1997: 29). Critique is thus understood as an articulation of counter-discourse, a kind of resistance towards and deconstruction of hegemonic governmental discourse (cf. Laclau 1993; Laclau and Mouffe 1985).

In order to add precision to and elaborate on his notion of critique, Foucault (1997) contended that government has three important anchoring points: Christianity, Law and Science. These all formulate certain truth claims and thereby govern society by subjectifying people in a particular manner. Foucault (1997: 32) argued that 'critique is the movement by which the subject gives himself the right to question truth on its effect of power and question power on its discourses of truth . . . critique would essentially insure the desubjugation of the subject in the context of what we could call, in a word, the politics of truth'. Foucault's conception of critique can be understood as a questioning of truth in order to avoid the individualization and totalization of modern power structures that regimes of government such as marketing prescribes (Foucault 2000a). This form of critique is thus dependent upon a detailed analysis of the regime of government that is the object of critique.

Marketing discourse

Based on Foucault's work, several approaches for analysing discourse have been developed (see Fairclough 1992, 2001; Laclau and Mouffe 1985; Phillips and Jørgensen 2002; Potter and Wheterhell 1987). Even though it is possible to see differences between them, they all share the idea that language and discourse do not only represent the world but they also produce the world. Discourse analysts thus have a performative[4] view on language and discourse. Generally discourse can be defined as 'a particular way of talking about and understanding the world (or an aspect of the world)' (Phillips and Jørgensen 2002: 1). Our particular conceptualization of discourse and discourse analysis is based on the work of Laclau and Mouffe (1985), where discourse is understood as rather fixed structures of signs that give meaning and determine what can be said within the particular institutional and societal domain that it regulates. But Laclau and Mouffe (1985) do not have a structuralist conception of discourse. Rather, one of their central ideas is that discourse is contingent. The discourse theory of Laclau and Mouffe (1985) emphasizes the fact that discourse is always characterized by struggles over meaning between different articulations.

Analyzing managerial marketing discourse as we do implies that we focus on traditions, discursive practices and technologies that directly or indirectly produce and reproduce its managerialism. We primarily (but not exclusively) analyse managerial marketing discourse through its representation in academic texts. Focusing on academic marketing discourse is in line with one of Morgan's suggestions for further critical marketing research (Morgan 2003). Accordingly, our main sources are not only scholarly articles and books that have problematized and redirected the managerialism of marketing but also the works of marketing historians, influential textbooks and texts produced by regulative organizations such as the American Marketing Association. This does not imply, however, that our critical discourse analysis addresses academic research only. Rather, by focusing on academic texts we believe it is possible to say something about managerial marketing discourse in general, an argument that would most probably be contested by most marketing historians. Adopting economics as their model, where economic theory is granted the role of 'driving' practice, marketing historians usually make a sharp distinction between 'theory' and 'practice' since they hold that marketing 'theory' has been unable to drive 'practice' (see Hollander et al. 2005: 32). This distinction between 'theory' and 'practice' is premised on the power/knowledge of a modernism and positivism that is prevalent within mainstream marketing research, holding that academic knowledge is able (and meant) to formulate general and objective truths about a material world independent of discourse. A logical function of this position is that 'practice' should strive to mirror marketing, economics or any other 'true' 'theory' (see Harvey 1990). Therefore 'theory' is posited as a driver of 'practice' and when 'practice' is found to not resemble 'theory', which often is the position held by marketing scholars (Brownlie and Saren 1991; Hollander et al., 2005; Hunt 1983, 1994; Wind and Robertson 1983) – despite the fact that the relationship between academic discourse and the marketing discourse operating in organizations is still yet to be systematically empirically studied (Marion 1993) – it is argued that the link between 'theory' and 'practice' is weak.

But the behavioural and social sciences are never purely scientific, as mainstream marketing scholars seem to believe. They are rather forms of 'expertise' closely related with certain professional roles such as those of psychologists, social workers, economists or marketers. In discussing psychology from this perspective, Rose argues that:

> By expertise is meant the capacity of psychology to provide a corps of trained and credentialed persons claiming special competence in the administration of persons and interpersonal relations, and a body of techniques and procedures claiming to make possible the rational and human management of human resources in industry, the military and social life more generally.
>
> (Rose 1996: 11)

We would claim that marketing, in the same way as psychology, is a form of expertise that has shaped organizations, their members and the society at large. However, since we perceive marketing as an expertise rather than a science in the positivistic understanding of the term, to us marketing will never have a totalizing effect on reality, unlike what many mainstream scholars seem to think. Organizations and their members will never be replicas of the prerogatives that academic marketing discourse prescribes, simply because its 'truth' is contingent, because other discourses make competing 'truth claims' and because actors have the possibility to resist marketing through drawing on or articulating alternative discourses (Covaleski et al. 1998; Kelemen 2000; Knights and McCabe 1999). Indeed, the few marketing scholars who have adopted a performative view of language and discourse, such as Cochoy (1998; see also Brownlie and Saren 1997), take the position that practitioner and academic marketing discourse are inter-mingled with each other and constitute a unified discourse. As Cochoy (1998: 217, 218, footnote 1) argues, marketing is a performative science – 'a science that simultaneously describes and constructs its subject matter' – and such 'sciences are truly disciplines, in the double meaning of the word: in their case, one cannot separate science from practice, the discipline–knowledge from the discipline–control since, by definition, these sciences arise in and trough practice'. Since neither 'practice' nor 'theory' is given a privileged position in this way, it is possible to see marketing as a unified discourse. Accordingly we wish to deconstruct the dichotomy between 'theory' and 'practice'. Several claims can be made in favour of our position: the persons that have redirected marketing discourse often have been academics *and* practitioners, central research streams in marketing are often founded on inductively generated (managerial) problems, and Fligstein (1990) has argued that the 'sales and marketing conception of control' dominated the management of the largest US firms at a time – from the great depression until the mid 1950s – when academic managerial marketing discourse was dominated by articulations of selling based in scientific management (see also Friedman 2005).

Outline of the book

The book is structured as follows. In the next chapter we relate our own project to a review of previous critical marketing research. In the third chapter we present our broader Foucauldian framework and deepen the presentation of the notion of governmentality from the present chapter including how we intend to use it in order to critically analyse marketing discourse. In the fourth chapter we relate our two most central methodological concepts, turning points and problematizations, to a presentation of Laclau and Mouffe's (1985) discourse theory. Since the work of Foucault and Laclau and Mouffe has been very rarely drawn on by marketing researchers, our presentation is rather broad. Our aim is to systematically introduce the Foucauldian and the post-Foucauldian research tradition as well as discourse theory to marketing in order to outline how it might inform marketing research broadly defined – not only our particular project. Based on the emergent methodological framework, our Foucauldian approach and our conceptualization of marketing as a managerial discourse, we make a distinction between three overlapping periods: 'Founding the power/knowledge of managerial marketing' (c. 1910–1960), 'Consolidating the power/knowledge of managerial marketing' (c. 1950–1985) and 'Elaborating the power/knowledge of managerial marketing' (c. 1975–present). These three periods are then described and analysed in the three subsequent (i.e. fifth, sixth and seventh) chapters. In these chapters we analyse the formation of marketing discourse within the respective periods through our discourse theoretical framework; and we examine the power that is promoted, the subjectivities that are prescribed and the technologies that are used through our governmentality framework. In the eighth and final chapter we summarize and further discuss our analysis, elaborate on our critique, outline the major conclusions and contributions and suggest directions for future research.

2 Critical marketing research

The review of critical marketing research (CMR) that we present in this chapter does not aim to give a complete account of the previous research within this field (see Alvesson 1994; Alvesson and Willmott 1996: chapter five; Brownlie et al. 1999; Burton 2001; Morgan 1992; 2003; Svensson 2003: first chapter, for other reviews of CMR). Rather, our reading has been informed by three demarcating criteria. First, we have searched for texts that explicitly focus on marketing discourse. Second, we have looked for research that examines how marketing is used or is intended to be used as a management device. Third (and obviously), we have reviewed critical research. The three criteria made us structure the review according to four research streams that we identified. We have labelled the first research stream 'postmodern marketing'. Within this stream postmodernism has been used to problematize the positivistic foundations of academic marketing discourse and to argue that marketing practices have turned postmodern. The second strand of research that we have identified is labelled 'critical consumption studies'. This body of research provides critical accounts of marketing discourse and practices but focuses on how marketing contributes to produce consumerism rather than managerialism. The third stream of research that we have reviewed is not explicitly rooted in the marketing discipline but nevertheless focuses on examining managerial practices that have commonalities with those prescribed by marketing discourse and on analysing how they are used to manage organizations and structure societal domains. We have labelled this research 'broader societal critique on the extension of customer-oriented managerialism'. The fourth and final stream is that which we call 'critical studies of the managerialism of marketing'. This latter research occupies the 'core' space that our three criteria define.

Postmodern marketing

With the publication of his excellent (and at times hilariously funny) book *Postmodern marketing* in 1995, Stephen Brown introduced the notion of postmodern marketing in a systematic way. The book also made Brown one of the most prominent postmodern marketing researchers, a position he has defended well since then through publication of a number of books (e.g. Brown 1998, 2006) and articles (e.g. Brown 1999, 2003; Brown et al. 2003) on the subject matter. Therefore we focus on Brown's work here, even though we are aware that other scholars have been influenced by postmodernism in their studies of marketing (see for example Holbrook 1993; Holt 1997; Firat and Venkatesh 1993). But what is postmodern marketing and what is its main contribution to the marketing discipline?

As Brown (1995) explains in his discussion, the term 'postmodernism' can signify many interconnected but also contradictory things. The concept of post-modernism is sometimes used to describe the particular characteristics of the historical epoch that we live in now – referred to as postmodernity; it also refers to certain movements and directions in art and literature that are considered typical of 'postmodernity' and also to certain philosophical and ontological positions which are central to postmodernist research. According to Brown (1995: 106–07, see also Brown 1999) such different signified are associated with the same signifier because they share certain key features: *fragmentation* (referring to the disintegra-tion and decline of established societal domains and disciplines of knowledge), *de-differentiation* (involving erosion of hierarchies and blurring of what were previously clear-cut boundaries between art and popular culture or between science and journalism for example), *hyperreality* (meaning that fantasy worlds and simulations such as themes parks, shopping centres or videogames are seen as real or even 'more' real than the material reality), *chronology* (corresponding to the concern with and the problematization of the history as an alternative to the modernist preoccupation with the future and progress), *pastiche* (referring to the mixing of established genres), *anti-foundationalism* (referring to the postmodern demise of orthodoxy and 'meta-narratives') and *pluralism* (a reminder that 'true' postmodernism is a synthesis of the six preceding categories). Thus, research, architecture, social movements, organizations and, indeed, marketing practices and research that are postmodern are characterized by these seven criteria.

Brown's work is massive and wide-ranging. In this context we shall emphasize what we see as his major problematizations of marketing. Brown (1995) has argued that academic marketing research should become postmodern and to some degree already has become postmodern. This is in opposition to mainstream marketing scholars who have attempted consistently to legitimize marketing as a func-tionalistic, objective, positivistic and (later) realist social and behavioural science (Hunt 1976, 1983, 1994). Arguing that marketing should and to some degree has become postmodern corresponds to an endeavour to move the discipline towards what Burrell and Morgan (1979) name the 'interpretative paradigm'. According to Burrell and Morgan (1979) the 'interpretative paradigm' shares an orientation towards stability and maintenance of the status quo with the 'functionalistic paradigm' which makes it weak in articulating a more radical social critique (Burrell and Morgan 1979; Morgan 2003). But it is also characterized by a subjectivist view of the organizational world, as opposed to functionalist approaches. Among interpretative approaches to research, Brown's relativist position towards ontology and epistemology characterized by anti-foundationalism and 'anything goes' mentality can be seen as extreme compared with interpretative perspectives closer to the functionalist approach. But Brown (1995) also argues that academic marketing research to some extent has already become postmodern since it is characterized by: fragmentation, which 'clearly underpins the academic reflections on the disintegration of mass markets [and] lies at the heart of the current enthusiasm for "micro-marketing", "database marketing", "one-on-one marketing", etc.' (Brown 1995: 140); hyperreality, exemplified by the many studies of shopping centres, theme parks, etc.; and pastiche, exemplified by investigations of time perception and anti-foundationalism expressed in the doubt against the utility of the marketing concept (Brownlie and Saren 1991). According to Brown (1999) this move towards postmodernism is even more salient for the marketing practitioner. Hyperreality for example is evident in practices such as the fantasy worlds of theme parks, videogames and personal selling. 'Reflect for a moment on the "pretence" of the typical service encounter, where the salesperson's adherence to a preordained script, rote responses to anticipated enquiries and heroic endeavors to fake sincerity can give the whole experience a not unpleasant but nonetheless unreal, illusory, slightly phantasmagorical quality' (Brown 1999: 35). Other examples that Brown (1995, 1999) refers to include the fragmentation of markets into smaller segments, the blurring of marketing boundaries (i.e. marketing messages infused to what on the surface seem to be 'journalistic objective texts', edutainment and interactive advertising) and pastiche in commercials represented by self-referentiality.

Critical consumption studies

Within consumer research, critical studies of marketing practices have been much more common than within managerial marketing research. Even though this stream of research focuses on consumption issues and consumption practices, it shows that within the formal boundaries of the marketing discipline it is possible to articulate a self-reflexive and critical discourse; managerial marketing, however, has seemed unable to articulate such a critique until now. The fact that this type of critical research has been published in leading journals including the *Journal of Consumer Research* signifies that it is very accepted within the field of consumer research. One important contributor to this stream of research is Barbara Stern. Stern has applied literary theory to advertising and consumption issues and her work has often been informed by a feminist critique (Stern 1989, 1991, 1996). An exemplary study is her Derridean deconstruction of the Joe Camel campaign: Stern (1996) undoes the definitive interpretations of that campaign and argues that the name 'Joe Camel' signifies both obedience and lust and thereby communicates an indeterminate identity that does not silence the repressed parts. Other examples of critical approaches in consumer research include Holt's (1997) poststructuralist take on lifestyle analysis, Borgerson and Schroeder's (2002) ethical analysis of visual representations as well as Holbrook and Hirschman's (1993) and Mick and Buhl's (1992) semiotic analyses of consumption practices.

Students of organizations have also analysed consumption issues (du Gay 1996; Hodgson 2002; Knights and Sturdy 1997). Hodgson's (2002) 'Know your customer' article is particularly interesting for this book since it explicitly focuses on marketing practices from the perspective of governmentality. More particularly, Hodgson analyses the deregulation of financial services such as pension insurances in the UK and the marketing practices they gave rise to. In a typical governmentality way, the deregulation of state welfare services is not seen as the state rolling back but rather as a change from a socialist to an advanced liberal tactic (Dean 1999; Rose 1999). Citizens are accordingly obliged to take more responsibility for their own lives and are encouraged not to rely on the welfare state to do this for them. The marketing communication used to advance this project uses the neoliberal rhetoric of free choice to legitimize this deregulation. The intra-organizational functioning of marketing within the financial industry is also changing in order to promote – and as an effect of – this governmentality. In particular Hodgson describes how these firms have implemented relationship marketing systems which 'store' personalized information about customers. This information is used by the customer service personnel to guide and control customers when the latter make use of their 'free' and 'unrestrained' agency. Hodgson thus positions marketing as a discourse of advanced liberalism that fosters government through and by freedom.

Broader societal critique on the extension of customer-oriented managerialism

A number of studies from outside marketing have examined how, in contemporary societies and largely under the influence of neoliberalism, the management ethos and customer orientation become combined in new ways to extend: from companies' relations outwards to internal relations (du Gay and Salaman 1992); from the private to the public sector (Clarke and Newman 1997; Fairclough 1993); from the cognitive to the emotional (Hochschild 1983); from caring for the customer to knowing the customer (Miller and Rose 1997).

From companies' relations outwards to internal relations

Du Gay and Salaman (1992) discuss how the 'sovereign customer' has become central to characterize not only the will to serve external customers but also the redefinition of internal relations within organizations. What they refer to are contemporary articulations of management that claim that there is a 'need to impose the model of the customer-supplier relationship on internal organizational relations', and that as a result 'departments now behave as if they were actors in a market, workers treat each other as if they were customers, and customers are treated as if they were managers' (p. 619). What they mean by customers being treated as if they were managers relates to the fact that customer satisfaction is understood as so critical to competitive success that the customer is like a sovereign whose will effectively rules. As we shall see this idea has kinship with the type of managerialism marketing prescribes. Du Gay and Salaman elaborate on how management is affected by briefly discussing how the forms of employee control are evolving as a result of the sovereign nature of the customer: these new forms of control function through stipulating behavioural standards and installing new technologies of surveillance while attempting 'to define and structure employees' subjective meanings and identities' (p. 621). But their focus is mainly on how this development has led to a new need for employees to be 'enterprising', connecting the situation within organizations with the broader society characterized by the dominant 'discourse of enterprise'.

From the private to the public sector

Clarke and Newman (1997) examine the emergence of what they call 'the managerial state' and show how the restructuring of the welfare state was undertaken in the name of the consumers of services. They also examine how the new managerialistic ethos of the public sector today is largely characterized by an attempt to 'speak for' and 'capture' the customer. In these times allegedly dominated by the sovereign customer, the customer has become the target for competing claims by different interests. The question in this contested terrain revolves around 'who can best "represent" what the customer wants or needs' (p. 116). Finding advantageous ways of representing the customer's needs is thus crucial for (public) organizations, giving rise to what Clarke and Newman call 'the politics of information'. But in addition to that, Clarke and Newman also identify another contested terrain around 'the politics of quality', that is, 'how to reflect what the customer wants in evaluations of organizational performance' (p. 1997: 116). The authors argue that these debates around quality have brought about quasi-competitive relationships between public organizations relating to different areas of welfare, such as schools or hospitals. Fairclough (1993) demonstrates that together with these quasi-competitive relationships found in the public sector, discourse about public institutions such as universities can be seen as increasingly marketized. Like du Gay and Salaman (1992), Fairclough sees this evolution as strongly influenced by the discourse of enterprise and the construction of more entrepreneurial institutional identities throughout society. As the institutions become more 'enterprising', so do the academics themselves: they tend to reconstruct their professional identities on a self-promotional basis. While Fairclough does not explicitly link his analysis to the advent of the sovereign customer, the programme materials and prospectuses he describes clearly show that universities, in virtually all their activities (from the academic conferences they organize to the undergraduate programmes they design), are now catering for 'customers'.

From the cognitive to the emotional

Hochschild (1983) examines how human feeling is being increasingly commercialized in contemporary societies and organizations. Although it is usually 'display' (e.g. a big smile that flight attendants are supposed to greet customers with) that is sold, Hochschild (p. 90) argues that 'over the long run display comes to assume a certain relation to feeling', because maintaining a difference between one's feelings and one's display of feelings will inevitably lead to some kind of 'emotional dissonance'. Corporate control over physical and emotional appearance is usually claimed on behalf of 'professionalism': the 'most professional' employee, in this context, is the one 'who most nearly meets the appearance code ideal'

(p. 103). As a result, it becomes more and more the rule in many 'professions' in all kinds of organizations that 'display work and emotion work are part of [the] job', because it is 'the customer's right to [receive] a sincere greeting and a sincere thank you' (p. 150). Courtesy and sincerity have become an integral part of the basic service that customers are entitled to expect: customer sovereignty thereby seemingly extends to the employees' feelings and emotions.

From caring for the customer to knowing the customer

Miller and Rose (1997) take an interest in how 'the subject of consumption' has been constructed by expert knowledge mobilized for the shaping and advertising of products. In particular they examine how changing psychological conceptions of the human being have affected advertising practice, by focusing on the Tavistock Institute of Human Relations (TIHR) which undertook a range of innovative psychological investigations, and worked extensively with advertising agencies between 1950 and 1970. While this study does not take place within the neoliberal context, it remains highly interesting in terms of its description of the emergence of an expert knowledge of the consumer/customer, and how this knowledge affected advertising and marketing practice. In particular the TIHR approach radically questioned existing marketing and advertising thinking by making it clear that: 'people did not know what they wanted; people did not tell the truth about their wants and dislikes even when they knew them; and one could not assume that individuals would behave in a rational way when selecting one commodity rather than another' (p. 4). Hence, it was needed to use psychological and psychoanalytic insights in order to understand and act upon consumer choices: TIHR experts could develop a knowledge of consumers, and in turn get to know customers better than they know themselves. This knowledge construed consumers as highly problematic and complex entities, but at the same time it no doubt contributed to the subjectification of consumers, by setting out in detail 'the habits of conduct which might enable one to live a life that is personally pleasurable and socially acceptable' (p. 32). However, while Miller and Rose thereby launch a project to study the consuming passions from a governmentality perspective, they do not examine in detail what this entails for the conduct of marketing professionals.

Critical studies of the managerialism of marketing

Judging from the existing reviews and general commentaries of critical marketing research (CMR) (Alvesson 1994; Alvesson and Willmott 1996: chapter five; Brownlie et al. 1999; Burton 2001; Morgan 1992, 2003), marketing has been comparatively much less influenced by the endeavour to critically analyse managerialism than other management disciplines such as accounting or human resource management. We have identified a handful of articles that can be considered critical studies of the managerialism of marketing. All of them constitute critical analyses of marketing discourse even though not all of them can be considered as clearly demarcated discourse analysis. Among the studies we have identified it is possible to make a distinction between: those focusing upon the ideology of the marketing management discourse and particularly on the alleged gap between this discourse and practice (Brownlie and Saren 1997; Hackley 2003; Marion 2006); critical analyses of marketing history (Morgan 2003); and critical analyses of service marketing (Skålén and Fougère 2007).[1] These studies have been informed by critical theory (CT) and Foucauldian perspectives and some of them combine perspectives.

The ideology of marketing management discourse

The critical reflections on marketing management discourse are in one way or another critical of the ideal of customer orientation that is quintessential to it, but their more particular focuses differ somewhat. Brownlie and Saren (1997) problematize the discourse of relevance that is central to marketing management research, that is, the notion that academic research should be able to prescribe how marketing practices ought to be carried out. Based on their performative view on language and discourse, Brownlie and Saren (1997) see several risks for the vitality of marketing management discourse. As opposed to postmodern scholars such as Brown (see particularly 2003), they argue that the aspiration for relevance has contributed and will contribute to make marketing management discourse more uniform and homogenous: they understand this as a crisis of representation (see also Brownlie and Saren 1991, 1995). The effects of this crisis, they argue, are manifold. First, with only one representation of marketing management, marketing will be inappropriate to address all the problems of marketing that exist in corporations. Contemporary organizations are diverse and differ substantially from one another, which implies both that the focal organization needs to approach the same problems from different marketing perspectives and that the approaches that different organizations need might vary substantially. Brownlie and Saren (1997: 148) thus argue that 'closing the perceived gap [between theory and practice] is not seen as a tenable route towards a more open and creative discourse which is tolerant of differences'. Second, the ethos that dominates managerial marketing discourse, which Brownlie and Saren see as being founded on the marketing concept, is likely to frame how people think about marketing. In academia this will have the effect that knowledge production will be framed by narrow mainstream boundaries that do not allow for alternative perspectives – the difficulty of publishing critical marketing research in academic marketing journals being one example of this. The actions and indeed the professional roles of professional marketers may also be defined by the narrow-minded ethos of managerial marketing discourse which will make them unable to see marketing issues from different perspectives. In sum this will produce unreflexive marketing scholars and practictioners. Third, whether marketing management discourse affects marketing practioners deeply or not, those knowledgeable of marketing management discourse will use it to legitimize their position and standpoint and as a rhetorical device to argue for furthering their own interests. Thus, it will be used as a means to silence other alternative marketing discourses that might shed light on the relevant problematics.

We have identified two other articles that have commonalities with Brownlie and Saren's (1997) in that they problematize the alleged relevance of marketing theory to marketing practice and the legitimacy and legitimization of marketing management ideology (Hackley 2003; Marion 2006). Hackley's paper focuses on rhetorical strategies and ideological control in marketing management textbooks. Hackley's ideology critique focuses on explicating the dominant discourse of ideological control in marketing textbooks in order to criticize it and to open it up for alternative interpretations. Based on the works by Eagleton (1991) and Alvesson and Deetz (2000), Hackley seeks to uncover how the textbook authors promote ideological control by naturalizing, normalizing, hegemonizing and instrumentalizing the central message of marketing management.

One central rhetorical strategy and source of legitimization in marketing management textbooks contingent upon the positive values associated with science and progress in modernism is the binary of theory/practice. The authors of marketing management textbooks legitimize their discourse by claiming its scientific status, by alleging its suitability for excellence in business practice and not least by articulating the theory itself as a practical theory. Indeed, as Hackley (2003: 1333) shows, authors of marketing management textbooks avoid the word theory and 'often [use] words like "tool", "framework" or "concept" to imply that marketing owns a special theory that is not a theory'. As Hackley argues this kind of logical contradiction becomes an ideological dilemma for the marketing management textbook authors; a dilemma that they have to solve at least superficially in order to retain the legitimacy that the binary of theory/practice gives to their discourse.

According to Hackley, the binary of theory/practice is supported by several ideological/rhetorical strategies. One such strategy is labelled by Hackley as 'bogus reflexivity'; it is used by textbook authors to mimic academic scientific discourse even though marketing discourse does not really qualify as this type of discourse. Another such strategy that is frequently used by textbook authors is to claim that marketing is very relevant for management practice. But Hackley turns this argument on its head by arguing that marketing writers invoke reality and relevance as a textual strategy 'to legitimize marketing management as a textual project . . . Academics are empowered by owning the conceptual technology (i.e. the rhetoric) of marketing. Managers may not be the prime beneficiaries' (2003: 1341, 1347). Other ideological/rhetorical strategies employed to support the theory/practice binary are the 'passion for definition' and the borrowing of 'scientific' terms from other academic disciplines that makes the text look scientific at least on the surface. One of Hackley's conclusions is telling:

> The respective rhetorical strategies of marketing texts of UK and US origin produce exactly the same effect. That is, the promotion of an unreflexive, normative, management consulting style of marketing management discourse based on 'core' concepts and constructed for easy consumption in education and training settings.

> (2003: 1335)

Marion (2006) conceptualizes marketing management as an ideology; he focuses on how it produces legitimacy and legitimization and on the role of critique. This conceptualization is as such a criticism towards marketing's managerialism similar to that articulated by Hackley (2003). Drawing on Ricœur (1975), Marion (2006: 246) combines an anthropological (Geertz 1973) and a Marxian definition of ideology. From the first conception he sees ideology as the 'common framework' or a system of 'shared beliefs' that 'delineates the range of expected behaviour in a particular context' providing legitimacy to someone who holds a position of power. Ideology provides the representations for the exercise of marketing management. From the second conception he sees ideology as claim of legitimacy by adding a supplement to spontaneous belief. The discourse of marketing management is also a distorted framework (through incantation and simplification) that produces legitimization as long as the gap between practice and ideal is not detected. In Marion's view the role of criticism is to make such gaps visible.

> [Marketing] produces legitimacy for marketing activities because it provides reasons to all market actors for accepting the way in which market economy is organized. The legitimacy of marketers stems from what those they interact with grant them by acknowledging their right to act: shoppers, customers, *as well as people in other departments of their company* . . . Marketing doctrine reminds us that, in a market economy, everything that is beneficial for the individual is also beneficial for the society, and that the one criteria for the common good is the general growth of the wealth, whatever or whoever is the beneficiary. Moreover, a *free* market and prospering consumption economy foster *freedom* and democracy.
>
> (2006: 248–9, emphasis added)

Marion thus reminds us in an elegant way that marketing is a source of legitimacy not only for the consumption society but also for the managerial society (cf. Clarke and Newman 1997). He also does this in a way that reminds us of Foucauldian analyses of governmentality. To Foucault (2000a) governmentality has as one of its main sources the social ontology fostered by the market economy and its discourse. Governmental discourse thus produces government through freedom by promoting growth and wealth and thus certain ways of behaving and being (see below and Dean 1999; Hodgson 2002; Rose 1999). But the ideology of marketing according to Marion also produces legitimization and primarily does this through the marketing concept that holds (falsely, as we will argue in the sixth chapter) that customer and company interests align and that marketing management is a managerialism that is superior to alternative managerial discourses (see for example Keith 1960; Kotler 1972; Levitt 1960). The role of criticism according to Marion (2006: 252) 'is to doubt the effectiveness of the production of legitimization by marketing ideology' and he illustrates this through the questioning of the concept of 'needs' and the 'theory of evolution' as articulated in marketing discourse. Marion also shows how criticism within marketing has been ignored or heard and co-opted – as Brownlie and Saren (1997) argue, marketing silences other voices –

and therefore it always has to be renewed. Marion also offers an interesting discussion on how criticism of the legitimization of marketing ideology is also dependent upon ideology. Ideology can only produce legitimization through providing reasons for accepting the marketers' actions. But this also constrains the actions of marketers. Therefore 'marketing ideology is seen as a pool of justifications useful both for marketers and criticism' (2006: 252).

Taken together, the works of Brownlie and Saren (1997), Hackley (2003) and Marion (2006) offer an insightful critique of the managerialism of marketing. Their deconstructions of the alleged scientific status of the managerialism of marketing and its performativity provide important input to our subsequent analysis.

Morgan's critical history

In the opening of his book on critical marketing, Morgan (2003) interprets the historical development of managerialism in academic marketing and in practice in a way that contradicts the mainstream version of this story. According to Morgan, marketing as an academic discipline was founded as a reaction against the monopolistic position that some key industrialists acquired in the late nineteenth century in the USA. 'Marketing was established as an academic discipline in the state universities of the Midwest with a view to developing systematic analysis of how markets were being distorted by these powerful individuals and corporations' (p. 113). Morgan refers to the institutional school in marketing and argues that its main purpose was to identify the major institutions that shaped the market (such as the state and major corporations) in order to marshal critique against how they prevented the market economy from functioning properly. Morgan (p. 113) thus argues that during its early days marketing had a 'critical perspective'.

The fight against 'big business' that marketing was involved in – according to Morgan – was eventually successful. Anti-trust law was passed in the period 1910–13 to break up the monopoly markets. Morgan argues that this changed the role of marketing, which found a place within firms in advising managers how to influence consumers on how to buy their products. Following Fligstein (1990), Morgan believes that marketing affected the overall management strategy very little in the 1910s and 1920s since the managerialism that was then practised in US firms was dominated by a production orientation. But, as market growth became more important to US companies, marketing scholars and practitioners started during the 1920s to blame this production mentality for hindering growth by downplaying what the customers really demanded. When competition became more intense, from the 1930s onwards, the general orientation started to change: as an alternative to productionism, marketing people advised the companies to be more customer oriented. In the 1950s the customer orientation that marketing had been increasingly promoting evolved into an explicit managerial strategy. Marketing scholars and practitioners argued that this was for the common good: eventually people got the products that they really wanted. However, as Morgan shows, practices and technologies for manipulating rather than serving consumers were developed and promoted in marketing. According to Morgan, marketing was trying to hide its real rationality under the rhetoric of doing well by giving people what they want. Morgan (p. 113) argues that 'marketing as an academic discourse shifted from being a critical perspective that showed how companies were exploiting consumers through their control of the market to being imbued with a managerial perspective, concerned to solve managers' problems'.

In our view this argument overstates the critical role of early marketing; Morgan himself (p. 123) acknowledges that his analysis of the formation of academic marketing discourse is 'preliminary and needs further development'. However preliminary his analysis is, he problematizes marketing in an original way and suggests a line of inquiry to follow. We certainly agree with Morgan (p. 123) when he suggests that there is a need for 'more critical analysis of the construction of marketing as an academic discourse', and we hope this book will be a valuable contribution in delivering this type of analysis.

Critical analysis of service marketing

A final study that is very relevant for this book is an article that two of us have written (Skålén and Fougère 2007). In this paper, service marketing in general, and the customer-perceived quality measurement instrument called the gap model (Parasuraman et al. 1985, 1988, 1994) in particular, are examined. The reason for singling out the gap model as the particular object of study lies in the fact that it has affected theory development as well as the practice of measurement in service marketing and that we believe it encapsulates the general spirit of contemporary marketing. The gap model takes as its point of departure the general idea that has been very central to the formation of service marketing discourse: that quality in service production not only is a function of the what that is produced (the product or the service) but also of how things are produced. It is argued that the customers evaluate both these dimensions of service production (Grönroos 1982). Therefore all types of personnel become a potential object of management in service marketing discourse; in order to reach business excellence, the general argument goes, the thoughts, feelings and emotions of the employees have to be managed. The gap model is an instrument designed to reach this particular kind of excellence since it is designed to act upon the actions of the employees by controlling and shaping them through 'general quality determinants'; for example, empathy, responsiveness and assurance.

The distinctive argument made in the paper is that, rather than bringing about excellence as it claims to, service marketing tends to produce *normal* organizations and individuals. This argument is based on an analysis informed by the notion of 'disciplinary power' (Foucault, 1977, 1981a) and more particularly the five steps of normalization that Foucault outlined in his *Discipline and Punish* (1977). Accordingly it is argued that the gap model based on the five quality determinants serves the purpose to 1) compare people with each other and 2) differentiate them from each other. Based on this comparison and differentiation the gap model 3) orders people in a hierarchy on the basis of their value as service workers – at least according to how the gap model defines value. The next step is 4) homogenization, which 'adds important aspects to the process of normalization. Indeed, employees will not be encouraged to maximize their service behavior, i.e. not try to produce as much empathy or responsiveness as they are able to ... The process of homogenization thus encourages a movement towards the middle of the normal distribution; it encourages people to move towards conformity' (Skålén and Fougère 2007: 121). The gap model also 5) marginalizes and excludes the people far from the centre of the normal distribution, accordingly defining them as deviant and abnormal people. These outliers are, however, of central importance to the process of normalization since they define the very dialectic of normality–abnormality. For it is indeed within the boundaries of this dialectic that the power/knowledge of the gap model in particular and service marketing in general should be located according to the argument made in the paper.

As a conclusion to this review of critical research relevant to the present project, we would like to point out that even though there is a quite rich and fast-growing literature on critical marketing, not so many studies focusing explicitly and specifically on marketing as a managerial discourse have been written so far. The existing works that critically take issue with the managerialism of marketing tend to mostly set a research agenda, preaching the need to thoroughly examine it, while not doing that in any greater detail (yet?) themselves. The present book is an attempt to address the wide research avenue laid out by authors such as Brownlie and Saren or Morgan, by looking at academic marketing specifically as a managerial discourse.

3 Power/knowledge, governmentality and government

In this chapter we articulate a precise position in relation to how we critically analyse managerial academic marketing discourse. Central to this position is the notion of governmentality, which surfaced in Foucault's work in the late 1970s. Even though his work explicitly addressing governmentality is limited to a few transcribed speeches with overlapping content (Foucault 2000a, 2000c, 2000d),[1] his various studies are increasingly being reconsidered and read as analyses of the governmentality of modernity (Smart 2002; Rose 1999). Foucault's work explicitly addressing governmentality was in progress when he died in 1984 (an unpublished book manuscript on the subject was among his literary remains, see Gros 2005). Therefore it is important not to lean only on his texts that deal explicitly with governmentality when outlining the concept. Above all, governmentality has to be interpreted against and related to Foucault's general understanding of power, knowledge, truth and subjectivity which is constitutive of much of his work as well as in relation to the very lively post-Foucauldian governmentality literature (e.g. Dean 1995, 1999; Rose 1996, 1999; Miller and Rose 1990; O'Malley et al. 1997; Townley 1994).

We open the chapter by presenting the notion of sovereign power which is opposed to Foucault's notion of power/knowledge. Then we turn to a review of central Foucauldian concepts and themes, after which we move on to consider governmentality. Finally, we introduce Mitchell Dean's framework for analysing government. This framework is a somewhat adapted version of the framework Foucault himself outlined in the second volume of the *History of Sexuality* (Foucault 1985a).

Sovereign power

Foucault is probably best known for his treatment of power. Clegg's (1989) review of the power literature shows that those conceptualizations of power that were most influential prior to Foucault's period of influence draw on the Hobbesian and Weberian sovereign – and agency-orientated – conceptualizations of power. What is central in this notion of power is that power holders have power over those who lack power and, consequently, that power is in the hands of certain people or institutions. An examination following such a conceptualization of power focuses on the 'what' of power; for example, what people in the name of power do against their will or the shift of power from one power holder to another.

Lukes (1974) distinguishes between three types of sovereign power. Lukes's (1974: 15, 11–12, emphasis taken away) first dimension of power 'involves a focus on behaviour in the making of decisions on issues over which there is an observable conflict of (subjective) interests' formalized as: 'A has power over B to the extent that A can get B to do something that B would not otherwise do'. Lukes's second dimension of power focuses on non-decision-making and particularly on how limiting the scope of the decision-making process through 'reinforcing [certain] social and political values and institutional practices' (Bachrach and Baratz 1962, quoted in Lukes 1974: 16) enables control of the agenda in situations of overt conflict. The third dimension of power that Lukes discusses includes covert use of power and the role that social structures and socialization have for action. Lukes argues that, through controlling the socialization process, power holders wield power over the formation of identities in societies. Accordingly, Lukes's framework of power emphasizes agency: through different means, individual or collective actors have power over other individuals or collectives. As we will see this characteristic – together with his materialist ontology and realist epistemology – differentiates Lukes's conceptualization of power from Foucault's.

Power, knowledge, truth and subjectivity

Foucault (1977, 1981a; see also Burrell 1988) rejects treating power as a commodity or as coupled with agency. Rather, he argues that, from the Enlightenment onwards, that is, during modernity, power has taken discursive shape – power is invested in discourse. The discourses which power is embedded in are forms of knowledge. Foucault thus postulates a break with positivistic epistemology and materialist ontology, which is a defining feature of modernist social and behavioural sciences. Foucault argues that scientific knowledge (e.g. psychology) is the example *par excellence* of discourses invested with power. Foucault's series of lectures on psychiatric power at the *Collège de France* in 1973–74 is illuminating in this respect (Foucault 2006).

Foucault (1977, 1981a) stipulates a close coupling between power and knowledge/truth and therefore prefers not to speak about power and knowledge but rather about *power/knowledge* in order to emphasize the interrelatedness between the two. This fundamental re-conceptualization turns alleged 'scientific' discourse, marketing in our case, into the very object of the study not the outcome of the study. Foucault differentiates between at least two forms of power/knowledge, namely 'disciplinary power' and 'pastoral power', which will be discussed later in the section on pastoral power. Here we outline his general notion of power/knowledge that provides foundation for these two specific types of power.

The discourse and the power/knowledge that the social and behavioural sciences produce not only represent the world but also produce the world: they are performative. And since the object of knowledge of these sciences is the human being, they explicitly or implicitly seek to shape the subjectivity of people by fabricating certain subject positions. When studying discourses of 'truth', Foucault thus does not focus on what was true and what was not. Rather he focuses on what possibilities 'truth' give to people in constructing the social world and what effects 'truth' has on the social world and particularly on the subjectivity of the people acting in this world (Foucault 1977, 1981a, 1985a). Psychology for example is about under-standing and theorizing human cognition, but it is not only a neutral representa-tion of this issue. Psychology also frames and controls people's understanding of their own and others' cognition and thus prescribes what are normal and abnor-mal thinking (Foucault 2003). Seen from this perspective the behavioural and social sciences are thus not bodies of 'abstracted theories and explanations, but . . . intellectual technolog[ies] . . . way[s] of making visible and intelligible certain features of persons, their conducts, and their relations with one another' (Rose 1996: 10–11). As we argued in the first chapter, the behavioural and social sciences, including marketing, are never purely scientific. They are also forms of 'expertise'.

The relationship between subjectivity and power/knowledge is not stable throughout Foucault's work, which has resulted in a distinction between his power period in the 1970s and his work on ethics in the 1980s. In fact this distinction was introduced and reinforced by Foucault himself. In his inaugural speech at the *Collège de France* in 1971 (Foucault 1981b), he looked back on his previous work and stated that it had dealt with power, even though the notion of power had not been explicitly used frequently. In the beginning of the 1980s he stated: 'it is not power, but the subject, that is the general theme of my research' (2000b: 327). However, these two periods should not be contrasted sharply. To some degree they are an effect of the rhetorics Foucault often used when reflecting upon his own work. But there is also a real shift in focus that needs to be taken seriously. During the 'power period' in the 1970s, subjectivity was theorized as contingent upon regimes of power/knowledge embedded in discourse, and later in the 'ethics period' in the 1980s the self-making of subjectivity came to the forefront. In works from the former period there is a structuralist tendency to treat subjectivity as more or less determined by power/knowledge, while in those from the latter period a space for the person's active construction of her/himself is opened up. The difference between these two periods should be seen as a shift of emphasis rather than a complete break: in his work on power Foucault was interested in the process of subjectification in discourse and power and later he focused upon how people construct themselves. Where to position oneself is thus dependent upon interest rather than theoretical conviction.

When analysing marketing, we focus upon the subject positions embedded in discourse and the discursive practices and technologies promulgated for making these subject positions a part of the self. We thus take into account Foucault's early focus on explicating the subjectivity immanent in discourse and the self-making of the latter period. However, we do not empirically study the self-making dimension. Instead we explicate what practices and technologies marketing has produced for accomplishing this through acting upon people's actions. This means that we look upon technologies such as targeting, measurement of customer-perceived quality, market segmentation, etc. from a completely different angle compared to mainstream marketing. Rather than contributing to developing these technologies, as is the focus in mainstream marketing research, we focus on what type of managerialism they presuppose and thus the possibilities they give to people in constructing themselves as workers or managers. This also implies a position in which forms of knowledge do *not* determine the subjectivity of people: we do not intend to determine whether marketing discourse actually fixates a particular subjectivity. Rather, we aim to pinpoint the type of subjectivity that marketing discourse *attributes* to managers and personnel and how – through what technologies and practices – this is meant to be done. As Dean puts it:

> The forms of identity promoted and presupposed by various practices and programmes should not be confused with a *real* subject, subjectivity or subject position . . . Regimes of government do not *determine* forms of subjectivity. They elicit, promote, facilitate, foster and attribute various capacities, qualities and statuses to particular agents.
>
> (1999: 32, emphasis in original)

One central aim of the analysis in this book is thus to explicate the subject positions embedded in marketing discourse. The position towards power that such an analysis implies manifests another important feature of power/knowledge analyses that sets them apart from mainstream analyses of power: that power not only restrains and controls people but also is productive and helps people to fulfil themselves. Power, from this point of view, is negative and positive, destructive and constructive. In addition, the negative and the destructive power effects of subject positions are played out differently compared to mainstream conceptualizations of power, which hold that power manifests itself in agency and through people having other people to do things against their will. In a discursive view of power, control can be understood as framing effects (Edenius and Hasselbladh 2002), which means that a certain subject position comprises a certain way of seeing – and accordingly acting in reality – and simultaneously rules out other ways of perceiving and acting. Consequently, subjectification and subjugation are closely related to each other.

Technologies and practices

What is inherent to regimes of power/knowledge is not only subject positions, but also technologies and practices for producing subjectivity. It is a central aim of our analysis to articulate the most important of these technologies and practices that marketing promotes at different periods in time. Following Rose (1996) we define these types of technologies as *human* technologies, which are distinct from intellectual technologies (see previous). In this book when technologies are mentioned without the qualifying notion – human or intellectual – it refers to the former. We understand (human) technologies in management discourse as detailed, often standardized examinations and methods (customer satisfaction measurement models, workplace attitude schemes, profit sharing and also 'softer devices' such as cultural engineering, mentoring, career development discussion, etc.) that promote a certain type of control of human behaviour. These technologies are often not in themselves framed as control devices by those who promote and use them but rather as neutral tools for 'getting the job done'. Technologies presuppose certain assumptions about human beings. These assumptions build on knowledge that is considered true, which infuses the technologies with power. But based on these assumptions technologies also produce 'true' knowledge, establish norms of appropriate behaviour, thinking and emotions, and offer approaches for regulating people towards these norms. Marketing segmentation might be taken as an example. Segmentation is not only legitimated as a managerial device through knowledge. It also produces contextualized knowledge regarding what kind of products the customers of a particular organization want. Practices are less detailed prescriptions regarding how things should be done or descriptions regarding how things should be acted upon, thought and felt about, but they work in the same way as technologies. The distinction between practices and technologies is fluid and blurred. Practices may be produced by and may produce technologies, but practices may also lack a 'technological foundation'. In such cases they may be regarded as specifications of broader ideals (Hasselbladh and Kallinikos 2000). The technologies of the self that are inherent in most other technologies and practices are the *confession* and the *examination* (Foucault 1977, 1997; Townley 1998) which will be discussed later in relation to pastoral and disciplinary power.

Much of Foucault's work and the analytical concepts that have emerged from it are based upon analyses of discourses that make truth claims about human beings (during modernity through positivism) and their performativity, particularly the subjectivity they foster. The subject is not understood as an autonomous and meaning creating entity but rather as contingent upon the subject positions embedded in discourse. In an analysis following such a conceptualization of subjectivity it is central to explicate the subject positions and also the technologies and practices promoted for establishing and fostering these subject positions. We argue that marketing is a discipline that seeks to make certain truth claims about and offer certain subject positions to human beings. But very few analyses have engaged in explicating the subjectivity that marketing attributes to employees and managers, the practices and technologies promoted to foster this subjectivity and how these practices and technologies are intended to accomplish this. This is what we set out to do in this book.

Governmentality

With this general understanding of power/knowledge, subjectivity and discourse, Foucault developed the notion of governmentality based on a study of what constituted the increasing governmentalization of society from the end of the fifteenth century (Foucault 1997, 2000b). In particular Foucault focused on the critical discussion revolving around Machiavelli's *The Prince* from the sixteenth century onwards. In reviewing this opposition to Machiavelli, Foucault did not focus on whether Machiavelli was interpreted 'rightly' (assuming that this could be determined) but rather on the implicit and explicit – and alternative to Machivellianism – notions and ideas of government that his opponents suggested.

The central problem for Machiavelli, according to Foucault, was that the link between the prince and his principality is always under threat. The reason for this is that there is no natural given connection between the sovereign and his land. This leads up to the conclusion that:

> This fragile link is what the art of governing or of being prince, as espoused by Machiavelli, has as its object. Consequently, the mode of analysis of Machiavelli's text will be twofold: to identify dangers . . . and second, to develop the art of manipulating the relations of forces that will allow the prince to ensure the protection of his principality, understood as the link that binds him to his territory and his subjects.
>
> (Foucault 2000a: 205)

The anti-Machiavellian literature had as its purpose to replace this orientation to government with something that Foucault names the 'art of government'. The common trait of this literature is the belief that there existed a gap between Machiavellianism and the practice of government: 'having the ability to retain one's principality is not at all the same thing as possessing the art of government' (Foucault 2000a: 205). 'The art of government' view is distinct from Machiavelli's position in several important ways. First, governing is not only knitted exclusively to the prince/sovereign but also to a lot of other subject positions (such as the head of the family, the teacher or the manager). We thus see a spread of government from one single governor to several governors. Second, government is not an activity aimed only to secure the rule of the sovereign, but rather an activity aimed to accomplish ends that are advocated inside most institutional domains, which means that government is spread within and across discourse and societal domains. 'The art of government' thus signifies a de-coupling of government from a governmental centre (the prince or the state) and a dispersion of government in society and discourse. In fact, many contemporary forms of political doctrines, such as neoliberalism, neoconservatism, communitarianism and 'the third way', intentionally downplay the traditional role of the state in government and instead promote managerialism, consumerism and the civil society as means of government (du Gay and Salaman 1992; Clarke and Newman 1997; Rose 1999). Accordingly Foucault 'implie[s] that, rather than framing investigations in terms of state politics, it might be more productive to investigate the formation and transformation of theories, proposals, strategies and technologies for the "conduct of conduct"' (Rose 1999: 3). The third and fourth aspects of 'the art of government' that set it apart from Machiavelli's understanding of government – the birth of the notion of the population and that of the economy – are engaged in a dialectical relationship. The dialectic between these notions makes it possible to change the rationality and object of government from securing the property and territory of the sovereign towards seeing the population, not as something to crush and repress, but rather as a resource to exploit and make use of: 'the care for the individual life is becoming

... a duty for the state' (Foucault 2000d: 404). Modern societies are thus preoccupied with promoting discourses fostering subjects that contribute to economic performance since this will contribute to the prosperity of the municipality, the region, the country, the supranational collaboration or whatever administrative units. This understanding provides foundation for the form of power that Foucault (1977, 1981a) labels 'bio-power' – 'the government of the social body' (Clegg et al. 2006: 53). Finally, these third and the fourth aspects are contingent upon what might be the most important displacement in relation to the Machiavellian conceptualization: that government is based upon and legitimated by forms of knowledge. It was the early schools of economic and statistical sciences that changed understandings regarding how wealth is created, the role the population and the individual subject play in this game and the understanding of government; this gave rise to scientific approaches to political economy that aim to produce and promote subjects and subject positions that contribute to economic performance. It is through a government embedded in discourse, regimes of truth and power/knowledge that productive subjects are meant to be produced: through objectifying the population and without the direct intervention of an agency. In Foucault's view (2000b), what the anti-Machiavellian literature from the sixteenth and seventeenth century argues for is the birth of a new form of government that can be characterized as government at a distance or economic government.

Mentalities of government and governmentalization

Against the background of this shift in the social ontology of government, Foucault coined the notion of 'governmentality', to which he gave two meanings. First, governmentality deals with how people think about governing, with 'the particular *mentalities . . . of government* and administration that have emerged since early modern Europe' (Dean 1999: 2, emphasis added). These mentalities are forms of knowing and thus rationalities that have given rise to a multitude of governmental apparatuses and practices. Governmentality from this perspective is the study of the collective and taken for granted governmental discourse or regimes of government – the particular kinds of regimes of practices that are used to govern oneself and others. To say that a mentality is taken for granted and collective means that it is a discursive construction perceived as the right way to govern a particular domain of society at a particular time and accordingly that it is very seldom questioned or problematized. Within the context of modernity, the most important force for legitimizing these mentalities and for producing their taken for grantedness has been the behavioural and social sciences. This is an argument that is not exclusive to Foucault: it has been put forward within several quarters of constructivist sociology, even though formulated somewhat differently (Berger and Luckman 1967; Bourdieu 1984).

But governmentality seen from this perspective is also the study of *governmentalization* – the dispersion of governmental activity across institutional domains and the spread of governmental rationality in discourse (Foucault 2000b). In our analysis of managerial marketing discourse, we will focus on explicating what governmental rationalities it has fostered, what governmental rationality eventually got a hegemonic position, and how and to what extent this/these rationality(ies) 'governmentalized'[2] managerial marketing discourse. As Townley (1998) has argued, Foucauldian analyses, particularly analyses of governmentality, should be inspired by 'depth' rather than 'binary opposition'. The latter approach, which has dominated analysis in marketing, 'reflects a modernist approach to knowledge . . . premised on the dualism of a knowing subject gaining knowledge of a known object' (1998: 192). An analysis informed by this standpoint focuses on the opposition between traditions and concepts and the move from one type of knowledge to another is often described as a paradigm shift in Kuhn's (1962) use of the word. In adopting the metaphor of depth, opposition will be downplayed. Instead, such aspects as continuity and consistency between traditions as well as elaborations and development of governmental rationalities will be emphasized. Central binary oppositions will be re-evaluated.

Pastoral power

The second meaning Foucault assigns to governmentality marks the emergence of a form and exercise of power/knowledge referred to as pastoral power (Foucault 2000b, 2000c). This meaning of governmentality 'is a historically specific version of the first' (Dean 1999: 16).

In organizing itself as a church, Christianity 'postulates . . . that certain individuals can, by their religious quality, serve others . . . as pastors' and this 'designates a very special form of power' (Foucault 2000b: 333). The word pastoral is usually related to Christian practices, but its function and its associated power relations have governmentalized many discourses and domains of the societal body since the establishment of the modern nation states. It is this 'secularized' form of pastoral power and the metaphorical use of 'pastor' that we have in mind here. In contemporary organizations, dominated by the discourse of rational organization theory (Jacques 1996), the pastor is reincarnated as the manager and his flock of sheep are made up of the employees s/he is supposed to manage.

As we pointed out above, forms of power/knowledge differ from sovereign power in several ways. But there also exist more specific differences between pastoral power and sovereign power. First, the pastor wields power over a collective of people rather than over a land. Pastoral power is thus based on a conceptualization of human beings as unique subjects with specific needs and wants and not as objects. As we will see later, pastoral power also fosters this historically contingent modern subject. Second, the pastor gathers together, guides and leads this collective. The object of pastoral power is thus the management of people by the pastor, who manages through her/his inner qualities which are superior to the inner qualities of the people of the flock. Third, in line with the religious metaphor, the objective of this power is to secure individual 'salvation' – not in 'the next world' though but in the present world. Salvation here takes on worldly meanings such as richness, health and self-fulfilment. Accordingly, Foucault (2000c) argues that pastoral power operates through a constant kindness vis-à-vis subjects rather than a constant submission. This means that pastoral power is always dependent on an implicit or explicit ethic since the kindness it promotes has to be qualified. Therefore, pastoral power should be seen as instrumental: through making people believe in a value system and through giving them rewards that are in compliance with it (and thus their beliefs), pastoral power will make people reproduce the rationality of the value system. In this way people are being governed without noticing it. Contemporary neoliberal and neoconservative governmental discourse has been analysed as forms of pastoral power (see Dean 1995, 1999; Hodgson 2002; Rose 1996, 1999). These forms of government which have been named 'advanced liberal government' and 'neoliberal government' foster the attainment of specific goals and values, such as health, richness, status and position, which thus become the object and aim of management informed by pastoral power. Such value builds up the normative ethos summarized in the nodal point of liberalism: freedom (Harvey 2005). Pastoral power in liberal discourse thus becomes a management of free people and their freedom through their *freedom* (Rose 1999). As the cultural critic Matthew Arnold argued: 'Freedom is a very good horse to ride, but to ride somewhere' (Arnold cited in Harvey 2005: 6).

Finally, pastoral power is dependent upon knowing the individuals' innermost thoughts so as to direct and lead them. Pastoral power thus depends upon the production of technologies and practices for making individuals talk about themselves and their innermost thoughts: it requires *confessional* techniques. That is why modern social and behavioural sciences, quasi-sciences and expertises have been given the role of developing such techniques. Obvious examples include psychoanalysis and counselling in the discourse of psychology (Rose 1996, 1999), self-assessment in Total Quality Management discourse (Quist et al. 2007) and customer-perceived quality measurement techniques in service marketing (Skålén and Fougère 2007). Through the outwardly confessional speech that these technologies stimulate it is possible to provide the kindness that the pastor – through the mediation of ethics such as neoliberalism and neoconservatism – believes is appropriate for his flock. But the technologies also become means of control since the pastor can know and decide if the sheep will be happy or not by continuing to live the same way they do. The type of freedom that neoliberal and neoconservative discourses of government promote, for example, is not an unconditional freedom, it is not anarchy. Rather, it is a freedom that promotes integration into a particular society. It fosters healthy and working subjects that can realize their freedom and themselves through consumption, physical exercise and education – not unhealthy and unproductive subjects dependent on welfare services. This type of discourse thus fosters 'active' rather than passive subjects (see Dean 1995; Rose 1999). As Rose (1999: 4) argues, 'when it comes to governing human beings, to govern is to presuppose the freedom of the governed. To govern humans is not to crush their capacity to act, but to acknowledge it and utilize it for one's own objectives'. Thus by acting on her/his flock the pastor can change it and thereby provide salvation and happiness to the people.

But the confessing subjects will also act on themselves. When speaking about themselves they will reveal to themselves what types of persons they are 'since the speaking subject is the subject of the statement' (Foucault 1985a, quoted in Covaleski et al. 1998: 297) and if they are not satisfied, in terms defined by the pastor informed by an external ethic, they will try to change themselves. Change is manifested in the speech through avowal. Confessional speech will thus not only serve as a device of control for who the person is but also as an indicator for who s/he becomes. Through series of confessions and avowals the person will move from one subject position to another. Discourses of pastoral power encourage and foster such confessions and avowals. In this book we will study if and to what extent marketing does this.

Pastoral power is thus a power that defines identity from 'the inside out' (Covaleski et al. 1998). Foucault (1977, 2000b) differentiated it from another form of power/knowledge labelled disciplinary power. The distinction between these two kinds of power is, however, far from clear-cut in Foucault's work even though some clear differences can be noted. Disciplinary power is a micro power that targets individuals, while pastoral power focuses on the collective or on the individual as a part of the collective. The operation of disciplinary power is dependent on the norm, which is embedded in different types of discourse and disciplines: scientific, quasi-scientific and expertise (Dean 1995, 1999; Rose 1999). The practices and technologies promoted by these types of discourse function as *examinations*, which Foucault (1977) sees as the 'technology of the self' associated with individuation through objectification (Foucault 1977, 2000b; see also Covaleski et al. 1998). Through examinations, people's actions become visible and detectable and thus known objectively, 'exemplified by the employee's reduction to a final score as, for example, graphic rating scales, or overall scores at an assessment center' (Townley 1993: 535). As an effect, examinations also reveal gaps between actuality and possibility, between the person's present state and the norm. This enables management and intervention of people by themselves or others and fosters a movement towards the norm. By closing these gaps between the actual self and the ideal self, the person becomes subjectified and subjected.

The objective of pastoral power and the discourses that legitimize it in con-temporary society is to manage the population so that it contributes to economic performance. But the invention of pastoral power does not mean that sovereign power is made obsolete. On the contrary, under pastoral power the problems of sovereignty become more acute than ever, but the problem is reversed: while it used to be about deriving 'an art of government from a theory of sovereignty', in the new era of government this 'art' is constituted by the political sciences and thus the focus of the problem becomes to 'see what juridical and institutional form, what foundation in the law . . . could be given to the sovereignty that characterizes the state [and not the monarchy]' (Foucault 2000b: 218). Sovereign power is thus made contingent upon and operates within the boundaries of power/knowledge.

> Accordingly, we need to see things not in terms of the replacement of a society of sovereignty by a disciplinary society and the subsequent replacement of a

disciplinary society by a society of [pastoral power]; in reality one has a triangle, sovereignty-discipline-government, which has as its primary target the population.

(Foucault 2000b: 219)

Seeing things through the lens of governmentality, there is a shift of emphasis but not a break or rupture, since existing forms of power, that is, sovereign power – the juridical and executive arms of the sate and other institutions – and disciplinary power – the power that subjectifies and normalizes the individual through objectification (Foucault 1977) – are recast to serve these bio-political ends, targeting the whole population.

We argue that the governmental rationality of managerial marketing discourse has been considerably elaborated since the birth of the discipline and that marketing includes several sometimes competing and contradictory governmental practices. Marketing has affected how people think and thereby are governed in many institutional domains (Brown 1995; Brownlie et al. 1999), in private firms (including service firms and manufacturing firms) (du Gay 1996; Hochschild 1983), in public sector organizations (Clarke and Newman 1997; Fairclough 1993) and in non-governmental organizations. In fact marketing has affected how people look upon and present themselves (Brownlie and Saren 1997). Despite this, marketing has not been approached from the perspective of governmentality. This book seeks to fill this gap by particularly focusing on the managerial rationality of marketing from the perspective of governmentality and the particular view(s) of power presented earlier.

Government

The notion of government as used in this book draws on the work of Foucault. This notion of government should be clearly differentiated from the notion of 'governance' – a term which definitely is on the agenda in contemporary society and social research (see Dean 1999; Pierre and Peters 2005). Foucault (2000a) defines government as the 'conduct of conduct'. With the first 'conduct' in this phrase, which comes from the verb 'to conduct', Foucault wants to imply that government is about leading, directing, guiding, etc. in a more or less deliberate way. But he also gives the verb 'to conduct' a reflexive meaning, that is, that government is not only about leading others but is also about leading oneself – it is about self-regulation. With the second 'conduct', the noun, Foucault refers to people's thinking, actions and emotions – the object of government. The 'conduct of conduct' thus means the deliberate direction of people's articulated set of behaviours. Dean defines government in the following way:

> Government is any more or less calculated and rational activity, undertaken by a multiplicity of authorities and agencies, employing a variety of techniques and forms of knowledge, that seeks to shape conduct by working through our

desires, aspirations, interests and beliefs, for definitive but shifting ends and with a diverse set of relatively unpredictable consequences, effects and outcomes.

(1999: 11)

A similar definition is given by Rose (1996: 12): 'government . . . is a way of conceptualizing all those more or less rationalized programmes, strategies, and tactics for "the conduct of conduct", for acting upon the actions of others in order to achieve certain ends'. We adopt the definitions of government given by Dean (1999) and Rose (1996) in this book, but in order to be meaningful and not subject to confusion they need to be qualified in several ways.

First, government is a deliberate attempt to regulate *human* conduct. Managerial discourses, among them marketing, have as their prime objective to articulate such attempts. Second, the use of *rational* should not be equalled with the specific form of rationalism dominating in the contemporary West and often referred to as 'Reason'. In fact, this is not the only rationality there is in the West and there are other rationalities operating in other times and spaces that an analysis of government takes into account. Rationality 'is simply any form of thinking which strives to be relatively clear, systematic and explicit about aspects of "external" and "internal" existence, about how things are and how they ought to be' (Dean 1999: 11). Rationalities are forms of knowing (Townley 1994). Third, the rational nature of government implies that it is linked to *moral* questions. The 'forms of thinking' and 'knowing' (the rationalities) that regimes of government are founded on are of a prescriptive nature (Foucault 1985a). They are forms of knowledge that offer 'truth' regarding how people ought to conduct themselves. Practices/technologies of the self and practices/technologies of government are thus tightly interwoven. Regimes of government can be considered as ethics rather than the objective truths they are often branded as (Dean 1999). From this perspective ethics can be conceived as regimes for the government of the self, as promoting action upon 'the self on self' (Foucault 1985a). Fourth, this understanding of the relationship between government and ethics implies that those governed are in some sense *free*, actors who are able to conduct themselves. As Dean (1999: 13) puts it, 'government is an activity that shapes the field of action and thus, in this sense, attempts to shape freedom'. This freedom also opens up spaces for resistance and critique by actors. It also gives actors the opportunity to govern themselves differently – to choose among governmental regimes. Therefore, and as noted earlier, certain regimes of government within the governmentality tradition, referred to as advanced liberal or neoliberal forms of government (Dean 1999; Rose 1999), operate through offering types of freedom to actors and regulating this freedom. They are packaged as ways to be free. Again we see how power/knowledge controls and enables simultaneously. Seduction, manipulation, discipline and normalization are on the other side of the same coin as fulfilment, empowerment, happiness and productivity.

An analytical scheme of government

In the remainder of this chapter we will outline Dean's analytical framework for studying government (Dean 1995, 1999) that will be used towards the end of the fifth, sixth and seventh chapters in order to structure and elaborate on our analyses. Dean's framework is an adaptation of the analytical typology that Foucault developed and used in his last two volumes of the *History of Sexuality* (Foucault 1985a, 1985b). In these works, which are usually considered as the most central in what is often referred to as Foucault's 'ethical' period, Foucault argues for a general connection between ethics and self-making but he does not explicitly connect this to a notion of government – even though he talks about clearly related issues such as bringing 'one's conduct in compliance with a given rule' and 'moral conduct' (1985a: 27, 28). In Foucault's view, the connection between ethics and the self should be studied by focusing on: what part of identity the individual constitutes as an object of moral conduct; the ways in which this moral conduct is made a part of identity; the identity this brings about; and lastly why this work upon the self on self is carried out. Foucault thus studies the relationship between ethics and subjectification by focusing on the ontology, ascetics, deontology and teleology of this problematic (Foucault 1985a). Dean also takes his point of departure in these four sequences. Dean's particular contribution is that he re-contextualizes and translates Foucault's typology into a language of governmentality and government – and it is this version of the typology that we draw on here.

Before presenting the typology, however, we would like to state how our usage of it differs from Foucault's and Dean's. They presuppose an actor who chooses what parts of the self are made an object of intervention, what technologies should be used to reconstitute identity, etc. as the object of study. Our analysis does not focus on actual instances of subjectification in social settings; it focuses on discourse. Our particular position on the concept of discourse is articulated in the next chapter but let us state briefly here that we focus on the subjectivity that academic marketing attributes to people – rather than the 'actual' subjectivities of professional marketers – and accordingly on the subject positions immanent in marketing discourse, on what technologies are promoted to accomplish the change of subjectivity and on who the target of this governmental rationality is. We thus use the typology as a 'grid' that we place 'upon' managerial marketing discourse rather than on the people that embody and bring about this rationality. This use is in line with Laclau and Mouffe's (1985) version of discourse analysis, which sees every object as constituted by discourse. Laclau and Mouffe (1985) do not differentiate between social and discursive practices, unlike Foucault, Dean and other discourse analysts such as Fairclough (2001).

After this short background to Dean's framework and the qualification of how we use it, let us now introduce it. As written previously, it consists of four sequences:

1. 'First, [governmentality] involves ontology, concerned with *what* [marketing] seek[s] to act upon, the *governed or ethical substance*' (Dean 1999: 17,

emphasis in original). In this book we conceptualize marketing as a management discipline and accordingly focus on the intra-organizational processes of government that marketing promotes and fosters.

2. 'Second, [governmentality] involves ascetics, concerned with *how* [marketing in our case] governs this substance, the *governing or ethical work*' (Dean 1999: 17, emphasis in original). In making this analysis, we focus on explicating the central technologies and practices that managerial marketing discourse promotes in order to accomplish the particular type of government envisioned. The technologies identified differ extensively from period to period in the history of marketing.

3. 'Third, [governmentality] involves deontology, concerned with *who* we are when we are governed [by marketing] . . . our 'mode of subjectification', or the *governable or ethical subject*' (Dean 1999: 17, emphasis added). What subject positions marketing offers to people is a major focus in the analysis. Foucauldian analyses of subjectivity have been taken up in a few critical analyses of marketing discourse. For example, two of the authors of the present volume, in their study of the gap model, a central customer survey technology within service marketing, argue that the latter 'has an extensive effect on the subjugation of people and thus on the production of subjectivity while at the same time reproducing human beings as objects of service marketing knowledge' (Skålén and Fougère 2007: 119). We will analyse how the development of marketing discourse fabricates distinct employee subject positions that make employees governable in a particular way.

4. 'Fourth, [governmentality] entails a teleology, concerned with *why* we govern or are governed [by marketing]' (Dean 1999: 17, emphasis in original). The reasons for the development of certain practices and technologies of government will be sought inside marketing. As with every managerial discourse that has been developed within the boundaries of the market economy, the central rationale can be argued to make this market economy work better and more effectively. But we will also explicate reasons not directly related to the idea of the market economy. Here we will focus not only on changes in the governmentality of marketing founded on articulations that are internal to marketing discourse, but also on discursive practices outside marketing – that is, competing managerial discourses and general changes in society.

4   Studying governmental discourse

In methodological terms, the endeavour that we undertake in this book can be described as a *critical discourse analysis* of managerial marketing. This chapter describes how we intend to accomplish this in four sections. The chapter opens by introducing the two major types of methodological principles Foucault developed to analyse discourse – archaeology and genealogy. Our analysis should be described as neither an orthodox archaeology nor an orthodox genealogy – it draws inspiration from both. In the second section we introduce our central methodological concepts: *turning points* and *problematizations*. Very generally, the former refers to shifts in direction of a discourse and the latter to what occurrences lead to these changes. We will, however, argue that the notions of turning points and problematizations as treated in previous research are too abstract for guiding concrete analyses of discourse. Therefore, the third section introduces the approach to discourse analysis outlined by Laclau and Mouffe (1985) referred to as *discourse theory* (Phillips and Jørgensen 2002), which provides a structure that can complement these two notions and qualify them more sharply. Discourse theory thus is the methodology that inspires our more detailed analysis of marketing discourse. We see the work of Ernesto Laclau and Chantal Mouffe as a specification of Foucault's position to discourse analysis – not as a substitute. In the fourth section, our periodization of marketing that will be deployed in the analysis is presented based on the turning points and problematizations approach contextualized by discourse theory.[1]

Archaeology and genealogy

The work of Foucault is usually considered as encompassing two overarching methodological approaches: 'archaeology' and 'genealogy'. The former type of inquiry focuses on illuminating and describing the unconscious rules of formation regulating the emergence of discourse in the human sciences. An archaeological study investigates what can be said and what it is that is being valued within a particular domain (Foucault 1972). The object of analysis in archaeology is discourse and the analysis of discourse is mostly neutral (not political). Genealogy also focuses on the formation of the human sciences and the expertise they give rise to, but this analysis is founded on the idea that this formation is intertwined with power relations embedded in knowledge (Foucault 1988). If archaeology is a more neutral history, genealogy is a critical history.

In his archaeological studies of medicine, social medicine, madness and psychology, Foucault used academic work as his prime material (Foucault 1967, 1970, 1973). In this sense our approach to discourse analysis has much in common with archaeology. But it also diverges from archaeology since we take a critical position towards marketing and since our ambition is to deconstruct marketing – not only to describe its formation and its ethics. Rather, and as discussed previously, we see our analysis of marketing and the subjectivities it prescribes as embedded in power/knowledge. But it also diverges in one important way from Foucault's genealogical position. In his genealogical work on crime and sexuality, Foucault (1977, 1981a, 1985a, 1985b) made a distinction between discourse and non-discursive dimensions of the social. Here, we analyse marketing based on its representation in academic discourse and do not directly focus on how marketing has been shaped by non-discursive forces. However, we would like to point out that we are not as far from Foucault as it might seem at first sight. In his genealogical work, Foucault analysed material aspects of the social *through* discourse, primarily texts. In fact, we argue that it is questionable whether one ever analyses non-discursive practices as long as they are mediated through and (re)constructed by discourse. With Laclau and Mouffe (1985) we argue that it is not necessary to make a distinction between material and discursive practices in order to be able to account for power relations. We perceive the social world as always mediated by and only conceivable through discourse.

> That does not mean that nothing but text and talk exist, but, on the contrary, that discourse itself is material and that entities such as the economy, the infrastructure and institutions are also parts of discourse. Thus, in Laclau and Mouffe's discourse theory there is no dialectical interaction between discourse and something else: discourse itself is fully constitutive of our world.
>
> (Phillips and Jørgensen 2002: 19)

The critical question in this perspective is rather if the sources that are chosen as the objects of analysis represent the discourse analysed in an appropriate manner. Our standpoint is that academic marketing texts do this for marketing discourse (see Chapter 1).

Foucault (1972) provided detailed methodological rules for archaeological analysis but not for genealogical analysis. Since our analysis includes the genealogical critical moment, Foucault's own work does not provide us with a detailed methodological foundation. Furthermore, we also believe that the post-Foucauldian governmentality literature has been weaker in developing detailed discourse analytic methods compared to furthering the theoretical legacy of Foucault. This is one important reason for us to take the discourse analysis of Laclau and Mouffe (1985) as our methodological foundation. We would, however, like to take our starting point in two concepts, turning points and problematizations, and later fuse them with the discourse theory of Laclau and Mouffe (1985). Turning points is only loosely connected to the work of Foucault (see 2000a, 2000b), but problematizations can be viewed as the overarching methodological principle in genealogical analysis.

Turning points and problematizations

Turning points and problematizations are our central methodological concepts. We will start this section by presenting the former, which should be seen as one of several periodization devices that have been used by historians in general, marketing historians in particular. This is evident from the work of Hollander et al. (2005), which has reviewed approaches to periodization in research on the history of marketing. Based on their review Hollander et al. argue that three basic techniques of periodization have been employed in studies of marketing history. One of them is the turning point approach which relies on identifying 'important turning points in the material itself under review' which can be 'significant changes in marketing methods, in economic conditions, and so on' (p. 37). They see this approach as the most appropriate periodization principle: 'Above all else, periodization should mark important turning points in time. Therefore, we believe that the most appropriate technique for periodizing marketing history is to use turning points in the material itself being studied' (p. 39).

Defining turning points as 'significant changes' is, however, rather vague and the notion needs to be qualified by taking into account the particular theoretical position guiding the analysis. In our case we look for turning points in the governmental and managerial rationality of marketing discourse and more precisely we look for changes, displacements and elaborations in, for example, the subject positions and technologies it promotes. We think that the general nature of a turning point has to be given a more precise meaning than is generally the case in historiography. Why does the course of direction for a particular discourse change? What is needed for this to happen?

In order to answer these questions we will introduce the notion of *problematizations* which can be considered to be Foucault's concept that refers to elaborations and changes in/of discourse. In the analysis we will use the notion of problematization as signifying the reasons and occurrences that lead to a realized or attempted shift in marketing discourse. This also enables us to connect our periodizing principle with our theoretical endeavour since the foundation for an analysis of government is to identify instances of problematizations of governmentality (Dean 1999; Rose 1996). Connecting turning points and problematizations in this way is not exceptional. In his writing on governmentality, Foucault himself frequently used the notion of turning points in a similar vein as we use it here (see for example Foucault 2000a, 2000b).

With problematizations, Foucault (1981a, 1997) means the way a regime of government is associated with questioning and interrogating the past and/or the present (Dean 1999; Rose 1996). This questioning might refer to a societal phenomenon, another discourse and/or the discourse itself. Since we primarily focus on academic marketing discourse, the problematizations we look for are often associated with the internal 'theoretical' debate in marketing between different and opposing positions. But these debates can be fuelled by discourses outside marketing; for example, general changes in society.

Problematization is a particularly central concept in Foucault's genealogical methodology. In genealogy it is central to reflect on the present time in history in order to question the self-evident and the familiar (Foucault 1988). A genealogy seeks to identify and illuminate significant developments leading to the present discursive order. Problematizations do not occur often and when analysing a discourse, it is pivotal to locate the time and context of a particular problematization. Rather than taking the standpoint in a general theory, analysing governmentality means to examine the particular instances when government is put into question (Dean 1999).

As Dean (1999: 27) puts its, 'a problematization of government is a calling into question of how we shape or direct our own and others' conduct. Problematization might thus equally concern how we conduct government and how we govern conduct'. A problematization may consequently be about how managers should carry out government and management of organizations according to prescriptions but also be about how managers and employees should manage and control themselves. The problematizations of regimes of government are based upon practices/technologies and the modification, displacement and elaborations of existing practices/technologies as well as inventions of new practices/technologies. Practices and technologies are prescriptive action and thought schemes based on knowledge/truth (see Chapter 3 and Foucault 1985a). Analyzing the practices and technologies that constitute the problematizations thus implies analysing the truths that they are founded on.

Problematizations in themselves should not be understood as a form of critique, at least not as how critique is understood here, that is, a matter of questioning the truths that constitute and provide foundation for regimes of government. Problematizations should rather be associated with the idea of cumulativity, a central goal with all modernistic knowledge production. In order to operate, cumulativity relies on the internal critique of the discourse, which makes problems and inconsistencies clear. The solving of problems and inconsistencies is equalled with important developments of a discourse and more particularly its governmental rationality: cumulativity is consonant with the modernistic notion of progress. The critical moment in analysing discourse, on the other hand, is constituted by explicating the governmental rationality that is elaborated on and manifested by problematizations; this is a prerequisite for 'not being governed so much' (Foucault 1997). Critique as we understand it is thus a problematization of the problematizations.

Discourse theory

Explicating the problematizations and turning points of managerial marketing discourse is thus the starting point for the analysis in this book. But problematizations and turning points can be considered as methodologically 'empty' concepts. To just say that the analysis should focus on turning points and problematizations of discourse is not enough. We also need to articulate how we intend to approach these turning points and problematizations more specifically and thus how we intend to unpack the managerialism of marketing discourse.

In this section we intend to develop a more precise methodological position by drawing on the discourse theory of Laclau and Mouffe (1985). Discourse theory will first serve to give the notions of turning points and problematizations a more precise meaning and a more steady base. Second, it will in itself provide the detailed methodological framework that we need for analysing the managerialism of marketing discourse in Chapters 5, 6 and 7.

Discourse and its formation

Let us start by recapitulating what we have already written concerning methodology. Our object of study is marketing *discourse*. Previously we have delineated how we perceive marketing (as a regime of government) and we have also argued that we will focus on the important problematizations and turning points within marketing. From the perspective of government that we have outlined we have theorized discourse as equivalent to regimes of power/knowledge and we have argued that discourse and language are intellectual technologies which make people frame the world in particular and distinctive ways. We have thus argued that discourses are performative – they do not only represent the world but they also produce it. But we have not systematically addressed the notion of discourse from a methodological perspective: we have discussed how discourse frames people's thinking and how it structures the social world but not what discourse is, what it is made of, how it changes, how it relates to other discourses, etc. In elaborating on our understanding of discourse and how to analyse it we take our point of departure in a much cited passage from *Hegemony and Socialist Strategy*, the most central work of Laclau and Mouffe:

> We will call *articulation* any practices establishing a relation among elements such that their identity is modified as a result of the articulatory practice. The structured totality resulting from the articulatory practice, we will call *discourse*. The differential positions, insofar as they appear articulated within a discourse, we will call *moments*. By contrast, we will call *element* any differences that is not discursively articulated.
>
> (1985: 105, emphasis in original)

This citation summarizes four of the most central concepts of Laclau and Mouffe's discourse theory – articulation, discourse, moment and element – and also indicates something about the basic relationship between them. Based upon Laclau and Mouffe, discourse thus can be 'understood as the fixation of meaning within a particular domain' (Phillips and Jørgensen 2002: 26). *Moments* are the building blocks of discourse. They are signs whose meaning is fixed because of their distinctness in relation to other moments. It is the practice of *articulating* that establishes this distinct relationship between moments and gives them their meaning. What constitutes a particular discourse is thus the total structure and network of relationships between moments established by articulations that fixate the meanings of moments. This understanding of discourse is theoretically distinct and rigorous and sets it apart from other indistinct usages of discourse as language in general or as the language use in a particular domain. In order for a discourse to exist there has to exist a structured and fixed relationship of meaning between the moments that constitute it.

Even though this definition of discourse is theoretically distinct, it is also something of an ideal-type definition since such fixed structures seldom exist. Laclau and Mouffe (1985) acknowledge this and argue that fixation of meaning is always *contingent*. Their understanding of contingency is based upon the introduction of the notion of *element*, defined as the signs whose meaning has not been fixed. By introducing the notion of element, Laclau and Mouffe thus relax the structuralism that is inherent in their definition of discourse. But this does not mean that they completely reject structuralism or that their definition of discourse should be understood as entirely idealistic. In the quote above, for example, Laclau and Mouffe define elements as 'not discursively articulated'. In order to account for articulation of meaning outside a particular discourse – for example, meanings that signs have had previously and meanings that signs are given in other discourses – Laclau and Mouffe introduce the notion of *field of discursivity*. A discourse is always constituted in relation to what it excludes and thus in relation to signs situated outside the discourse. This implies that a discourse might be undermined by elements in the field of discursivity: 'its unity of meaning is in danger of being disrupted by other ways of fixing the meaning of the signs' (Phillips and Jørgensen 2002: 27). Therefore a particular articulatory practice tries to turn elements into moments, thereby appropriating and fixing signs in the discourse.

Where does this take us? We understand Laclau and Mouffe's position as follows: it can be productive to picture and perceive discourse at a particular space and time as a temporary closure of meaning giving. But this closure – the transformation of elements into moments – is never complete, it is always contingent. Accordingly discourse can always be opened up and its meaning can be redefined. Exactly how 'closed' the language for a particular domain has to be in order to constitute a discourse about the domain it refers to is not determined by Laclau and Mouffe and it is of course hard and maybe not even constructive to set up such a rule. But they claim that 'any discourse is constituted as an attempt to dominate the field of discursivity, to arrest the flow of differences, to construct a centre' and they 'call the privileged discursive points of this partial fixation *nodal points*' (1985: 112, emphasis in original). As we interpret Laclau and Mouffe, discourse exists when meaning is structured around and is given meaning by one or a few nodal points (cf. Phillips and Jørgensen 2002). Nodal points are moments that have a heuristic position in the structure of moments that constitutes discourse. The implication is that discourse in the present study is defined as a relatively closed fixation of signs that refers to a particular domain in which no more than a few nodal points have a heuristic meaning giving position. If this closure does not exist for a specific domain, then there is no articulated discourse for this domain, which implies that the domain itself is arbitrary and blurred.

Our discussion hitherto enables us to refine our notion of problematizations and turning points. Translated into Laclau and Mouffe's language, problematizations include two operations: they open up discourse and they attempt to close discourse. Problematizations thus turn the moments of a discourse into elements. If the problematization does not successfully accomplish this, it cannot be considered to be a problematization but only an attempt to problematize discourse. When opened up, the particular articulatory practice inherent to all problematizations tries to turn the elements into moments and also to reconstitute the relationship between moments compared to how this relationship was arranged before the problematization. This second move is thus an attempt to reconstitute the meaning of the discourse. Problematizations directed towards nodal points have a greater potential to establish new relationships between the moments of the discourse. Even though problematizations always involve articulatory practices they do not need to be successful or realized in order for the problematizations to be considered problematizations. The attempt might be confronted with other articulatory practices aimed to secure the status quo or change discourse in other ways. But if the articulation of the problematization rearranges the discourse, then we are facing a turning point. Thus, problematizations are the occurrences that may lead to a turning point but they do not always do so. In subsequent chapters we will use the framework of Laclau and Mouffe to show how marketing became a managerial discipline and how its managerialism was rearticulated and changed at different points in time.

The contingent nature of discourse

When discourse is seen as contingent, discourse analysis centres on mapping the 'struggles' regarding the meaning that should be given to signs. These struggles are often organized around what Laclau (1990, 1993; Phillips and Jørgensen 2002) names *floating signifiers*, which are elements that are especially opened to attribution of meaning. Floating signifiers are signs that are parts of several discourses simultaneously and that are given a distinct meaning within each of them. Nodal points are often floating signifiers and this may seem paradoxical since we previously argued that nodal points are the privileged points that discourse is structured around. But a nodal point refers to the arrangement of meaning within one discourse while a floating signifier refers to the struggle of meaning given between discourses. A particular discourse on an abstract level aims to say something distinct about phenomena of central importance to the organization of a particular time and space and usually several discourses seek to do this simultaneously. Therefore, it is not so strange that nodal points and floating signifiers often coincide. Because of the antagonistic relationship between discourses, a nodal point of a particular discourse can be redefined, implying that the meaning of discourse will be changed from the outside. A particular discourse might thus be problematized by other discourses if one or several nodal points of the former discourse are also floating signifiers.

One example of a sign that simultaneously is a floating signifier and a nodal point is the notion of motor vehicles (Phillips and Jørgensen 2002). In the discourse of community and country planning, motor vehicles seem to structure the articulation of other moments; for example, that of shopping centres which, in contemporary community and country planning discourse, seems to be associated with localization outside city centres. In the global warming discourse, motor vehicles also play a central role as one major reason for the greenhouse effect but here motor vehicles are not conceived in terms of possibilities but rather as one of the big threats. Another example that is much closer to the topic discussed here is customer orientation, which is an underlying rationality in several branches of contemporary managerial discourse (see e.g. du Gay 1996), but is given a somewhat different meaning within them. Customer orientation is nevertheless central for structuring the meaning of different discourses.

In discourse theory, the concept of floating signifiers is thus used to analyse the struggle for the attribution of meaning between discourses and is thus closely related to Fairclough's concepts of interdiscursivity and intertextuality (Fairclough 1992). We will use the concept in this way when analysing how other discourses have impacted on and problematized marketing. But we also argue that the notion of floating signifiers sheds light over the internal struggle for attribution of meaning within discourses, particularly when a discourse is constituted and also when it is opened up and redefined. In the first instance we believe that the signs that eventually will turn out to be nodal points are open to attribution of meaning from different quarters inside discourse and that the floating signifiers turn into nodal points as discourse advances towards closure. We also argue that when discourse is problematized and thus temporarily opened up, the nodal points may be treated as kinds of floating signifiers since in such instances several articulations have the possibility to attribute meaning to the nodal point and thus to give the discourse a new direction. In these cases there are turning points and problematizations of discourse, which is a relatively rare occurrence.

Hegemony and deconstruction

Even though we understand discourse as contingent, the struggles for meaning may eventually end almost completely, which may lead to a closure where the fixation of meaning becomes taken for granted to the degree that it is perceived as given by nature. Laclau (1990; Phillips and Jørgensen 2002) calls discourses whose contingency have been 'hidden' in this way *objective*[2] in contrast to those that are contingent, which he calls *political*. The journey from political to objective discourse is mediated by *hegemonic interventions*, which are certain ways of perceiving the world leading to the establishment of *hegemony*, meaning that the worldview that a hegemonic intervention embeds comes to dominate a particular discourse. When a particular discourse is dominated by one such worldview it is called *hegemonic* or objective (Laclau 1990; Phillips and Jørgensen 2002).

If we again reflect upon the notions of turning points and problematizations from the perspective of discourse theory, we conceive hegemonic interventions as representing one important type of problematization. As argued previously, problematizations open up and *attempt* to close discourse. A hegemonic intervention is a problematization which by definition always manages to close discourse in a way that is in line with its inherent articulatory practice(s). It is thus a problematization that redirects the meaning of discourse and hence leads to a turning point.

It must, however, be noted that objective and hegemonic discourse is not the same thing. Even though hegemonic discourse is dominated by one way of framing the world, its hegemony has not completely institutionalized it. Struggles for meaning still take place. As long as the discourse's hegemony is intact, these struggles never succeed in challenging the existing order. But hegemonic discourse is always open to such challenges. When a discourse is objective, its hegemony is completely taken for granted, meaning that alternative articulations of its central meaning are impossible to articulate inside discourse. The hegemonic type should accordingly be situated between the political and the objective types and hegemony should be understood as operating between the hegemonic and the objective: it determines the degree of impact that the dominant worldview has on a particular discourse.

Both objective and hegemonic discourse can thus be referred to as being characterized by hegemony. What differentiates them is that the hegemony is total in the first case. It is, however, quite possible that hegemonic discourse may develop into objective discourse. This does not imply that objective discourse can never turn back into hegemonic discourse and eventually into political discourse. Rather, it implies, at least as we see it, that objective discourse can never be transformed like this from inside the discourse. But it can always be problematized through the signs it shares with other discourses – the floating signifiers – that is, be challenged from outside. In the analysis in subsequent chapters, we will analyse if managerial marketing discourse has been hegemonized by a particular governmental rationality and if this is the case, we will outline the substance of this rationality.

But our analysis of marketing discourse does not only aim to display its hegemony, it also aims to critically evaluate it. When objective and/or hegemonic discourse is analysed and discussed as we do in this book, the objective of the discourse analysis, according to Laclau (1993; Phillips and Jørgensen 2002: 56), is *deconstruction*. If the hegemonic intervention is the process that establishes hegemony, deconstruction is the activity that shows that the closure of discourse, and thus its particular network of relationships between its moments, could have been articulated differently. It seeks to show that objective and hegemonic discourses are contingent. In a technical language this means that the deconstruction seeks to turn the moments of a particular discourse back into elements. In a more common-sense language it is about questioning that which is taken for granted, self-evident and treated as given by nature. Deconstruction delivers the critique in the approach to discourse analysis that we have described here. Deconstruction can thus be thought of as a 'problematization of problematizations' or as 'reflexive problematizations'.

When we deconstruct the hegemony of marketing, we will articulate and make visible its internal logical contradictions. Hackley (2003), in his critical analysis of academic marketing discourse and particularly marketing management textbooks, calls such contradictions 'ideological dilemmas'. As he puts it, 'an ideological dilemma occurs where speakers must deal with a logical contradiction, which, if acknowledged as such, would rhetorically undermine the speaker's own positions and claims' (2003: 1334). One such dilemma that Hackley recognizes in academic marketing discourse is the contradictory claim that marketing is a scientific discipline with a rigorous and robust theory and that its scientific theory is weak. The former claim is made for legitimizing marketing as an academic subject and the latter claim is used for arguing that more research is needed in marketing and thus to open up for a particular contribution.

Interconnections

As may be clear by now, discourse theory has much in common with the Foucauldian framework presented and discussed in the previous chapter – there is thus no need for a distinct demarcation between 'theory' and 'method' in this book. For example, hegemony and governmentality, which must be considered to be central to the respective frameworks, fit well with each other. As we have argued previously, governmentality should be understood as collective governmental discourse that is taken for granted. Hegemony also refers to discourse that has been more or less taken for granted. What we have gained by adopting discourse theory is a methodological framework and concepts for analysing how hegemony/governmentality is established, changed and reproduced; the governmentality literature lacks these – at least in such a systematic and integrated form as in Laclau and Mouffe's (1985) discourse theory. To us discourse theory offers a concrete methodology for conducting the type of analysis and delivering the kind of critique that the governmentality literature sets out to do.

One other important connection between our 'theory' and 'method' is the notion of problematizations. From Foucault onwards, problematizations have been a central concept for analysing governmental discourse, signifying the ways through which a regime of government is questioned and/or questioning. With impetus from discourse theory, we have provided in this section the notion of problematization with a more robust methodological foundation and have given the concept a clearer methodological role. In the remainder of this chapter we will use the notion of problematization and the turning points approach to historiography to periodize marketing discourse, and thus provide the structure for the analysis of managerial marketing discourse in Chapters 5, 6 and 7.

Periodization

Delineating between historical periods is always arbitrary. Periodization is, nevertheless, a fundamental and necessary tool in historical analysis. When we identified our periods of marketing discourse, we were guided by an endeavour to delineate turning points in the governmental rationality of managerial marketing discourse. This approach implies that the traditions of research in marketing that have elaborated on, developed and perfected the managerialism of marketing – rather than those that have, for example, furthered the consumerist discourse within marketing – have been focused on.

Three periods

When the managerialism of marketing is analysed from a Foucauldian perspective, it is fruitful to argue for a distinction between three overlapping periods which we label: 'founding the power/knowledge of managerial marketing', 'consolidating the power/knowledge of managerial marketing' and 'elaborating the power/ knowledge of managerial marketing'. The major reason for this distinction is that important and fundamental changes in the managerialism of marketing discourse have taken place between these periods as regards the governmental rationality promoted, the governmental domain being aimed for and the governmental technologies and practices being promoted in order to achieve government. The shifts between the three periods which we have identified thus mark turning points and problematizations of the governmental rationality of managerial marketing discourse, but they also include important changes and elaborations. The last two periods coincide with the marketing management and the service marketing traditions of marketing research, which we both argue have contributed to reformulate and transform the managerialism of marketing. Our periodization thus coincides with periodizations made in some of the previous, more managerial historical research in the field of marketing (Vargo and Lusch 2004; Vargo and Morgan 2005; Webster 1992). This is quite natural since we focus on the turning points and problematizations of academic marketing discourse, which the shift from one research tradition to another may account for. The three periods will be described and analysed in Chapters 5, 6 and 7 respectively.

Sources

The focus on academic marketing texts in combination with our discourse analytical methodology centring on identifying turning points and the problematizations that lead up to them implies that our main sources are the texts that have contributed to problematize and redirect marketing discourse. This implies that we primarily focus on articles published in scientific journals and monographs written by professionals and researchers. It is indeed the case that many problematizations of marketing discourse have been initiated by professionals. The works of Wroe Alderson and Robert Keith at around the turn of 1960, for example, problematized previous articulations of marketing discourse and contributed to the establishment of marketing management. Another example of a professional involved in rearticulating marketing is Lynn Shostack, who contributed to the development of service marketing. This influence of professionals on the formation of academic discourse sets marketing apart from other academic disciplines. But this is not seen as a problem within marketing. Rather, the work of these professionals is published in academic journals or as monographs by academic publishers and is well integrated and considered as a part of academic marketing discourse. Besides leaning on articles and monographs, we base our description of marketing on works by marketing historians, on texts issued by regulative organizations such as the American Marketing Association and on textbooks. The latter category has sometimes contributed to problematize marketing discourse but they are also useful as sources for following changes and continuities. Philip Kotler's *Marketing Management*, for example, has been published in twelve subsequent editions.

It can be argued that our selection of texts is biased in several ways. Our selection can be accused of not covering everything that has been written in marketing. It must, however, be kept in mind that we focus on the managerialism of mainstream marketing and in order to do this we do not need to cover everything. Rather, it is important to focus on problematizations and turning points in terms of the discipline's managerialism. This book should thus not be read as a description of the 'whole' history of marketing discourse: this would probably be undesirable – and perhaps impossible – to accomplish in a single monograph, regardless of methodological focus. Another form of criticism that could be objected to our selection of sources is that we primarily base our description on texts of American origin. The fact is that marketing has first become institutionalized as an academic discipline in the United States, and that historically it has largely been an American discipline, written primarily by and for Americans about American issues. Reviewing the development of the marketing discipline by definition entails reading primarily American texts. However, it needs to be acknowledged that in recent years and particularly within service marketing, European scholars have also played a central role in redirecting the managerialism of marketing. The works of these scholars are of course also included in our review.

A word of warning

Our periodization has several commonalities with other reviews of marketing discourse (Morgan 2003; Vargo and Lusch 2004; Vargo and Morgan 2005; Webster 1992). Some of the previous research is characterized by a faith in progress. This is something that tends to characterize historical research that uses periodizations and it has (not very surprisingly perhaps) been a particular problem in marketing research.

> The history of marketing thought has fulfilled the prediction that periodization will tend to express its view of human progress. Overall, the literature sees marketing as moving from a crude state of intuitive action toward an increasingly informed and scientific discipline.
>
> (Hollander et al. 2005: 39)

We would like to warn against what we see as a misleading sense of progress and explicitly state that this book should not be read as such. Such an analytical style is not consistent with our analytical endeavour. Even though we will describe the development of marketing discourse, including how practices and technologies have come to be more perfected, elaborated on and how they have spread throughout marketing discourse, this does not imply that we celebrate this development or that we believe that the theories of marketing have become 'better' – in whatever meaning of the word. We merely seek to describe the differences in the managerialism of marketing discourse at different times. The normative analysis of marketing that we set out to accomplish is critical rather than managerially prescriptive and includes a deconstruction of marketing's managerialism instead of its celebration. Thus, even though our periodization has commonalities with more managerial accounts of marketing history, we adopt a completely different perspective for analysing this development.

5 Founding the power/ knowledge of managerial marketing

Marketing has its roots in very old trade practices, and the first examples of marketing thought can be traced back to Socratic philosophers. But it is only in the early twentieth century that marketing was born as an academic discipline. In this chapter we will describe the early articulations that led to the creation and institutionalization of the marketing discipline, thereby making it possible to establish its power/knowledge; we will discuss how articulations of marketing as a whole started emerging and competing for hegemony; and we will show how managerialism and a customer-driven governmental rationality rose in importance within certain streams of marketing, which made it possible for them to eventually characterize the dominant articulation of the discipline by the 1950s. We will especially focus on the most managerialistic articulations of marketing, which pertain to sales management, and describe the governmentality of marketing's managerialism in these articulations of selling.

Initial influences on marketing thought

There was much thinking about the impact of trade on society and the role of 'middlemen' through the ages, from ancient Greece to medieval times to the Enlightenment – and no doubt, in many other places and times before the establishment of the marketing discipline in the twentieth century. A brief overview of some of the main themes addressed by thinkers of different time periods relating to what was later to be called 'marketing' follows.

Ancient times

Many authors have tried to discuss where marketing originally comes from, and when it initially emerged. According to Herodotus (as translated by de Selincourt 1962), the first appearance of marketing dates back the seventh century BCE, when the Lydians, living in Asia Minor, used gold and silver as coins to go beyond barter and establish retail trade. This principle quickly spread to the West and soon replaced the less efficient systems of exchange that already existed around the world (Jones and Shaw 2002). It became clear quite early on that a civilization founded on retail trade could represent a threat to the social order and disrupt social relations:

in the fourth century BCE, Socratic philosophers expressed their worry as to the social impact of that system, in what Shaw (1995) argues was the earliest example of 'macromarketing thought'. Shaw explains that Plato, in particular, articulated a very elaborate understanding of why (marketing) intermediaries emerge in societies that aim to satisfy human needs through division of labour and market exchange.

Plato's views on these middlemen have been interpreted differently by different authors: while Cassels (1936: 130) understands Plato's position as benevolent towards these 'persons of excessive physical weakness who are of no use in other kinds of labor' (which he quotes from Plato's *Republic*) and opposes it to Aristotle's view of them as 'useless profiteering parasites', others (Kelley 1956; Steiner 1976) see Plato and Aristotle as equally hostile. What these authors nonetheless would probably agree on is that 'the great central problem of marketing, the problem of carrying through efficiently from the social point of view this final stage in the general production process, has remained essentially the same since it was so intelligently discussed by Plato twenty-three hundred years ago' (Cassels 1936: 129). We do not necessarily agree with this argument that marketing contributes to 'the social good'. Despite the fact the marketing is claimed by its advocators to be an empiricist and a positivistic discipline (Hunt 1976, 1983), marketing scholars have never really proven that there is a connection between marketing and 'the social good' (whatever that may be). Accordingly, we see the claim that marketing is able to produce 'the social good' as a rhetorical strategy that seems inconsistent with marketing's (alleged) positivistic core but that has nevertheless been used by marketing writers over the years to legitimize the existence and development of marketing. As we will try to show, not only is marketing discourse full of such internal inconstencies and logical contradictions (Hackley 2003), but it can also be seen as causing a number of social problems – rather than creating 'the social good' as its supporters usually claim.

A bias against marketing?

On the basis of their reviews of literature about trade from antiquity to more recent periods, both Kelley (1956) and Steiner (1976) contend that throughout history, functions that we would today associate with marketing have been considered immoral and of low social status. They root this idea of 'the prejudice against marketing' (Steiner 1976) in Plato's initial understanding of trade, which ascribes the role of trade intermediaries to those who are physically weakest. But what they fail to see, according to Jones and Shaw (2002), is that the choice of these types of people for these types of roles stems from the will to organize division of labour rationally, and not from a supposed bias against marketing functions. If anything, in Jones and Shaw's view, it is rather Kelley and Steiner who can be seen as biased in their selection of relevant literature: they deliberately exclusively focused their inquiry on views that were unfavourable towards trade and held that all value comes from the land. Where the bias lies is not for us to determine in this book; however, there is no denying that in many European societies in the past, trade was often not considered to be a noble practice – a practice that nobles, as rulers in society, would never indulge in. To us, the way that some marketing scholars try to relativize this fact probably serves as an attempt to underline the social value of marketing in order to further legitimize its existence and development in today's world.

In order to refute this idea of bias, and as a direct reply to Steiner (1976), Dixon (1979; referred to by Jones and Shaw 2002) shows how thinkers in all time periods have offered rational arguments for their discussions about trade issues, and how many of them have tried to display a balanced understanding of marketing, addressing both costs and benefits to society. He points out, in particular, that the marketer's beneficial social contribution was acknowledged not only by ancient Greek thinkers but also by church writers throughout the Middle Ages. There were, admittedly, concerns with potentially 'sinful' trade practices, but these more or less coincided with those that have also been condemned by law until today, and it was always 'clearly recognized that the fault lay in the man, not the activity' (Jones and Shaw 2002: 43–4). It is thus quite clear that, by the end of the nineteenth century, there had already been a rich body of literature discussing the impact of marketing practices on society in elaborate ways for a very long time. However, the substance of marketing – for example, what marketing is, how it is carried out, how it should be related to other functions in organizations and its strategic role – was still poorly articulated: nodal points that could structure articulations of its elements into moments were lacking. In the field of discursivity, signs signifying marketing practices and activities existed but the meaning of these signs was ambiguous. In order for a marketing discourse to be developed, the flow of meanings of the language of marketing had to be arrested and new signs needed to be developed. In short, closure was needed. The academics who first attempted to bring about this needed structuring of marketing as an object of study, starting to devote attention to marketing issues in the late nineteenth and early twentieth century, were mostly economists from the German historical school and the American institutional school.

The German Historical school and the American Institutional school

According to Bartels (1962: 13), the early marketing scholars (in the early twentieth century) had their roots in economics. Their initial articulations of marketing discourse were thus typically influenced by the ideas of classical economists such as Adam Smith, David Ricardo and John Stuart Mill, the neoclassical works of Alfred Marshall, and other developments by the Austrian 'marginalists' and some more modern economists. These early inspirations for marketing thought are confirmed by Dixon who identifies much impact on marketing coming from Marshall's *Principles of Economics* and from the contributions of Austrian economists Carl Menger, Böhm-Bawerk and Friedrich von Wieser who placed 'the individual decision-making process at the centre of economic theory' (Dixon 1999: 115). It is thus safe to say that since its genesis, the marketing discipline was framed by the rationality of liberal economics. We argue that this was important for the future formation of marketing discourse. Marketing would certainly have been articulated very differently if the works of Karl Marx, for instance, had had a major influence on academic marketing in its early formative period. However, while it is undeniable that economics determined to a large extent how these early scholars conceived of 'the market, value, production, government and business, the consumer, the role of business, the nature of man, social philosophy, and the state of the economy' (Bartels 1962: 13), it should be pointed out that their marketing work also signified something of a departure from mainstream theoretical economics. The idiosyncracy of early marketing thought can be explained by the important influence of a less known economic school, the German Historical school of economics.

Why were marketing scholars so influenced by this school? Jones and Monieson (1990) have investigated this issue and explain that during the nineteenth century it was common for American students to study in Germany where the universities were more practice-oriented professional schools with more academic freedom than in the United States and with more equality between students and faculty. The Historical School of economics became significant in the latter part of the nineteenth century and was positioned as a problematization of mainstream economic thought, which was deemed unable to address concerns raised by the spectacular economic growth that Germany was experiencing at the time. These concerns included 'poverty, industrial development, and development of a banking system' (Hildebrand 1848, quoted by Jones and Monieson 1990: 103). As a result, this German school of economic thought distinguished itself from classical economic theory through its use of historical methods, its pragmatic purpose and its idealistic foundations (see Herbst 1965). It was also a stream of economics that was clearly connected to the German tradition of social sciences, which was most influential at the time (Cochoy 1999).

In the 1870s, many German-trained economists came back to the United States and were hired by prestigious universities such as Columbia, Pennsylvania, Harvard, Johns Hopkins, Wisconsin and Michigan (Jones and Monieson 1990; Morgan 2003). These economists, led by Richard Ely, later founded the American Economic Association (AEA), which was to become extremely important in the development of the marketing discipline (see Bussière 2000). Ely, who became the head of the new School of Economics at Wisconsin, developed a view of economics inspired by his German training with as a central idea the need to combine 'book knowledge and practical experience' (Jones and Monieson 1990: 104). With his former students (especially John Commons) and other German-trained economists, he developed the Institutional school of economics (and later marketing) which can be seen as an 'American offspring' of the German school (Jones and Shaw 2002: 45). The influence of the German school on this early articulation of marketing meant that the initial focus, as understood by marketing historians, was on historical and descriptive topics (Jones and Monieson 1990) and 'the collection of marketing facts rather than the development of marketing theory' (Jones and Shaw 2002: 45).

The importance of American Institutional economists in the development of the marketing discipline is still very much visible in today's marketing. The four utilities concept, distinguishing between four different types of labour which all were understood to bring economic value in different ways (elemental, form, time and place), was imported by institutional economists such as Ely from the Physiocrats (Shaw 1994), one of the first economic schools of thought born in France in the eighteenth century. It was used by Ely and his students 'because it served to distinguish marketing from production, and at the same time demonstrated that marketing activities created value' (Jones and Shaw 2002: 46). While the four utilities concept has since then been dismissed in economics, it is clear that it has been very influential for the governmental rationality of marketing management, especially in relation to the conceptualization of the four Ps (Borden 1964; Shaw 1994; on the four Ps, see Chapter 6).

Birth of a discipline

When was marketing born as a discipline? There is no full consensus on that issue, but it is clear that by the 1910s there were elements of an institutional marketing discipline, and by the 1920s this discipline had already become significant in academia. The works of Robert Bartels (1962, 1976, 1988) on the development of marketing thought are particularly insightful in describing the early evolution of marketing discourse.

Early context, early articulations

According to Bartels (1962), the term 'marketing' came to be associated with an academic discipline in 1910, but there were books that can be considered as dealing with general marketing before, such as Crowell's (1901) *Report of the Industrial Commission on the Distribution of Farm Products*. Other authors see the emergence of marketing literature even before that, and Bussière argues that scholars such as Kinley (1894) and Hammond (1897) – the first to use the term 'marketing' 'in a manner consistent with current use' (Bussière 2000: 139) – introduced clear marketing contributions before 1900, within the framework of the American Economic Association. As for the geographical birthplace of marketing, while Bartels (1962) clearly sees marketing thought as having first emerged in the United States, as mentioned previously much of this early thought was strongly influenced by German scholars, and there is 'evidence that marketing courses were offered in Germany before those offered in American institutions' (Jones and Shaw 2002: 47). Now, there is no denying that the United States soon became an archetype of market economy in which marketing took on a much more important role than elsewhere (Cochoy 1999), and thus it can be safely argued that the most significant developments in early marketing thought took place in the United States.

As a result, Bartels's (1962) (and most other marketing historians') works overwhelmingly focus on American marketing practices and concurrent academic evolutions. With the notable exception of Harvard, all the main universities from which marketing thought emerged in the United States were from the Middle West: most significantly, Wisconsin, Ohio State, Illinois, Minnesota, and Northwestern (Bartels 1976). This can be explained by the fact that the first commercialization problems that were felt at the time had to do with the challenges with the concentration of population in urban centres and the specialization of rural zones in agricultural production (Cochoy 1999). Hence, the first economic domain that interested marketing was agriculture, and the first major marketing work was probably the above mentioned *Report of the Industrial Commission on the Distribution of Farm Products* (Crowell 1901), which included a detailed description of the supply chain of agricultural goods from producer to consumer (Bartels 1976). From this early focus on agriculture, marketing was to evolve (and governmentalize) much as the society it was born into, since the principal focus soon switched to industrial goods – and as we will see in Chapter 7, the discipline was much affected by a focus on services later on.

If we are to believe accounts provided by marketing historians, in these early days, the practice of marketing in companies tended to precede the rather descriptive developments in academia. At the time, when marketing was associated with 'science' and 'knowledge', it allegedly was not so much in connection to academic advances, but rather a matter of how certain marketing functions started defining themselves. In our understanding, however, marketing scholars played an important role in defining the relationship between different types of 'practical' knowledge and started to articulate and fixate the meanings of these different types in texts, which is a crucial step for turning a general language about something into a coherent discourse. In this way, 'practical' knowledge was objectified within the marketing discipline as academic knowledge and transferred to new generations of marketing practitioners who in turn presumably got to better understand marketing as a whole. In addition to academic marketing, research units dealing with market research within corporate marketing departments appeared around 1910 in companies such as Nabisco, General Electric and Kellogg, and they also contributed to articulate and formalize marketing practices (Cochoy 1999). The practice of market surveys, for example, was introduced in the industry as early as the 1910s (Strasser 1989), well before marketing became significant as an academic discipline – in the 1920s according to Bartels (1962). Earnest Calkins, one of the first advertising professionals, talked of his trade as a science, concerned with 'facts' and objective certainties (Strasser 1989). The claim that advertising was concerned with facts also meant that what was said in promotional material was supposed to inform the general public about issues of common interest: Colgate informed about dental hygiene, and advertisements by Gillette or Kodak were particularly didactic in showing how the products should and could be used (Cochoy 1999).

Even though the substance of these advertising practices was presented as informed by neutral and objective knowledge, this knowledge was used instrumentally in order to create needs for the respective products of these brands (Cochoy 2002). Educating humans, in this case consumers, is one way of governing them (Rose 1999). Teaching consumers how a safety razor could and should be used is complemented by the demonstration that shaving with that particular razor is desirable, and this naturally lowers the threshold for consumers to actually start to use it. It remains that there was an underlying argument that it was part of marketing's mission to be for the social good, and that this argument was transferred to early articulations of academic marketing, in which one of the claimed objectives was to 'clarify misconceptions held among the public' (Bartels 1962: 39). This argument is not as unproblematic and value-free as it seems. From our standpoint it can rather be interpreted as an instance of government. For defining what a misconception is in the first place a particular ethic is invoked rather than a neutral 'scientific truth'. The guise of neutrality found in the alleged purpose to 'clarify misconceptions' can be seen as a way to neutralize potential critiques seeing advertising as chiefly concerned with creating new needs, and thereby as a way to further the power/knowledge of advertising and marketing.

Advertising was clearly the aspect of marketing that gave rise to the biggest number of works early on (Bartels 1976), and this early literature was characterized by a strong focus on psychological factors – even though not to such an elaborate extent as was later to be developed at the Tavistock Institute of Human Relations (see Chapter 2 and the discussion of Miller and Rose 1997). But soon the approach to advertising became much broader, and the interdisciplinary book *Advertising: Its Principles and Practices* (Tipper et al. 1915), for instance, integrated 'economic, psychological, technical and artistic' considerations in the 'scientific' study of advertising (Bartels 1976: 37). In the 1920s, the structure of advertising thought was developed by a number of seminal authors such as Otto Kleppner, George Hotchkiss and Daniel Starch. In parallel with these authors developing theory and case-based study, more critical analyses of advertising practice and its economic and social impacts also were written – most notably by Floyd Vaughan and Roland Vaile – as there were accusations of 'deceptions and exaggerations cited in the Consumer Movement' (Bartels 1976: 43). Advertising as a object of study was relevant not only to academics and practitioners, but also very much to the general public, and in that sense it was a very distinctive aspect of marketing thought, not always directly connected to the development of general marketing thought within academia.

Bartels's decades

Bartels (1962: 158) divides marketing's early history into six decades: 'the period of discovery' (1900–10), 'the period of conceptualization' (1910–20), 'the period of integration' (1920–30), 'the period of development' (1930–40), 'the period of reappraisal' (1940–50) and 'the period of reconception' (1950–60). This periodization in decades seems a bit arbitrary and can be understood, like all periodizations (including our own), as rhetorical devices. It has also been criticized for causing confusion because each of the decades lasts eleven years instead of ten (Jones and Shaw 2002). However, one has to acknowledge that this ground-breaking work not only has been invaluable for marketing historians, but also problematizes approaches to the development of marketing in a highly insightful way. In discourse theory terms, we understand from the labelling of each period above (and from a closer reading of Bartels's discussions of them):

- that the initial twenty years of development (1900–20) were mostly devoted to isolated articulations of marketing from (mainly three) different perspectives;

- that the discipline integrated and developed during the next twenty years (1920–40), giving rise to different articulations of general marketing discourse competing for hegemony, seeking to turn elements into moments;
- that the next twenty years problematized marketing discourse, paving the way for marketing management (see Chapter 5).

Three competing approaches, one integration trend

By the 1920s three main perspectives had established themselves as the main approaches to marketing thought: the commodity approach, the functional approach and the institutional approach (Bartels 1962; Cochoy 1999; Jones and Shaw 2002; Sheth et al. 1988). Among marketing scholars it is widely agreed that these three schools were largely descriptive and non-managerial. In the first part of this section we will oppose this position by arguing that and showing how they can be perceived as forms of disciplinary power. We will also argue that in parallel with a movement of institutional consolidation of each of these schools of thought, there was a process of integration between them in order to construct marketing as a unified academic discipline.

The disciplinary power of the three traditional schools

The commodity school, focusing on goods, has had its origins traced to Charles Parlin's classification published in a *Department Store Report* from 1912, and has been largely developed by Melvin Copeland in the 1920s and Leo Aspinwall in the 1950s (Sheth et al. 1988). The objective of this approach was from the outset to develop a comprehensive classification system for commodities, with a broad inspiration coming from more established sciences such as biology (Rhoades 1927). It was believed that developing such a system would allow marketing to be recognized as a 'real' science. But another important concern lay in the need to be relevant to practitioners. It was thus crucial to systematically demonstrate that commodities could be grouped together into 'relatively homogeneous categor[ies] in which the same marketing procedures and techniques could be utilized for all products', with the eventual aim (or dream) of designing a 'grand "marketing cookbook"' (Sheth et al. 1988: 36). Among the many classification schemes that were developed in the early years of the commodity school, Copeland's (1923) was the most influential. It divided consumer goods into three categories: convenience goods, shopping goods and specialty goods.

The functional school, studying and classifying marketing activities, has been considered to originate with Arch Shaw's (1912) article 'Some problems in market distribution', and to include as important contributors scholars such as Louis Weld, H.B. Vanderblue, Franklin Ryan, Earl Fullbrook and Edmund McGarry (Sheth et al. 1988). It was extremely popular within marketing between 1920 and 1950, even more so than the commodity school. Like the latter, the functional approach ambitioned to gain legitimacy within both academia and the 'real world' of practitioners. As Sheth et al. (1988: 53) put it, while the commodity school was interested in the 'what' of marketing, the functional school focused on the 'how' question: 'the activities needed to execute marketing transactions'. Weld's (1917) classification of functions was arguably the most influential in the early period, describing the six functions of assembling, storing, assumption of risks, rearrangement, selling and transportation. The ultimate elaboration within this school was made by McGarry (1950), who improved earlier classifications by introducing the contractual, merchandising, pricing, propaganda, physical distribution and termination functions. In so doing he seemingly contributed to the death of the functional approach, which unlike the commodity approach is considered to be fully extinct today (Hunt and Goolsby 1988).

The institutional school, mainly concerned with describing and classifying the various organizations involved in marketing, is understood to have emerged with Louis Weld's (1916) book *The Marketing of Farm Products*. Many authors have significantly contributed to its development until the early 1970s: Ralph Starr Butler, Ralph Breyer, Paul Converse, Edward Duddy, Harvey Huegy, David Revzan, and more recently, scholars associated with the marketing management period such as Wroe Alderson (also associated with the functional school, and, as will be discussed extensively later, the marketing management period) and Bert McCammon. This approach developed in the 1910s as a result of consumer perceptions that the markets were being distorted by the powerful institutions that had most market power. Critical accounts of the period (Morgan 2003) suggest that oligopolistic business actors were doing everything to set prices and eliminate competition, with the help of a corrupt political class. While it seems that the institutional school initially emerged as an academic perspective in order to explicate and criticize how these few actors could shape the market according to their will, its focus soon turned to legitimizing the high prices that consumers were paying at retail stores as a result of moving to the fast-developing urban areas: the explanation, institutional marketers said, lay in the more elaborate marketing channels needed to organize the supply of these growing cities. What had initially promised to be a rather critical approach within marketing became another powerful justification for the existence and importance of the discipline. Thus, explicating – and thereby legitimizing – the role of middlemen in the economy was what pioneering authors such as Weld (1916) and Starr Butler (1923) mostly concentrated on, and many institutional authors writing in the 1930s and 1940s saw it as part of their mission to explain the need for a growing number of marketing people and institutions. With time, increasingly complex and dynamic articulations of the place of marketing in the economic order were developed in institutional works, and Sheth et al. (1988: 81) argue that the institutional perspective cannot be considered as having disappeared altogether in the 1970s since it has been elaborated on by the more behavioural 'organizational dynamics' school.

We would argue that rather than being purely descriptive, which is the common understanding within the marketing academia, these three schools are expressions of forms of power/knowledge and more particularly disciplinary power. In Chapter

3 we explained that power/knowledge controls people through framing and ordering reality in particular ways (see Edenius and Hasselbladh 2002 and Foucault 1970, 1972, 1977). The three early schools do this through classification: of marketing functions, commodities and organizations. Based on the work of Foucault, particularly *The Order of Things* (1970), Townley (1994: 30) argues that 'classification and tabulation operate through the process of comparison. Generally there are two systems of comparison: the creation of an order through a taxonomy, a sequence of descriptive language (taxinomia); or the establishment of an order through measurement (mathesis)'. The classification schemata developed by the three schools, such as Copeland's (1923) distinction between convenience goods, shopping goods and specialty goods or McGarry's (1950) distinction between six marketing functions – contractual, merchandising, pricing, propaganda, physical distribution and termination – are examples of taxonomies. Taxonomies can be seen as 'disciplinary technologies – at once both a technique of power and a producer of knowledge – which provide an order that simultaneously circumscribes a whole, and specifies its component parts' (Townley 1994: 31–2). The taxonomies offered by the three early schools framed reality but were also mechanisms for gaining knowledge about this reality. Let us exemplify this with Copeland's (1923) simple distinction between convenience goods, shopping goods and specialty goods. This taxonomy informs us that there are three types of goods that should be marketed in different ways. It thus aims to frame our thinking about goods and how to market them. But it is also an instrument for gaining knowledge. When we see a commodity, a car for example, it suggests that we should ask ourselves: is this a convenience, shopping or specialty good? If we, for instance, decide that it is a specialty good, then we also have informed ourselves and thus gained knowledge about what it 'really' is. As Townley (1994: 32) argues 'taxinomia . . . facilitate[s] management or governance. [It] provide[s] for the arrangement of identities and differences into ordered tables and create[s] a grid, a configuration of knowledge, which may be placed over a domain'. Let us now imagine that we are in the car manufacturing business and that we have concluded, based on the work of Copeland, that we are producing specialty goods. Then Copeland's taxonomy and the associated suggestions on how to market different goods provide possibilities for us to market our car.

In this way we can claim that the three early schools of marketing can be seen as forms of disciplinary power: the descriptions of organizations they prescribe frame managers' worldviews and foster certain norms regarding marketing. By comparing these norms with actual behaviour, gaps between actuality and potentiality, that is, between how marketing is managed and how it should be managed, are revealed. Disciplinary power is played out exactly through revealing and recommending closure of such gaps (see Foucault 1977; Townley 1994). We can accordingly claim that the three early schools are forms of power/knowledge that attempt to order and attempt at governing the world in particular ways. Then of course we cannot say anything about whether the reality really was ordered this way or not since we study text and not actual practices of marketing. But, as opposed to the common understanding of the commodity, the functional and the institutional schools, we can claim that they were managerial.

What remains true is that, unlike what later came to dominate managerial marketing articulations, the three early schools did not explicitly articulate a notion of customer-oriented managerialism. Accordingly they did not provide any detailed discursive practices and technologies for establishing customer needs and demands as the point of reference for the design and development of organizations in general and for the product and services they offer to the market in particular.

No closure yet

Another important feature of the three early schools is that they largely developed in parallel, and could not really be considered articulations of marketing as a whole but rather isolated articulations of different parts of the problem. It can be argued that none of the three schools really had the potential to become hegemonic within the emerging marketing discourse, since none of them were able to arrest the flow of meanings. Within the commodity school, the main terms of the most established classifications still lack clear definitions today, despite permanent elaborations. In addition, the relationships between the elements of the commodity approach are specified in a way that is '*contingent* upon the diversity and individual differences among consumers' (Sheth et al. 1988: 48, emphasis in original) as well as 'the possible change in any consumer's behaviour over time' (Sheth et al. 1988: 49). In short, the understanding of the classifications invites such flexibility of interpretation that, depending on how different consumers define them, products can be classified in any of the categories. This makes it difficult to fix these classification systems as established moments serving as foundations for a solid articulation of marketing. The functional school suffered from similar shortcomings. It was particularly 'weak on forming a nomological network among the concepts' and did not go 'beyond the listing and categorization of functions' (Sheth et al. 1988: 57). Besides, there was no real attempt to understand the interdependence between the different functions, whose impacts were assessed in isolation of one another. In discourse theory terms, it can be argued that the functional school's classifications of functions merely consisted of 'elements'; in the mid-1930s, as many as fifty-two different functions had already been identified by many different authors, as shown by Ryan (1935). Some of these elements (as developed by McGarry in 1950) were later to be borrowed and turned into moments by McCarthy (1960), with the popularization of the four Ps of marketing. While the institutional school was undeniably better structured and specified than the other two traditional schools, it also had fatal shortcomings. The most significant reason for its inability to become a credible articulation of marketing as a whole probably lay in its lack of interest in some of the most important marketing issues that emerged within marketing, such as 'market satisfaction, product innovation, and conflict and power issues among the channels of distribution' (Sheth et al. 1988: 84). Considering how the institutional approach initially was born out of dissatisfaction of consumers with high retail prices, it is surprising that the school failed to develop much articulation of these issues, and question power in marketing channels in particular.

Another reason why the three traditional schools failed to be convincing as articulations of marketing as a whole is that in all three schools, the consumer/customer, while a central reference point, was conceptualized as rather passive. One important reason behind this was that the inspiration for the three approaches was chiefly based on economic principles and took very little consideration of organizational, social and psychological variables. The institutional school was the only one of the three that was inherently interactive, acknowledging 'the interdependent relationships between the sellers and the buyers' (Sheth et al. 1988: 73), and was thus less biased towards suppliers than the commodity and functional schools. But it lacked a behavioural dimension – which was later provided by the 'organizational dynamics' school. All three schools definitely contained a managerial element, but it was weakly elaborated and did not seem to be the main focus in these different articulations.

The way the three schools developed has to do with how people with different training and experience were each bringing what they could to the study of marketing as a hitherto unexplored territory (Grether 1988). Quite soon, however, the one school that was most clearly leading to generalization, the functional school, contributed to an integration of the approaches (Cochoy 1999). In his *Principles of Marketing*, Frederick Clark (1922) broadened the discussion on the general functions of marketing, borrowing from authors representing the different approaches and combining their insights into one of the first coherent general descriptions of marketing (Bartels 1962; Cochoy 1999) – although it can be claimed that Louis Weld (1916) had also used insights from the other two schools while introducing the institutional approach in his seminal work on farm products. Thereby there was a passage from an 'era of isolated pioneers' to 'a discipline about to be organized' (Cochoy 1999: 102). The functional school played an important part in this integration process and it can be argued that it had the advantage over the other two between 1920 and 1940 (Hunt and Goolsby 1988) when the three main articulations (commodity, functional and institutional approaches) were competing for hegemony within marketing discourse. But for the idea of a marketing discipline (and discourse) to make sense in the first place, there was a need for further institutional integration. The development of marketing into a discourse in Laclau and Mouffe's (1985) sense, requiring that there exist a structured and fixed relationship of meaning between the moments that constitute the discourse, needed the marketing discipline to become more institutionalized in American academia and society.

Institutional integration and the logic of attelage

In order to describe the integration process of the marketing discipline in the first half of the twentieth century, Cochoy (1999) introduces the notion of '*attelage*'. *Attelage* is a French noun that literally means 'harnessing', although it does not only refer to the process of harnessing but can also signify 'harness' itself or the result of harnessing, that is, 'carriage'. In typical post-Derridean French fashion, Cochoy plays with that polysemy as well as another derived meaning of the verb '*s'atteler à*' – which means 'to get down to' something. According to him, this double meaning provides insight into the integration processes through which the marketing discipline went. First, using the term *attelage* 'attracts the attention to the deeply individual roots of the processes at stake',[1] since before associating themselves, the pioneers of marketing thought 'first got down to their tasks' individually (Cochoy 1999: 118), often in fairly isolated ways, as pointed out earlier. Second, using that term emphasizes the 'eminently dynamic nature' of the integration, since the process of *attelage* can be seen as 'not only adopting a plural and solidarity-driven configuration, but also joining those who, before you, have already endeavoured to develop together, harnessing yourself to the convoy along the way'[2] (Cochoy 1999: 118).

By studying this logic of *attelage*, Cochoy not only concentrates on how marketing actors integrated together within academia, but he also examines how the pioneers of the marketing discipline were simultaneously 'harnessing themselves' to such driving forces as economic growth in the business world, Taylorist successes in the industry, the spectacular development of American universities, the implementation of business schools, the creation of associated degrees, and the rise in social status of the executive class. So the development of a marketing discipline through this logic of *attelage* was closely linked to a number of important societal changes; early marketing discourse in turn was characterized by an interdiscursivity (Fairclough 1995) involving articulations emerging in these different academic, business-related and broader societal processes – as will be shown later concerning the influence of scientific management on marketing, for instance. These *attelage* effects, however, were often local, implicit and sometimes counter-productive. For example, Cochoy (1999) argues, spreading to many universities and delivering many degrees was not only a good thing for the discipline, in that the contents of marketing knowledge and training initially varied considerably between places. What was needed in order to institutionalize the discipline further was a way to move from *attelage* – 'the free and local harnessing between some individuals' – to association – 'the formal gathering of the members of one community' (Cochoy 1999: 119).

The role of the American Marketing Association

The marketing discipline integrated from different groups. According to Agnew (1941), the very first meeting that was significant in this integration process took place at the annual convention of the Associated Advertising Clubs of the World, in 1915 in Chicago. It gathered twenty-eight teachers of advertising, invited by George Hotchkiss from New York University, and sought to address the questions of 'what constituted advertising and what should be included in a study of advertising' (Agnew 1941: 374). From then on, there were regular meetings and this group of advertising scholars kept growing each year. In parallel, Louis Weld was also instrumental in the early integration process of the marketing discipline. Two years after the publication of his breakthrough textbook (Weld 1916), he gathered some five or six scholars from different universities in the United States who were interested in marketing (among whom was Frederick Clark) for an informal dinner at a meeting of the American Economic Association in Richmond (Weld 1941). Starting from that event, a marketing interest group 'grew fairly rapidly, and was soon important enough to get a place on the Economic Association's program for round table discussions of marketing' (Weld 1941: 381). In 1923, this group attended the meeting of the National Association of Teachers of Advertising, which led to the founding of the National Association of Teachers of Marketing and Advertising (NATMA) (Agnew 1941). From then on, a newsletter called the *Natma-Graphs* was sent out to the members of the NATMA, sent by then secretary of the association Nat Barnes. In 1933, the NATMA was changed to NATM, since advertising came to be understood as included in general marketing. Two years later, the *Natma-Graphs* were transformed into a journal, the *National Marketing Review*. Meanwhile, Nat Barnes had also been instrumental in the setting up of a new organization, the American Marketing Society (AMS), in 1930, and its associated journal, the *American Marketing Journal*, first issued in 1934, that is, one year before the first volume of the *National Marketing Review* (Agnew 1941). These two journals were short lived since they were merged in 1936 into what became the *Journal of Marketing*, and soon afterwards came the birth of the American Marketing Association (AMA) in 1937, as a result of the merger between the NATM and the AMS.

It can be argued that it is with the formation of the AMA that marketing history as such started (Cochoy 1999). From that point, the discipline began growing exponentially: between 1937 and 1947, the amount of AMA members quadrupled from 584 to 2,300 (Applebaum 1947). The AMA is undeniably the reference point for when marketing clearly became one discipline rather than different isolated approaches: the AMA provided the institutional apparatus for defining marketing, developing its conventional language, giving visibility to the main developments within the discipline (through appropriate AMA publications and especially the *Journal of Marketing*) and distinguishing the participating actors (AMA members from both business and academia) (Cochoy 1999: 125). It was through the institutionalization made possible by the AMA that marketing discourse became powerful. The main articulations that already existed could thereby start competing for hegemony within general marketing discourse.

Instrumentalizing the Great Depression: marketing's managerialism in the 1930s

The Great Depression of the 1930s, disastrous as it was for business, represented a great opportunity for marketing to establish its centrality in getting the market economy back on track (Cochoy 1998, 1999; Fligstein 1990). Business people, greatly confused by such a never-seen-before crisis, were literally desperate to find new understandings of how it happened and, more importantly, creative suggestions for ways out. Hence, they were most receptive to new managerial articulations of market dynamics. This certainly helped the young, not-quite-yet-integrated marketing discipline, to define its new agenda, an agenda that was to be explicitly managerialistic, providing solutions to individual companies. This agenda was clearly announced, in light of the New Deal, in the foreword to the first issue of the *American Marketing Journal*, in 1934:

> 1) All of us realize that extremely important problems in business during the next decade or more will almost certainly fall in the field of marketing and distribution. 2) As this first issue goes to press, the National Recovery Administration and the Agricultural Adjustment Administration are making bold attempts to hasten the return to prosperity. 3) Whatever may be their ultimate success and accomplishment, they will certainly have made a lasting impression upon business thinking. 4) Under the descending spiral of the depression, business men have developed a frame of mind which makes them willing to accept leadership along lines which a few years ago they would not have been willing to consider. 5) The Administration assumes that steady employment and adequate wages are of first importance in providing a mass market for our mass production, and the nation is united in a great practical effort to put this conception into universal operation. 6) The results will be watched closely by marketing executives, who will give greater attention to data on wages and hours, as indices of sales possibilities . . . 7) The purpose of the *American Marketing Journal* is first of all to present worthwhile material which will be of interest to those in charge of marketing operations in business operations. 8) In other words, we hope to be one factor in helping to sell the results of true market research to management. 9) One of the troubles with much business research is that its practical results are seldom placed before management in such a way that they can be used in modifying the methods of buying and selling commodities.
>
> (Editors of the *American Marketing Journal* 1934,
> as quoted by Cochoy 1998: 206)

We can see that in the formulation of this agenda: a link is established between the economic problems and questions of marketing and distribution (1); marketing initiatives are positioned within the framework of national efforts for a return to prosperity (2), because these will undoubtedly affect business thought and practice in the future (3); this is a unique opportunity for the marketing discipline to extend its power/knowledge reach because businesspeople are desperate for new managerial initiatives (4); the driving force towards prosperity will clearly be consumption, and the whole nation, including business actors, will be committed to important efforts in order for people to be able to consume (5); this state-led process provides an interesting laboratory for marketing practice in order to evaluate sales possibilities (6); the role of the journal (i.e. academic marketing) will be to help marketing departments from business in taking advantage of these new sales possibilities (7) and establish marketing practices (especially market surveys) as central to management, thereby attempting to frame the managers' minds through the power/

knowledge of marketing (8), in a prescriptive way meant to be applicable to companies and affect business practices (9). This is very clearly a managerialistic project, demonstrating at once the importance of the discipline for local managerial practice and the global (or at the time 'national') relevance of such a marketing approach from the societal viewpoint, as it anticipates (and to some extent performatively contributes to) the developments towards a more extreme consumption society in which citizens/consumers are co-opted and become driving actors of the market economy (Baudrillard 1970). In this long citation we can clearly see an attempt at founding a unified power/knowledge of marketing as a managerial discipline.

Hence, the Great Depression, and the New Deal as a response to it, contributed to the development and integration of marketing, in that a clear and managerial agenda for the discipline could be formulated under these conditions of possibility. Some authors (especially Fullerton 1988: 122) see the switch from an 'era of origins' to an 'era of refinement and formalization' of marketing thought as occurring around 1930, and such a periodization can make sense to the extent that the institutional integration of marketing made a great deal of progress, as we have seen, during the 1930s. And unlike what most marketing historians usually claim regarding marketing before the Second World War, a clear and explicit managerialism characterizes the agenda formulated above. However, was such a managerialism entirely new in 1934? The shift that occurred in the mid-1930s seems to have been in terms of making the hitherto implicit managerialism of marketing explicit. This explicitness in the managerial argument can be seen as a problematization of previous approaches rather than as an indication of a 'paradigm shift' to come. Indeed, after further scrutiny, it seems that the managerialism of marketing in these early times, including prior to the 1930s, was always present (although not dominant), but has been consistently downplayed in retrospective historical studies describing the development of the discipline.

The strangely overlooked importance of scientific marketing management

This tendency to downplay the managerialistic dimension of marketing literature before the late 1940s is especially striking when it comes to the place of scientific marketing management in the reviews concerning early marketing thought. Jones and Shaw (2002: 55) acknowledge that 'it is surprising there hasn't been more historical study on the influence of Scientific Management'. In a sense, it seems to us that one of the reasons for this is the need for ratifying the argument that a 'paradigm shift' occurred around 1950 (as in Grönroos 2007; Vargo and Lusch 2004; Webster 1992), following an allegedly largely descriptive (i.e. non-managerial) early marketing thought almost exclusively characterized by works from the three traditional schools. We would argue that this argument underestimates the managerial significance of much early marketing research, as we will see below.

Early marketing thought at Harvard

The Harvard Graduate School of Business was founded in 1908, 'based on a vision of business as a profession, an art and a science' (Jones and Monieson 1990: 106). As in other universities that were influential early on in the development of marketing, the first marketing scholars at Harvard came from economics. Frank Taussig and Edwin Gay especially were major early thinkers of marketing based at Harvard. Like other academic marketing pioneers, both Taussig and Gay had studied in Germany and used the insights from the Historical school (see previous). While Taussig was more influenced by the neoclassical works of Alfred Marshall, Gay was most enthusiastic about the views of his German professor in Berlin, Gustav Schmoller, especially to the extent that they allowed for a 'belief that economics could be made into a real social science by being brought into close relation with psychology, ethics, history and political science' (Heaton 1949: 12). Being the Harvard Business School's first dean, Gay had to decide on what had to be taught as part of business education. He articulated his initial understanding of business activity as divided into 'two fundamental functions of industrial manage-ment [production] and commercial organization or marketing' (Gay 1908, quoted by Jones and Monieson 1990: 107). The industrial management side was to be taught with reference to what had acquired most 'scientific' legitimacy regarding production at the time, that is, Frederick Taylor's approach to scientific manage-ment. The course that addressed the marketing side was taught by Paul Cherington and was titled 'marketing' as early as 1914 (Jones and Monieson 1990: 108).

This course in marketing was made consistent with the Harvard Business School view of business as profession, art and science. In order to be able to address these three distinctive characteristics, Gay (1908, quoted by Jones and Monieson 1990: 108) advocated teaching not only 'the fundamental principles of business system' but also 'the art of applying them after investigation, to any given enterprise' through 'a laboratory-system of instruction'. It was thus clear to him from the onset that teaching marketing should not only be about describing commodities, functions and institutions, but also, and most importantly, about applying managerial prin-ciples to individual firms – so goodbye to the claim that all early marketing was characterized by a lack of prescriptive and firm-centred insights. The initial emphasis on a laboratory method for teaching and studying business led to the well-known trademark of the Harvard Business School, the case approach, rooted in the German background of Gay and others, and in particular their interest in historical study.

In parallel to this highly original (at least at the time) case-based teaching, Harvard's early marketing scholars were also quite distinctive in the problems they studied. Unlike the research being done in the Middle West and especially at Wisconsin, research at Harvard was interested in 'the problems faced by individual marketing managers', and, as Arch Shaw put it, the '"how to" of marketing' (Jones and Monieson 1990: 109). In order to study the latter, Shaw asked for help from Frederick Taylor himself, whom he invited to Harvard to give lectures in his course (Cochoy 1999; Jones 1997). So there was definitely a clear managerial dimension in the early marketing scholarship developed at Harvard.

The functional school and scientific management

Discussions of the three traditional schools by today's marketing scholars (see e.g. Vargo and Lusch 2004; Webster 1992) often present early research efforts in marketing as mainly descriptive, dealing with existing (i.e. there to be described) commodities, functions and institutions. While this view is valid to some extent, it does not follow that descriptive, neutral-looking knowledge is non-managerialistic, which it is often claimed to be. As we showed earlier, the substance of this research, such as the grids and typologies for classification of goods and marketing functions can be seen as examinations that objectify reality. As such these typologies have potential power/knowledge effects since they may frame the thinking of the subjects that use and believe in them. Furthermore, seeing the three schools as descriptive only is somewhat misleading. The functional school, especially, can be claimed to have been influenced by an explicit managerialism, that of scientific management. As discussed earlier, Arch Shaw is usually considered as having initiated the functional approach with his 1912 article 'Some problems in market distribution' (Sheth et al. 1988). In this article he tried to develop general principles about the functions of middlemen through a 'laboratory method in the form of a historical, statistical study of the role of merchants in the British economy' (Jones and Monieson 1990: 109). While the influence of scientific management thought on this article may not seem very obvious at first sight based on this brief description, the way Shaw has been inspired by Taylor and his followers (including his seminal research on problems in market distribution) has been underlined by many scholars (Jones 1997; Usui 2000).

In order to understand what was promoted in marketing works drawing on scientific management, we need to discuss Taylor's works at some length and examine what type of power they entail. Let us first recall the four principles, all addressing changes in the management function, that Taylor (1911) believed would make organizations more efficient. First, Taylor (p. 36) believed that the management should 'develop a science for each element of a man's work'. In order to develop 'scientific' knowledge about work, Taylor prescribed time and motion studies of actual work tasks. The use of the stopwatch to time work tasks was central to this practice. But it was also central to experiment with different ways of doing the particular job in order to find more efficient ways, which remained the main explicit aim of scientific management. Finding 'the one best way' often entailed doing the concrete practical shopfloor work (e.g. how to shovel coal, how to carry heavy pieces of iron, how many breaks to take, etc.) in many different ways. The outcome would be that the one best way would eventually be established, leaving no room for rules of thumb. The results of the time and motion studies – the most efficient ways for carrying out work – were then to be translated into formal rules aiming to govern work and the division of labour particularly. In order for this to really happen, Taylor (p. 36) prescribed his second and third management principles. The second principle held that management must 'scientifically select and then train, teach, and develop the workman' and not leave the training and teaching to the workmen themselves, which Taylor believed had been the case in the past. The third principle prescribed that the management should 'heartily cooperate with the men so as to insure all of the work being done in accordance with the principles of the science which has been developed'. Taylor then concluded in the fourth principle:

> There is an almost equal division of the work and the responsibility between the management and the workmen. The management take over all work for which they are better fitted than the workmen, while in the past almost all of the work and the greater part of the responsibility were thrown upon the men.
>
> (p. 37)

In their analysis of Taylorism, Clegg et al. (2006: 46, emphasis in original) argue that 'after Taylor, the individual workman need not exist merely as a creature of habit, tradition or craft but could become an *object* of scientific knowledge and a *subject* produced by the application of that knowledge'. What Clegg et al. imply is that scientific management is a form of disciplinary power. We agree and argue that Taylor's four principles of management illustrate this very well. The starting point for disciplinary power is that human beings are turned into objects of scientific study (Foucault 1977). This is also the starting point for Taylor's management principles; the first principle prescribing that management should 'develop a science for each element of a man's work'. Then the operation of disciplinary power is dependent on practices and technologies for gaining knowledge about reality. Foucault (1977) refers to the technologies of the self associated with disciplinary power as examinations. Through examinations the world can be known and studied objectively. As previously mentioned, the practice that Taylor prescribed for studying work scientifically was time and motion studies and the technologies such as denoting and coding and the use of the stopwatch associated with it. Yet examinations are not only used to study how things work, but are also used for establishing norms for how things ought to work. Such norms are established through experimenting by doing the human exercise studied in many different ways and then finding out the best way of carrying out a particular operation in relation to an overall norm such as efficiency. As we have seen, Taylorism prescribes that management should conduct such experiments in its quest for efficiency. The most efficient ways are then transformed into rules for how to do the work, that is, norms. When actuality and possibility have been established in this way, disciplinary power reveals gaps between the actual and the ideal – in the case of Taylorism between the current way and the ideal way of carrying out a particular work task. In order to close such gaps, humans have to be changed – this is how disciplinary power is exerted. Such changes might be achieved through applying means of government and management; for example, training and education (Rose 1999), as prescribed by Taylorism. For studying ideal ways of carrying out a particular task, such as a work operation, does not only generate norms but also gives ideas on how to carry out the work and so suggests how humans need to be trained and educated in order to change. Thus, by studying the most efficient ways for carrying out work, strategies for how to change the workforce so that they work more efficiently can be derived. This is why we agree with Clegg et al. (2006: 60) in their contention that 'F.W. Taylor . . . stands as a representative example of the forms of disciplinary power that shaped modern management'.

Shaw's (1951) early functional work, as published in 1915 in a book with the same title as his 1912 article, was described in an advertisement from the Harvard University Press as 'an attempt to do for distribution the work of standardization that Scientific Management has done for manufacture' (Jones 1997: 155). In the book, there are many discussions of how the principles of scientific management can help if implemented to address the problems of market distribution. According to Jones (1997), Shaw had already embraced the ideas of scientific management by 1900, when he founded a monthly magazine titled *System*: before his seminal contribution to marketing thought, he wrote several pieces, there or in other outlets, to advocate the application of scientific management in business in general and marketing in particular. Although marketing historians disagree as to the extent to which Shaw's project was an application of scientific management into marketing, there is consensus on the idea that Shaw's central notion of 'system' was very similar to scientific management in its demand for standardization and formalization (Usui 2000). In addition, while his functional work is not always considered to be managerial and positioned on the micro level of individual firms, some authors have pointed out that his thought as a whole (including his functional approach) 'can be evaluated as management oriented' (Hashimoto 1972, quoted by Usui 2000: 133), with a distinctively micro perspective (Mitsuzawa 1988, referred to by Usui 2000). It is clear that his repeated use of 'the machine metaphor' (commonly used in management thought; see Morgan, Ga 1980), which is a central and defining feature of his approach in his 1915 book, was meant to look for ways of improving marketing efficiency and not just to describe 'the motions of marketing' (Jones 1997: 153).

Hence, it appears to us that the functional school was more explicitly managerial than is usually admitted in broad retrospective studies of the evolution of marketing thought. This impression is confirmed by Sheth et al. (1988: 56), who point out that 'the four Ps of product, price, promotion and place are actually only derivatives from earlier classification systems presented by functional school theorists, such as Shaw, Weld, Ryan, and especially McGarry'. The functional school definitely was animated by scholars who had prescriptive objectives dealing with the 'how to' of marketing. Now, this is particularly important since this school is considered to have 'won' the early contest with the commodity and institutional schools, growing much faster than them between 1920 and 1940 and becoming much more applied by the end of the early marketing thought period (Hunt and Goolsby 1988). It seems as though some of the elements introduced by functional school scholars were about to become moments when the school, mature as it was, died and thus opened the way to a more modern approach that completed the transformation into moments through a new terminology (such as the four Ps), in the marketing management articulation of marketing discourse.

Charles Hoyt and scientific sales management

Not all the marketing works that were inspired by early scientific management were from the functional viewpoint. A number of the early marketing thinkers who imported ideas from Taylorism had an engineering background, and they brought their interest in efficiency and standardization into the emerging marketing discipline. The main domain of marketing practice that was identified as needing this systematic way of organizing was clearly sales management. And the pioneer of scientific sales management was Charles Hoyt, a Yale engineering graduate from 1894, who had spent more than fifteen years as a sales representative before becoming a consultant and deciding to use his sales experience and engineering training for writing a textbook on this topic, published in 1912. Hoyt admired Taylor a great deal, all the more so since his personal trajectory, with experience from basic practice early on, was similar to Taylor's (Cochoy 1999).

The starting point of Hoyt's discussion of scientific sales management was his contention that, at the time when he wrote his 1912 book (and its 1929 sequel), there were two kinds of sales managers: on the one hand, the 'old-fashioned sales manager', who 'believes absolutely in securing results through the sheer force and brute strength of his own personality' (1929[1912]: 10), and on the other hand, 'the sales manager who believes in method' (p. 11). Hoyt's description of the modern sales manager follows:

> One of the most successful sales managers of my acquaintance has often said that in selling, method is 80 per cent, and men or salesmen only 20 per cent. He does not mean by this that one need not have good men. He means that the methods under which these men are employed and directed are the most important factors. He believes in making a sales plan, or in sales planning, and then in working that plan. He has the same idea as the exponents of scientific management, such as was developed by Frederick W. Taylor. These men believe that most of the responsibility is up to the management, and not up to the men.
>
> (p. 11)

We would argue that the subject position of the 'old-fashioned' sales manager is an expression of sovereign power since 'he' (he is always referred to as a male in Hoyt's writings, and we will use the corresponding form for the sales manager – and the salesman – throughout our discussion of these works) supposedly secures results through his own 'sheer force' and 'brute strength' while the 'new' type of sales manager, believing in 'method' – that is, the scientific management method – is an expression of disciplinary power. It is possible to advance this argument if the two types of power are related to the two types of subject positions along a few central dimensions that differentiate sovereign power from disciplinary power. We think that this argument is valid also because this scientific management articulation can account for changes in the general structure of power in managerial marketing discourse at the time.

As discussed in Chapter 3, in the sovereign theory of power, power is in the hands of someone while disciplinary power is embedded in discourse. The statement about the 'old-fashioned' type of sales manager can be interpreted as though it is the sales manager who has power over the salesman as an effect of his position. It is also possible to argue that the subject position of the 'new' sales manager was articulated as relying on the power/knowledge embedded in scientific management in order to control the salesman. Furthermore, it can be argued that the 'new' sales manager was normalized by the power/knowledge of scientific management, since he valued the rationality of these types of control technologies.

A second distinction between sovereign power and disciplinary power is that the former is advocated upon issues of overt conflict and is accordingly dependent on its visibility in order to have effect but allows those over whom it is exercised to remain in the shades. The latter imposes a principle of compulsory visibility to those who are objectified by and subjected to it but is in itself invisible. Foucault makes this point very clearly in *Discipline and Punish*:

> It is the fact of being constantly seen, of being able always to be seen, that maintains the disciplined individual in his subjection. And the examination is the technique by which power . . . instead of imposing its mark on its subjects [as sovereign power do], holds them in a mechanism of objectification.
>
> (Foucault, 1977: 187)

The articulation of the subject position of the 'old fashioned' sales manager presupposes that there is an overt conflict between the manager and the salesman. By using his 'brute strength' and 'sheer force', the manager exerts a power that is very visible to each and everyone and this visibility is in fact the *raison d'être* for his use of power since force and strength must be visible in order to provide power. Through imposing his mark on the salesmen, the sales manager will be able to lead. The 'new' sales manager on the other hand uses his power through the application of technologies imported from scientific management. These are seldom made visible in themselves. In fact, the control technologies recommended to sales managers by scientific sales management – for example, concealed microphones and mystery shoppers (Canfield 1940) – were to a large degree defined by their invisibility. Furthermore the power of the disciplinary practices that were given, such as training, compensating and setting sales quotas are also invisible: they are never framed as forms of power.

The third and last distinction between sovereign and disciplinary power that we use to distinguish the two subject positions from each other has to do with the means and effects of power. Sovereign power makes people do things against their will: it is coercive. Disciplinary power operates through examinations embedded in discourse and subjectifies: it can coerce *and* empower. The defining feature of Hoyt's 'old' sales manager is that he relies on force in order to get the salesman to do what he wants. It is thus possible to see him as an expression of sovereign power. But why does he have to rely on force? The answer to this question we find in the view that Hoyt believes this type of manager to have of salesmen – and perhaps employees in general – as obstructing, opposing and battling the will of the manager (cf. Taylor 1911). Therefore, the sales manager has to use coercion in order to control them. On the other hand, the 'new' sales manager relies on the disciplinary power of scientific management. Its technologies do not only coerce but also empower. Attaining sales quotas for the salesman for instance might imply some form of coercion in the demand to work harder than the salesman would like. But it may also empower the salesman with prestige and bonuses. Furthermore, working hard may mean developing a 'selling attitude', which empowers the salesman in his professional role. But why does the 'new' sales manager rely on the examinations embedded in scientific management discourse rather than on coercion? Again, we must deduce the answer from the implicit view of the salesman that informs the subject position of the 'new' sales manager. This subject position posits salesmen not as explicitly obstructive but rather as idle, unenterprising and passive. By gathering information about the very details of the salesman's physical and mental expressions, it will be possible to control and direct him through detailed instructions – see the classic description of Schmidt in Taylor (1911). The objectification of the salesman that these technologies of control are designed to produce may eventually result in a salesman who is framed by and takes for granted the scientific discourse on selling, thereby behaving in accordance with it without noticing it.

Thus, Taylor's principles of scientific management were meant to be central in the articulation of the new approach to sales management. Hoyt pointed out that while the application of Taylor's ideas to manufacturing '[had] resulted in mass production, in greatly increased input per worker, in a lowering of the cost to manufacture', at the same time selling was still characterized by costs that '[seemed] constantly on the rise' and the fact that 'additional volume [was] secured, if at all, in small quantities and at an expense not warranted' (1929[1912]: 17). What was needed within sales management, he contended following Taylor's articulation of scientific management, was a 'complete mental revolution on the part of both workmen and management' (1929[1912]: 21). The goal was to do to salespeople what Taylorism had done to workers: first, placing them under the direct expert control of a specialized management unit, and second, internalizing their training (Cochoy 1999: 110). Salespeople were to be considered as an integral part of the company's personnel, that is, as much so as workers and other employees. This process was quite explicitly designed to have normalizing effects, not only in terms of integrating the salespeople as subjects to management but also in terms of standardizing their jobs, thereby affecting their subjectivities, in order to 'get above-average performance from average men by scientifically managing their productivity' (La Londe and Morrison 1967: 10). The idea of salespeople being 'average men' contrasted with many early approaches regarding selling as an art that as such cannot be taught and should be left to gifted individuals (e.g. Maxwell 1913).

For Hoyt, one way of 'selling' his scientific approach to business (and society) was to underline what a 'win–win' situation the implementation of Taylorist principles would entail: he claimed that 'the method should insure maximum advantage for all concerned', with the salesman earning maximum wage, the consumer spending less money, and the manufacturer and the distributor making 'a better profit for themselves' (Hoyt 1929[1912]: 32). Although the impact of scientific selling in general – and Hoyt's works in particular – on business practices is hard to evaluate since systematic empirical studies are lacking, it is interesting to note that the period when scientific selling was one of the dominant articulations within managerial marketing discourse, from the 1920s to the late 1940s, coincides rather perfectly with the time Fligstein (1990) argues that the 'sales and marketing conception of control' dominated the management of the largest US firms. Fligstein (1990: 10) defines conceptions of control as 'totalizing world views that cause actors to interpret every situation from a given perspective' – a definition not very far from how we perceive, with Foucault (1977), how discourses invested with power/knowledge operate on people's subjectivity. According to Fligstein (1990) the 'sales and marketing conception of control' not only made managers focus on finding, creating and keeping markets but also manage the sales and marketing function through using scientific management. That scientific selling and 'the sales and marketing conception of control' may 'coincide' in time and substance in this way is surely not purely coincidental. Rather, it can be argued that a similar managerial marketing discourse was represented in academic literature and shaped the practice of selling from the early 1920s at least up till the late 1940s (see also Friedman 2005 for a similar argument). Scientific selling thus certainly contributed to restructuring business organizations and to integrating salespeople more deeply into the workforce, thereby monitoring their actions more extensively and thus having stronger disciplinary effects on their subjectivities. However, Hoyt's was not the most complete application of scientific management to marketing: a more systematic approach was to be articulated, fifteen years after Hoyt's breakthrough textbook, by Percival White.

Percival White and scientific marketing management

In the early 1920s, Arch Shaw was among the marketing scholars who were keeping an application of scientific management to marketing on the discipline's development agenda, with 'a pamphlet entitled "Picking the 'One Best' Marketing Plan"' published in 1921 (La Londe and Morrison 1967: 11). Another notable work seeking to apply Taylor's insights to marketing was Cowan's 'example of scientific marketing procedure', which was published in the *Bulletin of the Taylor Society* in 1924, and which introduced the concept of 'market segmentation' (Cowan 1924, quoted by La Londe and Morrison 1967: 11) well before this concept became a moment within marketing discourse when it was 'reinvented' by Wendell Smith in 1956 (see Chapter 6). But it was Percival White who extended the scientific marketing management endeavour most significantly and developed a systematic project out of it. In 1924, together with Walter Hayward, he wrote that even though 'it is doubtful . . . whether marketing can be reduced to a routine so precise as that of production' as made possible by Taylor's scientific management, 'both production and marketing are most efficient when best coordinated' (White and Hayward 1924: 4, quoted by La Londe and Morrison 1967: 11), thereby laying out his project of a fully integrated scientific marketing management.

He went on to write his groundbreaking book titled *Scientific Marketing Management: Its Principles and Methods* which was published in 1927. This book is remarkable in many ways. After discussing 'the wastes in marketing' in the introduction, White formulated the rather prophetic argument of the book as follows:

> The thesis of this book is that the beginning and the end of all marketing problems is the consumer. The consuming public is therefore discussed at length, in order to make clear the broader situation in its broader aspects. How the requirements of the consuming public are catered to by business constitutes the other half of this problem, and this subject is treated in the second chapter of this section.
>
> (1927: 19)

White's objective was clearly to place the consumer at the center of all marketing problems. For example, White (p. 110) identified eight 'basic marketing functions', 'all of which were focused on service to the customer' (La Londe and Morrison 1967: 12). But beyond that, he also wanted to place marketing at the center of the organization, claiming in his introduction that 'marketing is primary and all production depends ultimately upon the demand of the market' (White 1927: 3). Admittedly, he rooted this centrality of marketing in insights from business practice of the time. Similarly to Hoyt's dichotomy of old-fashioned and new sales managers, he introduced a distinction between 'two types of Marketing Organization' (p. 59): the first, labelled – and dismissed as – 'the older type', corresponded to companies where products were developed only to the extent that they were 'closely related from a production standpoint'. The second, 'newer' type, on the other hand, '[was] characterized by the conscious attempt to build a line which shall meet the requirements of one market, regardless of whether the manufacturing equipment required for this purpose [was] available within the company's own factory' (p. 60). In this type, which White acknowledged was 'rarer' at the time, it is clear that, in a reversed relationship, manufacturing becomes subjugated to marketing, and, in White's (p. 60) own words, 'the manufacturer assumes a sort of jobbing function'. For this type of marketing organization to work properly, the initial efforts needed to be devoted to market research, which was presented as indicating 'the requirements of consumption, both actual and potential' and allowing the manufacturer to 'no longer torture his imagination or resort to his overworked guessing ability in order to devise new ways of tickling the consumer's fancy' (p. 17).

White's work, of course, was as much about describing this evolution as about promoting its advent: there was a performative dimension in his prophetic claims about marketing taking precedence over competing articulations of management. Going even further than Hoyt, he pointed out that the marketing practice that 'will bring success, in the largest and most enduring sense' is the 'most ethical' one, that is, that 'which is best for all concerned' (p. 98). He also transposed the Taylorist idea that scientific management unites employers and workers and makes their 'real interests' the same (Cochoy 1999: 115) to marketing, by claiming that:

The system depends upon a nicely balanced relationship between producer and consumer, whereby each party is benefited. Just as one of the basic aims of scientific management was to promote a better relationship between the company and the workman, so the primary objective of scientific marketing should be to promote a better relationship between the company and the consuming public.

The system of scientific marketing assumes that production exists in order to serve consumption . . . [It] is based on the theory of finding out what the consumer wants and then giving it to him . . .

Production exists in order to serve consumption, and for no other purpose. Man does not consume in order to produce; he produces in order that he may consume.

(White 1927: 99, emphasis in the original)

This citation clearly shows that a customer-driven governmental rationality was already made very explicit. In order to make it possible to implement his scientific principles of marketing management, White introduced a departmentalization of marketing activities corresponding to the division of marketing between different functions: market research, marketing planning, marketing training, selling, advertising, service, credits, marketing accounting, and a number of secondary marketing functions. By doing so he clearly drew on previous articulations of marketing from the functional approach. What White mostly tried to do was to formalize (in great functional detail) how all the departments were meant to be organized, and how they should be coordinated with one another. He did not invent entirely new managerial practices and technologies; rather, he described already existing practices and inscribed them within a fully integrated and coordinated system. For instance, he classified the existing market data collection practices according to three types of data – 'data for purposes of classifying markets and consumers', 'data for purposes of measurement', and 'data of market preferences' (p. 154) – but did not explicitly show how the advocated systematic analysis and interpretation of these data was to be used in market segmentation. His main concern was to design a system that would be optimally efficient, emulating within the organization the changes in market conditions. In typical Taylorist fashion, he wrote in many occasions of the need for the 'elimination of waste'. For example, he lamented the way that 'salesmen's territories' were typically organized in the United States according to state boundaries, and instead promoted 'a system based on careful analysis of the market, the methods of transportation, and the salesman's ability' (p. 176) in order to optimize each salesperson's territory.

Particular as White was about the details of a scientific management of marketing activities, his framework did not give birth to a broadly defined marketing subject. This is understandable since the system he proposed was based on scientific management, and in particular the central principle of division of labour: the 'objective knowledge' he developed entailed the subjectification of highly specialized professionals contributing to scientific marketing management, not subjects who would be considered 'marketers' in general. As a result, the marketing training he envisioned was meant to define extremely specialized roles, with as little over-lapping of duties as possible. In the example of salespeople's jobs, he put forward that it would be necessary for salespeople 'to unlearn many practices which are commonly taught' since the goal of the salesperson should not be 'to sell the most goods possible at a given moment, but to set up the satisfied customer as the objec-tive' (p. 183). Since labour was meant to be so specialized, the importance of thinking about the customer varied considerably across different job descriptions, and salespeople were those who were naturally meant to be most customer con-scious. The importance of demand was central throughout the organization, but in most departments – and for most executive roles – it was expressed in more macro, market-level ways. A notable exception was the service department, where 'a higher-principled relationship with customers' (p. 242) was meant to be developed.

It can be argued that by discarding the most common practices of the time as 'old' and presenting emerging phenomena as desirable for all parties, White attempted a kind of hegemonic intervention, not only coming from scientific management into marketing, but also from marketing into general management. This hegemonic intervention attempt was not very successful initially, and his work has seemingly been forgotten by many subsequent marketing scholars even though his approach was very modern and in many ways visionary of the future of marketing through his stress on 'marketing management' and the centrality of the consumer (and customer) to marketing and of marketing to the organization. Beyond his contribution to marketing, his prescriptive managerial discourse was also one of the first appearances of 'the visible hand of managers' (Cochoy 1999): the idea that markets are not only working according to the 'invisible hand' economic principle, but that they can also be managed. This entailed a strong subjectifying potential, although it is unclear whether White's writings alone were influential on the managerial practices of their time. Whether they had a strong performative influence or not is difficult to determine, but in hindsight this seminal book certainly looks almost prophetic. In that sense, it looks as though it was an important general contribution to the existing managerial disciplines. It also seems that this one book made it possible for ideas from scientific management to be applied throughout American capitalism, with the Taylorist technologies of control targeting all participants in the market economy, from the worker to the consumer (Cochoy 1999).

Announcing the triumph of managerialism

By the 1940s, the institutionalization of marketing as a science was completed, a process in which the American Marketing Association was central, as we have seen. This made it possible for Hugh Agnew to conclude his *Journal of Marketing* essay on the early history of the AMA in the following way:

> In the future, we may hope for a very high degree of perfection in the develop-ment of scientific procedure in research in which the American Marketing

Association will certainly lead . . . What we need most is to get some basic principles which shall be the guidance for marketing processes. We need an Adam Smith in marketing . . .

We have passed the place where we teach only what business does. We do not hesitate to criticize business where it is inefficient in method or uneconomic in purpose. Those members who are practitioners, with few exceptions, are no longer satisfied merely to get the answer the "boss" wants. Rather they have reached the position where, if their answer is the one the boss wants, they are dubious of their own accuracy.

(1941: 379)

Thus, it is clear that within mainstream academic marketing circles in the early 1940s, scholars were interested in having an impact on managerial practices and not merely in describing these.

No clear hegemony yet

We have questioned the tendency of certain marketing scholars (such as Keith 1960 and Levitt 1960) to retrospectively reinvent the discipline's past in order to make it possible to present a sort of teleological view of the development of marketing: as Marion (2006: 256) puts it, 'the past is "open" to interpretation' and is 'rewritten according to the new prescription – in other words, the error of the past *versus* the new and "real" marketing to be adopted'. However, this does not mean that there was already in the early 1940s an articulation of marketing as management that was widely accepted in academic marketing circles. To sum up where the marketing discipline stood at the end of the 1940s and beginning of the 1950s, we can put forward that:

- marketing was strongly institutionalized both in business, where marketing departments were the rule in important companies, and in academia (largely thanks to the American Marketing Association), where it was becoming possible to refer to it as a 'science';
- none of the early competing approaches to marketing had become hegemonic, mostly because of the inability of any of these three approaches to cover all issues relevant to marketing within it – however, the functional school had outgrown the other two schools quite clearly;
- concurrently to the growth of the functional school (and to some extent in connection to it), a managerial aim was becoming increasingly central to marketing scholars;
- how this managerial aim was to be fulfilled, however, remained to a large extent unclear – theoretical attempts to apply scientific management principles to marketing had probably been introduced in a too sudden and radical way, requiring too extreme changes in both the conceptualization of marketing in theory and the practice of marketing in business.

As a result, while it is clear to us that many of the retrospective analyses of the early marketing thought have greatly underestimated the managerial dimension that was present in those early times, it remains that marketing's managerialism was not yet articulated enough – that is, scattered elements of managerialism had not been turned into moments yet – and the power/knowledge of managerial marketing remained rather weakly elaborated. For instance, it has been argued that market segmentation and even the marketing concept were widely practised at the time and before then (Fullerton 1988; Hollander 1986) but these technologies had not yet been established in these terms in marketing theory – Shaw (1916) used the term 'market contours' instead of 'segments', and Cowan's (1924) use of 'segmentation' was not immediately caught up by marketing scholars – nor had these practices yet been made key moments of a comprehensive articulation of marketing. Therefore, even though managerialism, a microfocus on organizations and an interest in consumers and customers were very common at the time in both practice and academic theorizing, the governmentality of marketing discourse was not much affirmed yet in terms of influencing the subjectivities of all marketing professionals. If marketing was becoming a profession (Agnew 1941), all marketing practitioners were not affected by the academic discourse in the same way. The subfield of marketing that was most subject to the customer-driven governmental rationality of marketing in those times was undeniably selling.

Selling as the first target of marketing's managerialism and governmental rationality

The period between 1930 and 1950 has been referred to as the 'sales era' by some notable marketing authors (see Keith 1960; Kotler 1967; Levitt 1960). Sales practices at the time have been claimed to be hard-sell-oriented, with not much concern for customer wants. As a result, it has also been argued that 'true marketing' only appeared (seemingly out of nowhere) after 1950. It should be clear from the previous review that there is a great deal of contrary evidence to this thesis. As Fullerton (1988: 120) points out, while it is true that before the 1930s 'some of the sales manuals in use then emphasized dominating the buyer to the point of mesmerization', they were not particularly representing the dominant view, since other literature 'stressed a problem-solving, consultative approach and warned against the short-sightedness of the squeeze sell'. In a similar vein, Friedman (2005) shows, in his historical analysis of salesmanship in the United States (particularly focused on the latter part of the first half of the twentieth century), that caring for the relationship with the customer was central to selling in businesses characterized by repeat buying. During the Great Depression, it was soon understood that trying to understand buyers and their particular needs was crucial to companies and their salespeople. The notion of 'consumer engineering' was introduced then, putting consumer needs at the centre of the process of designing and selling products (Sheldon and Arens 1932, referred to by Fullerton 1988).

It remains that the first marketing function that was systematically affected by the interest in consumer needs and wants was selling. It is understandable since 1) in the company, salespeople were the persons who were in direct contact with customers, 2) their 'performances' were seen as more easily measurable, and 3) it had become possible to monitor them better since they had become employees of the company – as Hoyt (1912) had been suggesting early on. Hence, the emerging new governmental rationality, based on the satisfaction of consumer needs rather than the 'art of selling' or the 'selling personality' (Ivey 1925, summarized by Bartels 1962: 88), influenced sales(people) management a great deal well before 1950. The idea of division of labour, central to scientific management, explains why it was possible that such a strong governmental rationality affected so significantly one function of marketing while remaining more marginal within other functions. It is thus within selling that a customer-driven governmental rationality first became dominant – but, in the absence of an established signifier (such as 'customer orientation') that could crystallize this rationality as a nodal point, it was what we shall call merely an 'underlying signified', expressed through various articulations of a broad interest in the customer needs and wants.

The governmentality of early marketing thought as expressed in selling

So far we have been reviewing early marketing thought and analysing it by drawing on the language of discourse theory and a Foucauldian power/knowledge understanding. We will now move on to our more focused governmentality analysis of early marketing thought. Because of the fact that selling was the only marketing function that was clearly and systematically affected by the new 'customer-driven' governmental rationality before 1950, we will focus on articulations of selling and sales management. We will spell out the governmental implications of early discourse on selling by drawing on the analytical scheme that was outlined in Chapter 2. We are thus going to address the following four questions: 1) what is being governed; 2) how is government achieved; 3) who do we become and 4) why we are governed in this way.

What is being governed (ontology)?

As we have hinted earlier, by the 1940s the only subject position that had been clearly re-framed by marketing's emerging customer-driven governmental rationality was the selling function, since it was understood to be closest to the customer. Thus, the people who were subjected most to the notion of satisfying the customer's needs during the early days were sales staff. Even though there were isolated articulations of marketing management as the main strategic issue for the firm well before the first formulation of the marketing concept (most notably by White 1927), these remained marginal within the emerging marketing discipline and were seemingly forgotten or deliberately downplayed by many subsequent managerial marketing scholars. In addition, a strong differentiation in terms of interest in different aspects of the market between different marketing functions was legitimized by the principle of division of labour inherent in the scientific management inspiration of these isolated articulations, which made it possible to present selling as more interested in the customer than other functions.

The employees from the company dealing with sales were not only salespeople per se, but also sales managers. For instance, much of Hoyt's (1912, 1929) articulation on scientific sales management was targeted at changing the work of sales managers. As Hoyt put it himself, there were not only 'two kinds of salesmen' (1929[1912]: 3) but also two kinds of sales managers, an 'old-fashioned' one and one 'who believe[d] in method' (1929[1912]: 10–11). As a result, sales managers were also subject to the governmentality of early sales management discourse. Hoyt's work was also claimed to be targeted to all managers and executives in the firm (as put forward in the foreword by Barton 1929), but generally speaking, the new articulation of sales management that emerged in the first half of the twentieth century can be understood to have mostly influenced the works and subjectivities of salespeople and sales managers.

How is government achieved (ascetics)?

During the 1930s, previous, naïve sales philosophies – contending that aggressive salespeople would be successful – were strongly questioned by the marketing discipline. This questioning began as early on as the late 1910s when widely held notions – for example, holding that 'selling cannot be taught' – started to be challenged (Whitehead 1917). However, many training programmes and textbooks remained more concerned with salesmanship as being the persuading of the customer to accept the salesman's viewpoint and purchase the goods (see especially Ivey 1937). Scholars more clearly positioned within the marketing discipline took issue with the notion that selling lay in imposing the salesman's will upon the customer: Jones and Comyns (1918), for instance, held the view that selling should be viewed as a 'warm, man-to-man affair' and treated the salesman as an employee, 'a unit of the selling organization' (Bartels 1962: 88). At the core of the discussion about the nature of selling as fundamentally either a matter of persuasion or a more balanced man-to-man process wherein the whole organization is represented lay the contrasting views of salesmanship as an 'art' – that is, Douglas (1919: 4) writing about 'the methods of artistic persuasion' – and the 'scientific' conceptions of selling.

The first highly significant articulation of these scientific conceptions of selling and sales management was produced by Hoyt (1912, 1929), as discussed earlier. However, unlike White (1927) and his much farther-reaching conceptualization of scientific marketing management, Hoyt's views were far from isolated in the 1910s and 1920s. Hence, in the first issue of the *Bulletin of the Taylor Society*, H.W. Brown (1914) wrote about 'scientific management in the sales department' and 'proposed a system in which management routed the salesmen rather than allowing salesmen to route themselves' (La Londe and Morrison 1967: 10). Six years later, members of the Taylor society decided to arrange a meeting for selling executives because they felt that sales management was in need of re-organization; 105 executives met in New York on 25 June 1920 and discussed how to efficiently coordinate production and selling. During the debate, it was suggested that 'the planning of future projects [was] the job of sales engineering', while 'the planning of present projects [was] the job of production units' (Freeland 1920, quoted by Cochoy 1999: 107). Henry Dennison, who was present at the meeting, concluded his speech by stating that Taylorist principles can be applied within selling, especially regarding planning and sales quotas (Dennison 1920, referred to in La Londe and Morrison 1967). In the following years, the *Bulletin of the Taylor Society* featured many more articles on sales management – or rather, as it was more often referred to in that publication, sales engineering. Another important contribution within scientific sales management in the 1920s was Lyon's (1926) book *Salesmen in Marketing Strategy*, which, La Londe and Morrison (1967: 11) argue, can be seen as both an application of Taylorist principles to selling and an early articulation of something that looked a lot like what later came to be known as the marketing concept.

Thus, the scientific management perspective to selling progressively gained ground in the 1920s and became the dominant one in the 1930s when it was claimed that the economic crisis made it necessary to act in a more rational way (see Cochoy 1998). The introduction of notions and practices from scientific management into marketing discourse as early as during the early 1910s has especially contributed to the setting up of new and productive methods of dealing with sales jobs. These methods have entailed control technologies such as 'setting sales quotas, and . . . training, compensating, stimulating, supervising, and evaluating the performance of salesmen' (Bartels 1962: 204). A telling example of the new scientific approach to selling was Canfield's (1940) methods of studying and controlling the function of the salesman: 'he used concealed microphones, he had investigators posing as buyers, he recorded salesmen's traveling time, and he measured their foot travels with pedometers' (Bartels, 1962: 92). The marketing discipline's claim to scientific knowledge, which became significant during the 1930s, aimed not only to make salespeople perceive these new technologies of control and discursive practices as appropriate and contributing to the optimization of their work, but also to encourage managers and executives to accept more and more of the managerialistic marketing notions as legitimate and well suited to their work.

Who do we become (deontology)?

As stated earlier, during the first half of the twentieth century, marketing's emergence as a managerial discipline and a scientific field was mainly designed to affect salespeople. The new rational discourse on the optimization and control of selling performances – through 'training, compensating, stimulating, supervising and evaluating the performances' (cf. earlier) – aimed to make salespeople more accountable for their performances and thus more competitive, in the sense that it was understood as providing incentives for them to improve their productivity quantity-wise, become more inclined to compete with others, and seek to be better than them in understanding and caring for the customer.

According to Bartels (1962: 85), this led salespeople to become 'heroes of the business world', although one may wonder whether their lives were any the better for it. However, if we are to believe Bartels (1962), not only were they competitive, but there was also a sense that their selling of products was for the common good. Indeed, being a good salesman was no longer considered a matter of the 'ability to sell goods to people who did not need them'; on the contrary, it became a matter of the 'ability to sell goods at a profit for the mutual benefit of buyers and sellers' (Bartels 1962: 90). This was to a large extent rooted in Hoyt's (1929[1912]: 32) claim that introducing scientific management methods to selling and sales management 'should insure maximum advantage for all concerned'. At that time, marketing discourse envisioned 'customer-interested' salespeople, and since they were also becoming increasingly seen as employees who were well integrated into the organization, the idea of a general customer orientation for the organization was implicitly present.

Why are we governed in this way (teleology)?

The teleological implications of the 'newer' – as opposed to 'old-fashioned' in, for example, Hoyt's (1912, 1929) rhetorics – sales management articulations developed during early marketing thought are to be understood in terms of Hoyt's (1912, 1929) claim of maximum advantage for everyone: by using scientific and systematic methods for managing sales and salespeople, and thereby 'reducing the percentage of cost to sell', Hoyt (1929[1912]: 32) argued, the salesman would earn maximum wage, the consumer would spend less money, and the manufacturer and the distributor would make 'a better profit for themselves'. Hence, even though Hoyt's endeavour was chiefly about sales management, it not only expressed the ambition to improve the efficiency of the selling function, but also, more generally, claimed that through such an improvement, all the actors involved in the consumer society would be better off. There was a clear ethical dimension in this view of a more scientific sales management as beneficial to the whole of society, and, once all involved would come to believe that this was indeed a sound rationale, they would all be convinced of it being for the better good, and thus commit to working according to its guiding 'scientific' principles.

In order to reach such an aim, then, a 'scientific approach' needed to direct sales management, with the purpose of managing the sales department as efficiently as possible. This in turn was to be done by 1) monitoring salespeople more efficiently and thereby improving their performances, 2) assessing consumer and customer needs through valid methods of market research, and thus 3) training (or should we write governing) salespeople to be 'customer-interested' – that is, to use results of market research in their selling practice, and to not rely chiefly on 'selling skills' in order to persuade by 'petty means' but rather to try to find out what customers need before going about the sale itself. This is how a customer-driven governmental rationality came to characterize the dominant articulation of selling.

Whether early marketing scholars, sales managers and salespeople believed strongly in Hoyt's prophetic claim that the whole society would benefit from this new organization of selling is difficult to determine, but within the dominant academic discourse on sales management by the 1940s, it is clear that this ethos of being more efficient and customer-interested for the good of society was central. It is, however, important to deconstruct the clear ethical dimension put forward by Hoyt and White – the notion that the selling and marketing practice that would be most efficient and successful would by definition be the 'most ethical' one because it would be 'best for all concerned' (White 1927: 17) and that a scientific (read Taylorist) approach to selling and marketing would make the 'real interests' of both the company and the consuming public the same. We see two main ways in which this claim on behalf of the common good can be illuminated as displaying 'false consciousness' at best – and deliberate deception at worst.

First, the agenda exposed in the foreword of the first issue of the *American Marketing Journal* in 1934 (see p. 62) clearly was as much strategical as it was founded on a genuine attempt to find a way out of the Great Depression that would be best for all. If anything, it is not so much marketing which can be proven to have been the solution to the crisis as the crisis itself which was instrumentalized in order to legitimize the existence and enable the development of the marketing discipline. It was quite explicitly stated in that foreword that in the face of the Great Depression, a new 'frame of mind' made people 'willing to accept leadership along lines which a few years [earlier] they would not have been willing to consider' (Editors of the *American Marketing Journal* 1934, quoted by Cochoy 1998: 206). Taking advantage of this new 'frame of mind' open to new perspectives was what the editors of the *American Marketing Journal* attempted to do in order to obtain universal consensus on the idea that society should be seen as before all a 'mass market' and that marketing should be understood as the discipline most needed to make sure that such a mass market be made to work for the good of society as a whole.

Second, the emerging managerialism already – and increasingly explicitly – found in a number of works within marketing and selling meant that while the whole of society – that is, 'the consuming public' (cf. White 1927: 99) – was allegedly meant to benefit from the spreading of a managerial marketing perspective within all firms, those who would be taking care of implementing this great social progress were going to be (marketing and sales) managers, not benevolent philanthropes. It is relatively doubtful whether managers can generally be considered the actors who are in the best position to serve the common good since their first allegiance should go to the owners of their company and consequently their prime objective should be to maximize profits and share value. Now, it is fairly clear that in an exchange relationship, maximizing the profits of one particular actor tends to be done to some extent *at the expense* of the other party in the exchange, or at least that neither party in the exchange can increase its benefit without affecting the other party somewhat negatively. That is why we feel that making marketing a managerial discourse, and thereby placing it in the hands of managers in companies, cannot as such deliver the promised maximization of the benefit for the whole society.

6 Consolidating the power/ knowledge of managerial marketing

In the previous chapter we demonstrated that managerial articulations of marketing discourse were gradually gaining momentum from the early 1910s to the late 1940s. This is thought-provoking since the common view in mainstream marketing is that this early period of marketing thought was descriptive and anti-managerial (see e.g. Vargo and Lusch 2004; Webster 1992). Our analysis also revealed that the descriptive and alleged anti-managerial articulations of marketing discourse in fact could be analysed as forms of disciplinary power. Furthermore, based on an analysis of the discourse of scientific selling we argued that marketing discourse was changing from being founded in sovereign power to being based in power/knowledge, disciplinary power in particular. However, by drawing on discourse theory we argued that marketing thought was not yet articulated around a clear nodal point. Rather we claimed that several articulations were competing for hegemony, including some more managerial articulations.

The increasing importance of managerialism during the early period paved the way for a major turning point in marketing discourse around 1960 which will be focused on in this chapter. This was accomplished within the boundaries of *marketing management discourse*, particularly through the discursive practice of *the marketing concept*, its associated technologies and the governmental rationality of customer orientation it prescribes. In this chapter we will present our interpretation of marketing management discourse, its turning points and the problematizations that lead up to them by drawing on discourse theory. In addition we will analyse it as a form of power/knowledge. The analysis of the change of power base from the preceding chapter will be continued and so will the analysis of the governmental rationality of managerial marketing. Towards the end of the chapter Dean's framework (Dean 1995, 1999) will be used to draw together the analysis and to deconstruct marketing management discourse.

The marketing concept: one meaning – two histories

Laclau and Mouffe (1985) conceptualize discourses as consisting of several articulations competing for hegemony. Academic marketing discourse from its birth in the early twentieth century and well into the 1950s can be described as such a struggle between competing and, to a certain degree, contradictory articulations. As discussed in Chapter 5, some articulations of marketing discourse in the early period were characterized by an explicit managerial rationality related to a central interest in the customer, especially within scientific sales management but also in some more general elaborations of the functional school informed by scientific management. With the launch of the marketing concept at the end of the 1950s and in the early 1960s a similar type of managerial rationality was articulated more forcefully and was broadened to be applied to a range of managerial problems and workplace subjectivities. The marketing concept was thus articulated as an overall strategic governmental rationality.

We open this section by presenting the foundation of the marketing concept in the work of Wroe Alderson. Then we analyse the meaning and the substance of the marketing concept through the lens of our Foucauldian and discourse theory framework. We structure this analysis by giving two historical backgrounds to the articulation of the marketing concept. First, we give the mainstream version that still dominates in marketing discourse. We must emphasize from the outset that we do not agree with this version. As we hinted already in Chapter 5, it reinvents rather than accurately describes previous research. It is nevertheless important to describe mainstream versions since their power/knowledge still frame most of the research that is conducted within the boundaries of marketing management and marketing broadly defined. Second, we present an alternative version of the history of the marketing concept holding that the mainstream version is founded on historical-material claims that are impossible to maintain.

Foundation of the marketing concept

Textbook authors (Brassington and Pettitt 2000; Jobber 2004; Kotler and Keller 2006) often give credit to managers, researchers and consultants such as Keith (1960), Levitt (1960), McKitterick (1957), Borsch (1957) and Drucker (1954) for the articulation of the marketing concept. However, this version is contested by marketing historians who usually attribute this seminal articulation to Wroe Alderson. This is, for example, the case in Jones and Shaw's (2002: 39) account; they argue that 'with the publication of Wroe Alderson's (1957) *Marketing Behavior and Executive Action*, the modern era of marketing began' (see also Bartels 1988).

Alderson grounded his marketing theory in functionalism. He acknowledged kinship between his own functionalism and the functional approach presented in Chapter 5 but used the notion of function as a theoretical and abstract term – not empirical. Drawing on the work of Parsons, von Butterfly, Winener and others, Alderson (1957: 16) defines functionalism as the 'approach to science which begins by identifying some systems of action, and then tries to determine how and why it works as it does'. In the spirit of systems theory Alderson perceives marketing as an organized behaviour system and draws attention to the principle of interpreting its parts in the light of how they serve the system.

If we turn to the managerial implications of Alderson's writings, which he himself sees as the final goal with his marketing theory, his point of departure is taken in three concepts: opportunity, effort and management.

> [Opportunity and effort] refer to the same thing as demand and supply, but they reflect a more dynamic view of the relationship as seen by the marketing organization itself. The term 'opportunity' is more specific and more narrowly defined than the broad concept of 'demand'. It means demand for the particular products or services that the individual firm is prepared to provide [. . .] The term 'effort' designates the activities which a firm puts forth to serve its market. While it pertains to supply, it is a more dynamic concept than supply because it relates to a set of activities rather than to a quantity of goods [. . .] The third major concept in this approach to the market is management or the skilful direction of effort in relation to an understanding of demand.
>
> (1957: 355–6)

Alderson argues that the executive has an organizing, operating and symbolic function. These three functions of management are not exclusive to Alderson's argument, they were actually well established when Alderson wrote his major works in the 1950s and early 1960s (see Barnard 1938; Mayo 1933, 1945; Taylor 1911). The originality of Alderson's work, from a management theory point of view, lies in his suggestions regarding what governmental rationality the management of firms should be guided by. According to Alderson (1957: 445) executives are 'marketing men first of all' and 'management should not lose sight of the fact that the values achieved in production rest to a large extent on marketing decisions and marketing effort'. This position is, however, somewhat nuanced in Alderson's discussion about the relation of marketing to finance, production and engineering. From this discussion it becomes evident that in some situations Alderson gives primacy to finance, production and engineering over marketing. It is in fact possible to read some parts of Alderson's work as giving rules for how managers should choose between different managerial rationalities and thus how they should govern themselves and others. As we will see later, this type of more nuanced argumentation is completely lost in the literature that popularized Alderson's work.

But what is the essence of the governmental rationality of marketing discourse as articulated by Alderson? In Alderson, we do not find the same catchy phrases as we do in the writings that popularized his work. But it is nevertheless clear that Alderson argues in favour of a managerialism guided by the needs and the wants of customers. If we return to his use of the terms 'opportunity' and 'effort', at the beginning of his discussion on managerialism in marketing, we can note that in Alderson's articulation both opportunity and effort should be segmented but that 'this process begins logically with the evaluation of market opportunity' (1957: 357). It thus seems as though the needs of the customer should set the boundaries for what the firm should offer the market, which is central to the governmental rationality of the marketing concept. Many of Alderson's examples from his own consultancy practice also show how problems have been solved through investigations, which has provided a picture of what the customers want and need and has served as a starting point for producing goods adapted to these wants and needs. According to Alderson, management from a marketing perspective thus implies finding out what the customers want and need and in turn giving them what it is that they want and need.

The history of the marketing concept: the mainstream version

The main problem with Alderson's work when it comes to informing concrete management practice is that it is complex and abstract. Alderson's followers did not only prescribe customer orientation, but they also acted accordingly: their way of writing as such was customer oriented and therefore the texts they produced managed to popularize and simplify Alderson's thought.[1] One of the more influential of these texts was Robert J. Keith's article entitled 'The marketing revolution'[2] (1960), which represents the governmental rationality of the marketing concept very well and introduced the historical periodization that still dominates in mainstream marketing today.

At the time of writing, Keith was executive vice president of Pillsbury (a manufacturer of bakery products), which he had joined in 1935. It is by drawing on his experiences from Pillsbury, which allegedly 'ha[d] followed a typical pattern . . . in the evolution of the marketing concept' (Keith 1960: 36), that he unfolds his argument. It must, however, be maintained that Keith himself presents no justification for his claim that it is feasible to generalize from the Pillsbury case to the economy at large. According to Fullerton (1988: 110), 'the traditional picture of the Industrial Revolution painted by economic historians tends to substantiate' Keith's claims even though, as we shall see later, Fullerton himself disagrees with Keith and articulates an alternative view.

According to Keith (1960), Pillsbury in its 'marketing revolution' had gone through three 'eras'[3] dominated by production, selling and marketing. We perceive these eras as constituted by three different regimes of power/knowledge referred to as 'concepts' struggling for defining the floating signifier (Laclau 1990, 1993) 'management' in distinctive and, to a large extent, contradictory ways. Each of these regimes of power/knowledge is structured by distinct nodal points framing the management of Pillsbury quite differently, thereby furthering the divergence between different managerial aims. The first was the 'production-oriented' era, which was characterized by a managerial rationality that took its point of departure in what products the company could produce and not in what the market wanted and needed. The production era was thus dominated by a managerial rationality within marketing often referred to as the 'production concept' (see Kotler 1967; Levitt 1960), holding that businesses should focus on high production efficiency, low costs and mass-distribution. Production and the product are thus central nodal points within this type of managerialism. According to Keith, Pillsbury did well during this 'production era' since then the demand for its products were high, which made demand stimulation and thus marketing efforts not needed. The second era constituted by another managerial discourse that came to inspire management at Pillsbury was the 'sales-orientated era'. Guided by this governmental rationality Pillsbury established 'a commercial research department to provide [its managers] with facts about the market' (Keith 1960: 36). This era was dominated by a managerial rationality often referred to as the 'selling concept', holding that customers will buy the products of a company only after massive commercial campaigns that will stimulate interest in their products (see Levitt 1960; Kotler 1967). Selling thus is the nodal point of this type of managerialism.

Keith's third era is named the 'marketing-oriented era'. This is the era that is built up by the governmental rationality of the 'marketing concept'. According to Keith (1960), Pillsbury entered this era in the early 1950s. During the period from the beginning of the 1950s to the time when Keith wrote his article, Pillsbury developed, Keith argues, a more flexible organization: the managers at Pillsbury experienced that 'research and production could produce literally hundreds of new and different products' (p. 37). Pillsbury experienced for the first time a situation where it 'needed a set of criteria for selecting the kind of products that [it] would manufacture' (p. 37). In order to respond to this new situation, a new management function was created – marketing – as well as a new department – the marketing department. 'This department developed the criteria which we would use in determining which products to market. *And these criteria were, and are, nothing more nor less than those of the consumer herself*' (p. 37, emphasis in original). The nodal point of consumer/customer orientation is thus at the centre of the power/knowledge of the marketing concept and its introduction marks, according to Keith (p. 35), a 'virtual revolution in economic thinking'. Keith formulated the shift in managerial rationality that the marketing concept introduced at Pillsbury and, in his view, in most other organizations at the time as well, as stated very forcefully in the introduction to his article:

> No longer is the company at the center of the business universe. Today the customer is at the center. Our attention has shifted from problems of production to problems of marketing, from the product we *can* make to the product the consumer *wants* us to make, from the company itself to the market place.
>
> (p. 35, emphasis in original)

Another early and influential treatment of the marketing concept is Theodore Levitt's (1960) paper 'Marketing myopia'. In accordance with Keith, Levitt believed that previous forms of managerialism had made managers focus too much on production, research and development, and selling while neglecting marketing, at least marketing as understood by Levitt. This led him to argue that marketing became 'myopic' and accordingly to redefine the managerial rationality of marketing. This new rationality of managerial marketing is articulated forcefully in comparison to selling:

> The difference between marketing and selling is more than semantics. Selling focuses on the needs of the seller, marketing on the needs of the buyer. Selling is preoccupied with the seller's need to convert his product into cash; marketing with the idea of satisfying the needs of the customer by means of the product and the whole cluster of things associated with creating, delivering, and finally consuming it.
>
> (Levitt 1960: 50)

In Levitt's words, shifting from a selling-orientated view on marketing to a marketing-orientated view on marketing makes marketing less myopic, redirects marketing efforts and broadens the scope of marketing. In addition it makes the marketing enterprise look less egocentric and fairer since this shift makes marketing focus on the needs and wants of customers not sellers. As we interpret Levitt, the power/knowledge of what he perceived as previous articulations of marketing had made companies focus too much on their own needs, an argument that we nuanced in Chapter 5 when we argued that the governmental rationality of the marketing concept was embedded in the discourse of selling in marketing much earlier than 1960. From Levitt's standpoint, however, it was necessary to rearticulate the role of marketing in line with the customer orientation of the marketing concept.

> What does customer orientation involve? . . . For the present, let me merely suggest what appear to be some general requirements . . . [The company] has to adapt to the requirements of the market, and it has to do it sooner rather than later. But mere survival is a so-so aspiration. Anybody can survive in some way or other, even the skid-row bum. The trick is to survive gallantly . . . No organization can achieve greatness without a vigorous leader who is driven onward by his own pulsating *will to succeed*. He has to have a vision of grandeur, a vision that can produce eager followers in vast numbers. In business, the followers are the customers. To produce these customers, the entire corporation must be viewed as a customer-creating and customer-satisfying organism. Management must think of itself not as producing products but as providing customer-creating value satisfactions.
>
> (Levitt 1960: 56, emphasis in original)

The most important issue for Levitt is thus that executives base their strategies in the governmental rationality that the marketing concept prescribes. Other early formulations of the marketing concept were offered by Drucker (1954), Borsch (1957), McKitterick (1957) and Alderson (1957). McKitterick, in his famous version, argued:

> the principal task of the marketing function in a management concept is not so much to be skilful in making the customer do what suits the interests of the business as to be skilful in conceiving and then making the business do what suits the interests of the customer.
>
> McKitterick (1957: 78)

It is important to note though that marketing management did not constitute a complete break with the mainstream of previous marketing thought. Particularly the functional and the institutional approaches have still been given quite a lot of importance in the marketing management textbooks that, according to Bartels (1976), have dominated the market since the middle of the 1960s. For example, McCarthy, in his revised edition of *Basic Marketing: A Managerial Approach* (1964), includes a chapter on wholesaling discussing 'possible wholesaling functions' (see pp. 530–74) at length. Another example would be Lazer and Kelly's *Managerial Marketing: Perspectives and Viewpoints* (1962), which includes a whole section labelled 'the *functions* of marketing management' (emphasis added). In these and other early marketing management textbooks (e.g. Howard 1957; Kotler 1967), the functional and institutional approaches to marketing are, however, rearticulated to serve as a means for furthering the project of marketing management and realizing the managerialism of the marketing concept. But this is not particularly difficult, since there is no basic contradiction between marketing management and previous articulations of marketing, at least in our view.

A clear hegemony

The pioneers of marketing management perceived early marketing research as synonymous with the functional, the institutional and the commodity schools of thought and only acknowledged a few pioneering managerial articulations of marketing such as the work of Alderson (1957). Accordingly, many of them believed that they were part of a collective that invented customer-oriented managerial marketing and thus that they turned marketing from a macro-orientated descriptive discourse to a micro-orientated managerial discourse. This is a view of early marketing thought still embraced by most mainstream marketing scholars. Accordingly, researchers such as Levitt and managers such as Keith and McKitterick (whether intentionally or not) downplayed and reinvented previous articulations of managerial marketing. Downplaying and reinventing the contribution of earlier research is, as Brownlie and Saren (1997) and Marion (1993) suggest, a rhetorical strategy that is often used within marketing for researchers to position and legitimate their works.

However, it remains possible to argue that the early contributions to marketing management discourse in the late 1950s and early 1960s defined the marketing concept more clearly and stringently and described its managerial rationality and its practical usefulness in a more persuasive and convincing way compared to previous research (Fullerton 1988; Hollander 1986). This crystallization of the marketing concept within marketing discourse, rather than the alleged development of a new meaning of customer orientation, made possible the consolidation and unification of marketing discourse around the marketing concept. From our discourse theoretical perspective (Laclau and Mouffe 1985) we thus propose that the marketing concept became the *nodal point* of marketing management discourse at the beginning of the 1960s. Through its customer-oriented managerialism, the marketing concept turned elements of marketing discourse, such as the four Ps and marketing segmentation (to be described later), into moments which infused them with a customer-oriented governmental rationality and changed their meanings. These moments were clustered together into a discursive totality held together by the marketing concept, and accordingly turned marketing into a clear managerial discourse. The rules for what was considered good research were altered. As Hollander suggests: 'the dominance of the marketing concept, as a prime paradigm for marketing academics, tended to divert scholarly attention away from some of the social and macroscopic implications of marketing activity' (Hollander 1986: 23).

That the marketing concept still is one important nodal point of marketing management discourse is evident if contemporary marketing management textbooks are studied (see for example Brassington and Pettitt 2000; Jobber 2004; Kotler and Keller 2006), since they all take their point of departure in the marketing concept. It is in particular interesting to note that Kotler, in his *Marketing Management* textbook, has included a description of the marketing concept in his opening chapter from the first edition of the book in 1967 to its twelfth edition in 2006, and that he still founds his discussion mainly on Keith (1960) and McKitterick (1957) (as well as on Borsch 1957). Treating the marketing concept as a nodal point thus seems to make sense; the marketing concept can also be understood as a hegemonic intervention (Laclau and Mouffe 1985) and thus as a problematization that constituted a turning point for managerial marketing discourse.

The myth of the production era: an alternative history

Keith's (1960) distinction between a production, a selling and a marketing era has been widely cited and accepted as an accurate historical account within marketing. Its power/knowledge has influenced the historical treatment of marketing, the focus of marketing research and in fact the self-identity of the marketing discipline.

However, as Marion (2006: 256) puts it, 'the acknowledgement of eras in Keith's fashion is not a work of historiography, it is the rhetoric of a project. A prophecy which, like any prophecy, is made to have an effect on the future'. It was indeed successful in that respect. But Marion (1993) reads Keith's paper more as a pamphlet and as a part of Keith's personal career development, and argues that the marketing concept was materialized at Pillsbury only after Keith became executive president in 1966. More fundamentally, Fullerton (1988; see also Hollander 1986), as a result of detailed historical studies, argues that Keith's eras do not correspond with what happened in reality. In particular Fullerton contends that the production era is a myth. Fullerton (1988) is able to show that four claims that have been central in maintaining the notion of a production era are false. The production era has been characterized by those who have discussed it as 1) a time when demand increased faster than supply, which 2) made redundant conscious demand stimulation, and thus 3) marketing too as well as 4) marketing institutions outside the focal firm, such as advertising agencies and marketing education. Fullerton marshals arguments against all these claims. The notion of the production era ignores that from 1870 to 1930 (when the production era supposedly took place) 'competition was intense in most business, overproduction common and demand frequently uncertain' (p. 111) which makes it impossible to argue that demand increased faster than supply at this point in time. Demand stimulation was thus needed. Accordingly, 'marketing efforts [were] made by numerous manufacturers and other producers' and 'new marketing institutions outside the manufacturing firm' grew dynamically (p. 111). This leads Fullerton to conclude: 'The production era concept is clearly untenable. No such era existed' (p. 117), which implies that there never was a shift from a production to a selling to a marketing era. Despite this strong objection, 'textbook authors systematically resort to this illusion of reality to make people believe (often by calling on their common sense) that the change has taken place in certain companies (American, Japanese, etc.) . . . and that we cannot escape the revolution now in progress' (Marion 1993: 150). This tendency of textbook authors 'provides an entirely false sense of progress . . . It clouded [and still clouds] the profession's eyes to how little basic progress had been made in solving fundamental micro and macro problems' (Hollander 1986: 23).

From the materialist perspective on history writing that Fullerton adopts it has to be acknowledged that his critique is effective. It is important to note though that many marketing scholars use a similar conceptualization as Keith (1960), but they do not necessarily perceive it as a historical periodization only. According to our Foucauldian interpretation they rather, as we have argued earlier, present different managerial rationalities such as 'the selling concept' prescribing focus on selling through sales promotion and marketing communication, 'the production concept' emphasizing efficient production and 'the marketing concept' promoting management with a customer orientation (see Kotler 1967; Kotler and Keller 2006; Levitt 1960).[4] These researchers thus articulate the conceptualizations as distinct management discourses that presuppose distinct ways of managing and controlling organizations and their members. This usage of the terminology is not the target of Fullerton's materialistic critique.

However, Fullerton also discusses the articulation of the production, the selling and the marketing concepts, and differentiates between them. The way we interpret his discussion, these managerial rationalities were developed in tandem and have coexisted. According to Fullerton there is no fundamental opposition between them and the reasons why the different rationalities were developed: they were simply needed simultaneously. Fullerton traces the rationality of the marketing concept all the way back to sixteenth-century Britain. The reasons why this rationality emerged so long ago simply lie in the fact that competition, overproduction and flux in demand have been common problems for at least the last 500 years. Therefore demand stimulation by producers has been common, which made producers adapt their offerings to what the customers asked for.

Fullerton's argument is convincing. The production, the sales and the marketing concepts have informed practical business for a long time. But when academic and expert discourses were formed focusing on the same problematics – for example, Taylorism about production issues, scientific selling about issues that have to do with selling and marketing management about managerial marketing issues – the managerial rationalities inherent to the concepts were articulated more distinctively which made the contradictions between them more obvious and explicit. For these managerial concepts or rationalities prescribe more or less contradictory types of management, advising management to focus on production, selling and marketing respectively. Therefore, introducing the marketing concept to managerial marketing discourse, can, from a discourse theoretical position, be seen as an attempt to articulate the floating signifier *management* in line with the governmental rationality of managerial marketing, and thus as an attempt to order general management discourse, including the subject positions it entails and the ordering of organizational reality it envisions, accordingly. As Laclau and Mouffe

(1985) argue, discourses are always struggling with each other about defining the meaning of floating signifiers in ways that are in line with the rationalities that the discourses involved in the struggle prescribe.

But the signifier 'management' is not only a common floating signifier for all management discourses, it is also a nodal point in or closely associated with central nodal points of these discourses. In marketing management discourse for example, the marketing concept prescribes the type of customer-oriented management that this discourse promotes – as opposed to production- and selling-oriented manage-ment which are prescribed by discourses such as Taylorism and scientific selling. When floating signifiers are similar to or closely associated with the privileged signs that structure the meaning of the moments building up discourses, that is, nodal points, discourses are sensitive to problematizations and attacks from other discourses through these floating signifiers/nodal points. Indeed, if one management discourse is able to articulate the floating signifier 'management' in a more convincing or 'successful' way than those other management discourses it competes with, it will better its position and thus gain more influence at the expense of the others and might eventually hegemonize general management discourse. The articulation of scientific management, for instance, is an example of a successful problematization of general management discourse. Scientific management thus constituted a hegemonic intervention and led to a turning point in general management discourse.

The marketing concept, in a similar way as the production and selling concepts, can thus be seen both as an attempt to hegemonize general management discourse and as a 'proactive' strategy for protecting marketing discourse from problematiza-tions articulated within the boundaries of competing quarters. Against the background of this discourse theoretical interpretation, it is understandable that both in the pioneering works of marketing management discourse and in most contemporary textbooks, marketing notions are articulated as the superior way of managing organizations. By arguing for this superioriority, the authors try to defend marketing against competing notions from other discourses and thus aim to put their own discipline, and indeed their own work, in a good position. From a discourse theoretical perspective the dichotomization of the marketing concept with other management concepts in marketing textbooks thus has very little to do with whether it is a more accurate description of reality than other management concepts. The marketing concept should rather be considered as important ammunition, maybe the most powerful ammunition that marketing has hitherto developed in the discursive war for domination with other management discourses.

The marketing concept, the cold war and McCarthyism

From a discourse theoretical perspective, the reasons for the articulation of Keith's eras and thus the crystallization of the marketing concept in managerial marketing discourse around 1960, despite the critique levelled by Fullerton (1988) and others, can thus be interdiscursively (Fairclough 1992) explained. On the other hand, Fullerton (1988) effectively opposes the reasons given by Keith, Levitt and other pioneers of marketing management for the articulation of the marketing concept. What other general issues, other than the dynamics between different management concepts, may account for the crystallization of the marketing concept in marketing discourse at around 1960? We can find an answer in Tadajewski's (2006) analysis of the ordering of marketing theory through the influence of McCarthyism and the Cold War. Named after Senator Joseph McCarthy's search for people believed to be Communist sympathizers, McCarthyism was a period characterized in the USA by a strong anti-Communist and pro-American (govern)mentality. It is usually seen as having lasted between the late 1940s to the late 1950s even though many commentators believe it still influenced the US society long after that.

> Marketing was not immune to the influence of McCarthyism and the Cold War ... Central to the general atmosphere of the time was the demand for academic research to be geared towards the promotion of American interests, aimed at keeping America economically strong in the face of the ideological appeal of Communism, whose main attraction was seen to be its promise to redistribute wealth more equitably through society ... In this environment, desirable forms of academic labours were those that could contribute to the undermining of Communist propaganda by promoting American democratic goals in the international arena by bolstering the image of the United States and capitalism against the propaganda produced by those allied against America and Judeo-Christian values.
>
> (Tadajewski 2006: 171–3)

In a similar vein as the Great Depression in the 1930s created a demand for innovative advanced liberal solutions such as customer-oriented managerial marketing (see Chapter 5), the political climate of the 1950s stimulated a similar demand, even though the reasons for it were quite different. As was the case in the 1930s, marketing scholars were not late to seize the opportunity to further the interests of their discipline through elaborating on its managerialism (Cochoy 1998).

The general ordering of reality in the pro-American atmosphere was also supported by more direct interventions of academia in the name of McCarthyism, which also contributed to the elaboration of managerial marketing. As Tadajewski (2006) shows, the principal philanthropic foundations in the early 1950s – the Carnegie Corporation, the Rockefeller Foundation and the Ford Foundation – were, through their funding of the social sciences, accused of furthering socialist thought. In light of the political climate of McCarthyism, this gave rise to a highly problematic situation for the foundations. As a response to the accusations, the Ford Foundation, which played a particular role in funding marketing research, started to use different labels for describing their funding strategy: it claimed that what it funded was *behavioural* – not *social* – science. Through this discursive move the Ford Foundation distanced its funding strategy from the textual similarity between social science and socialism. But Tadajewski (2006) also argues that this textual change informed action that contributed to order marketing theory differently. The Ford Foundation demanded that research that it funded should be carried out in 'scientific', 'objective' and 'verifiable' ways and thus stimulated a move towards logical positivism/logical empiricism. Tadajewski (2006) carefully describes how, apart from funding research projects in marketing based on these principles, the Ford Foundation funded seminars in mathematics, sponsored professorships of marketing (for example Wroe Alderson's chair) as well as changes in undergraduate and postgraduate marketing education. It also sponsored a variety of publications to provide teachers of marketing with recent advances in marketing theory. All these educational activities aimed at furthering the positivistic and managerialistic agenda, which affected many marketing scholars. As Tadajewski (2006: 181) convincingly shows by referring to Staelin (2005) concerning the influence of the Ford Foundation programme at Harvard, 'those taught by first generation Ford Foundation scholars – Frank Bass, Ed Pessemier and Philip Kotler – were influential in training what [Staelin] calls the second generation of Ford scholars', who have been very instrumental in consolidating marketing's scientific (read: positivistic) status.

As we know from the governmentality literature, 'government is achieved through educating citizens, in their professional roles and in their personal lives' (Rose 1996: 75–6). That education and training are fundamental technologies of government is in fact central to the very idea of performativity, to Foucault's notion of power/knowledge and to the coupling between knowledge and the constitution of subjectivity. Indeed, if a collective of people, such as the academic marketers at Harvard referred to by Staelin, is taught how to conduct quantitative research but not qualitative research, this not only makes them more inclined to do quantitative research but it also makes them inclined to think as quantitative researchers because they really lack the ability to think as qualitative researchers. Their subjectivities are centrally defined through this quantitative orientation and ethos: they *are* and perceive themselves as quantitative marketing researchers. At Harvard and in Staelin's days, there were perhaps some 'closet qualitativists' who managed to educate themselves in qualitative research and thus tried to resist the pressures from the quantitative quarters. But these persons, if they existed, probably had a tough time. Eventually their professors and peers probably became aware of their 'difference' – papers must be published and manuscripts need to be handed in to supervisors. Then it is possible to imagine that several means of power could be used to get them back on the 'right track'. Sovereign power could be invoked by cutting funding for instance. Pastoral power could be used by explaining to the students that quantitative research was really the right way: diverting from this way would surely lead to frustration, a non-productive career and the problems it may cause. The power/knowledge of positivism could be invoked to legitimize the pastors' advice. Professors could thus use their privileged position as interpreters of the 'scripture' to guide and lead their flock of sheep. The managerialistic research agenda was most probably furthered in similar ways, in order to convince the few 'lost sheep' who made it all the way to doing research in marketing at Harvard without being fully normalized by the all-dominant quantitative and managerialistic ethos. Having Frank Bass, Ed Pessemier and Philip Kotler as teachers does not really provide the best conditions for developing a critical or at least reflexive view on the limits of quantitative research. Possibilities for developing into a critical scholar did not exist. Doing managerialistic research and shaping managerialistic scholars was the objective of the funding from the Ford foundation – and thus a prerequisite for getting funding in the first place. The quantitatively trained students were turned into managerialistic scholars well armoured to further the pro-American ideals of McCarthyism without reflecting upon them.

Through the influence of McCarthyism, the vision of the philanthropic foundations that was informed by a new 'modern' ethos was gaining momentum and this, together with the general political atmosphere of the Cold War, deeply affected the development of marketing theory and the marketing academic discipline. When viewed through modernistic discourse, 'knowledge production is valued according to its contribution to the consistent, controlled change and progression of the US economy and those abroad, the meter of which was economic growth' (Tadajewski 2006: 178). It is not very surprising that in this context the marketing concept was articulated more clearly and came to dominate managerial marketing discourse.[5]

Where does this take us?

The governmental rationality of the marketing concept fosters customer orientation. We maintain that the substance and the meaning of the marketing concept have almost never been seriously debated. Rather, the meaning of the term has been surprisingly stable since its early formulations of marketing management discourse (see Brownlie and Saren 1991). On the other hand, as we have shown, the mainstream account of its discursive and material history suffers from serious shortcomings and inaccuracies. What attitude towards this latter issue shall we adopt from the perspective of the ontological and epistemological position we have adopted (i.e. that of Foucault 1972, 1988; Laclau and Mouffe 1985; Rose 1999)?

For us it becomes important to determine what version of the history of the marketing concept is considered as accepted in marketing discourse, since the accepted version, which is not necessarily the one that corresponds best with the material reality or the articulation of some discursive position, is the one that has influenced the ordering of marketing discourse most. Otherwise it would be impossible for us to analyse what subject positions marketing discourse promotes and what governmentality marketing fosters. As Rose (1999: 29) has pointed out, studies of governmentality are concerned with 'analyzing what counts as truth, who has the power to define truth, the role of different authorities of truth, and the epistemological, institutional conditions for the production and circulation of truths'. From this perspective it has to be maintained that the mainstream version has impacted on marketing discourse most. This is the view that most scholars seem to hold (including the critics) and the one that is presented in textbooks (Brassington and Pettitt 2000; Jobber 2004; Kotler and Keller 2006). It thus captures what marketing scholars accept as the truth and thus the power/knowledge of academic marketing discourse better than Fullerton's – or our own – rereading.

One must keep in mind though that the aim of critical discourse analysis is not only to present an interpretation of the discourse studied but also to deconstruct it.

When deconstructing marketing management discourse, which we turn to towards the end of this chapter, studies such as Fullerton's and our own rereading can be helpful. In this particular case Fullerton's work and our own critical analysis give impetus to the interpretation that we briefly touched upon earlier: that the early marketing management scholars, seemingly through ignorance (whether intentional or not), downplayed early contributions to managerial research in marketing discourse in order to upgrade their own contributions. These accounts also make it possible to defeat marketing on its own positivistic grounds. Based on Fullerton's and our own analysis, we can argue that the 'habitus' of marketing research is anti-scientific since it accepts shallow and anecdotic descriptions such as Keith's as truths rather than rigorous, evidence-based positive research as it claims to (see e.g. Hunt 1976, 1983).

Towards an ethical project?

When the marketing concept became the nodal point of marketing discourse, it meant (in our terminology) that the governmental rationality – and thus the ethic – of customer orientation that it promoted, governmentalized managerial marketing discourse. The governmental rationality of customer orientation was accordingly articulated as needed in all parts of the focal organization. Keith illustrated this reasoning well:

> Marketing permeates the entire organization. Marketing plans and executes the sale – all the way from the inception of the product idea, through its development and distribution, to the customer purchase. Marketing begins and ends with the consumer. New product ideas are conceived after careful study of her wants and needs, her likes and dislikes. Then marketing takes the idea and marshals all the forces of the corporation to translate the idea into product and the product into sales.
>
> (1960: 37)

It is plausible to interpret the governmentalization of marketing discourse by the ethic of customer orientation as a move from promoting disciplinary power to emphasizing a neoliberal form of pastoral power (see Chapter 3 and Foucault 2000a, 2000b). As we argued in Chapter 3, the rise of governmentality and thus pastoral power is dependent on economics and the role it ascribes to the population and organizations in creating wealth and progress. The knowledge, expertise and indeed the worldview that the discourse of the market economy embeds changed the rationality and object of government from securing the property and territory of the sovereign towards seeing the population, not as something to control and repress, but rather as a resource to exploit, control and make use of (Foucault 2000d). This implies that discourses that produced and promoted 'happy' and productive subjects with the ability to contribute to economic performance, such as Taylorism and Human Relations, have been articulated. Control and management in governmentality is thus advocated through the creation of the happy self which is a more productive self than the repressed self and a self that becomes happy by being productive since productivity is rewarded monetarily. To show that this happy self is also a controlled self is one of the major aims – and strengths – of governmentality analysis.

The ordering of marketing as an academic discipline was very much influenced by economics but different articulations of economics frame the world differently. As we have shown in Chapter 5, the institutional, the functional and the commodity approaches to marketing were influenced by the German historical school of economics which was articulated as a reaction to classical liberal economics and did not prescribe an explicit managerialism. Classical economics was among other things accused of being unable to address the poverty that the industrialization gave rise to and therefore the German institutional school granted state intervention a more significant role in the economy.

On the other hand, it is quite possible to argue that marketing management and earlier managerial articulations of marketing, and thus customer-oriented articulations of marketing in general, were more influenced by classical and neoliberal economics. The central idea of the governmental rationality of the marketing concept, for example, is precisely that organizations should produce what the free unregulated market 'orders' them to produce. One prime goal for the marketing academia within marketing management, framed as we believe it was by the power/knowledge of economic liberalism, thus became to develop the practices and the technologies that allowed organizations to collect information about the market and not to describe the functions, institutions and commodities composing it. Accordingly, articulating the marketing concept is dependent on whether a free market can exist and is also supportive of the idea of a free market. The marketing concept is thus supportive of the idea that people are able to realize their freedom in the market place and thus that the market is a good mechanism for distributing and creating happiness, health, wealth and status (Marion 1993, 2006). Marketing management discourse thus presupposes and promotes a liberal governmental ethic which has been seen as kinds of pastoral power in previous research (Dean 1995, 1999; Rose 1996, 1999). In addition, we would like to claim that marketing management discourse presupposes that organizations should be managed in accordance with this liberal customer-oriented ethic. The pioneers of marketing management all emphasized this. McKitterick (1957: 78) for example claimed that 'business' has to be 'skilful in conceiving and then making the business do what suits the interests of the customer', Levitt (1960: 56) argued 'that the entire corporation must be viewed as a customer-creating and customer-satisfying organism' and Keith (1960: 37) contended that customer-oriented 'marketing permeates the entire organization'.

Furthermore, marketing management discourse turns the manager into a pastor who, through her/his superior inner qualities, is given the role of leading and guiding his flock of workers. Levitt (1960: 56), for example, argues that every business organization needs a 'vigorous leader' who in turn needs to be guided by a 'vision of grandeur' in order to make the 'entire corporation . . . a customer-creating and customer-satisfying organism'. Accordingly, the 'vision of grandeur' needs to be informed by the ethics of customer orientation since it should contribute to the final goal of making organizations more customer oriented. The subject position of the manager in marketing management discourse is thus given the role of interpreting the 'dictate' of customer orientation and what it can mean for the organization and the workers that s/he is appointed to lead. This corresponds very well with the schemata of pastoral power where certain persons are given the privileged position to interpret 'the right way' (Foucualt 2000a, 2000b) because of their inner qualities. In marketing management discourse, as the above quote from Levitt (1960) illustrates, managers are also given the role of guiding, and govern the personnel in a way that aims to lead up to them embracing the ethics of customer orientation and becoming a part of 'the customer-satisfying organism'. The subject position of the manager in marketing management discourse is thus given the role of governing and managing themselves and the personnel in line with the ethic of the marketing concept. As a result, the managers and the workers will be fulfilled and happy: the company will make a good profit and the personnel will be monetarily rewarded. Articulating the subject position of the manager and worker in this way is very much in line with what pastoral power prescribes (Foucault 2000a, 2000b).

However, as we know from the governmentality literature, pastoral power is dependent on confessional techniques in order to be effective. The pastors need to know the innermost qualities of the workers that they are appointed to lead in order to make sure that the eventual fulfilment/happiness promised may come about. To really be able to govern and manage, the pastor needs to govern 'from the inside out' (Covaleski et al. 1998). In order to correct the souls of the flock of sheep, the pastor has to know their innermost thoughts and who they really are. In addition, the workers themselves need to know who they really are through confessing and avowing this to themselves in order for them to be able to govern themselves. This type of reflexive self-regulative government is another central feature of the operation of pastoral power (Clegg et al. 2002). The texts of the pioneers of marketing management which we hitherto have concentrated on, however, do not include any extensive descriptions of such confessional technologies.

We thus conclude that it can be argued that marketing management turned marketing from a disciplinary project into an ethical and pastoral project. But before we give a more definitive interpretation concerning this assertion we need to analyse if the technologies associated with the marketing concept are permeated by a customer-oriented ethic, if they promote confessions and if they foster a management from 'the inside out' and self-regulation, central features of pastoral power. We turn to this question in the next section.

Technologies associated with the marketing concept

The marketing concept in itself does not give much advice regarding how to accomplish the managerialism it prescribes. The logical question then becomes: according to marketing management discourse, how should organizations integrate the governmental rationality of the marketing concept with their operations? We would argue that three interrelated human technologies – *market segmentation, targeting* and *the marketing mix* – are designed to accomplish this. The aim with segmentation is to divide the market into demarcated parts (segments). Targeting refers to the organization's activities of choosing what particular segments to focus its efforts on, that is, what segments to target. The aim of the marketing mix is to guide managers about what marketing operations should be used for a particular targeted segment. A marketing mix can consist of several elements (Borden 1964). Today McCarthy's (1960) four Ps – product, place, promotion and price – seem to have been institutionalized within marketing regarding what elements marketing mix decisions should be informed by.

Even though these technologies are given as the most important for making the governmental rationality of the marketing concept useful in practical management they were not originally developed to serve this purpose. Rather, all three technologies started to be developed early on in the development of marketing discourse. However, when the governmental rationality of customer orientation became more central to marketing discourse by the end of the 1950s, the practical importance of segmentation, targeting and the marketing mix became more evident. Accordingly, when the marketing concept became the central nodal point of managerial marketing discourse, these technologies where turned into its most central moments. Much attention was given to these technologies by marketing scholars from the early 1960s onwards, which made them more elaborated and infused with the customer-focused type of managerialism prescribed by marketing management discourse.

Market segmentation as a managerial technology

In his review of marketing segmentation research, Wind (1978) makes a distinction between 'a priori segmentation design' and 'clustering-based segmentation design'. In the former design, managers decide in advance on what basis the segmentation should be made (Wind provides loyalty and customer type as examples), while in the latter design, clustering technologies determine segments by analysing the data set (Wind provides benefit need and attitude as examples of clustering variables). In his latest (twelfth) edition of *Marketing Management*, Kotler differentiates between bases for segmenting consumer and business markets. When it comes to segmentation principles for consumer markets, a distinction is made between geographic, demographic, psychographic and behavioural segmentation (Kotler and Keller 2006). This can be compared with the segmentation principles of Alderson (1957), who also differentiated between consumer and business markets, and for the latter between geographic and demographic variables. The conclusion can be made that the substance of the mainstream of segmentation has not been changed that much since the 1950s. The major changes have been made in statistical applications, survey construction etc., but this has not changed how segmentation is intended to function as a managerial technology, which we focus upon here.

Perceiving marketing segmentation as one of the central managerial technologies of marketing management discourse is supported by previous research. For example, in his review article on segmentation research referred to above, Wind (1978: 317) argues that: 'segmentation has become a dominant concept in marketing literature and practice. Besides being one of the major ways of operationalizing the marketing concept, segmentation provides guidelines for a firm's marketing strategy and resource allocation among markets and products'. In addition, recent scholars with a more critical perspective on marketing have also seen segmentation as one of the 'cornerstones of marketing management' (Firat and Schultz 1997: 183). Segmentation can thus be treated as one of the major technologies for turning the managerial rationality of customer orientation that the marketing concept prescribes into practice.

In the context of marketing discourse, segmentation must be seen as one particular approach to conducting market research. Kotler and Keller (2006: 102) define market research as 'the systematic design, collection, analysis and reporting of data and findings for a specific marketing situation facing the company'. Based on Wind (1978) we argue that it is possible to distinguish between two types of power/knowledge informing market research: 'convergence' and 'adaptation'. The first type prescribes that market research should be used to affect the wants and needs of the customers so that they converge with the line of products that the focal organization offers: the market, and not the focal organization, is thus made the object of intervention and change. Since marketing management scholars perceived previous marketing research as anti-managerial and macro orientated (see previous) they believed that this perspective on marketing research was dominating in marketing discourse prior to the marketing management period.

Wendell R. Smith (1956) adapted theories on segmentation into the language and rationality of marketing management discourse (he did not invent segmentation though, contrarily to what is claimed by some mainstream marketing management scholars). Smith argued:

> In some cases . . . the marketer may determine that it is better to accept divergent demand as a market characteristic and to adjust product lines and marketing strategy accordingly. This implies ability to merchandise to a heterogeneous market by emphasizing the precision with which firm's products can satisfy the requirements of one or more distinguishable market segments.
>
> (1956: 4)

The adaptation type of power/knowledge embedded in Smith's articulation of segmentation thus prescribes that organizations should transform themselves and the products they offer guided by the demands of the market. Since this rationality is central to the marketing concept segmentation became a means to accomplish the managerialism that the marketing concept prescribes. Therefore marketing segmentation was given a more central position in marketing management discourse compared to previous articulations of marketing.

Segmentation slipped into marketing management textbooks published around 1960 (see Howard 1957; Lazer and Kelly 1962; McCarthy 1960). In these textbooks, segmentation was not clearly knitted to the managerial rationality of the marketing concept. It is reasonable to say that Kotler (1967) was the first textbook author who really understood the implications of the governmental rationality of marketing management and rearticulated his notion of segmentation accordingly (cf. Brownlie and Saren 1991). However, this did not mean that market research technologies based on convergence were banished from marketing management discourse, quite the opposite. Judging from marketing management textbooks published around 1960 (see Howard 1957; Kotler 1967; Lazer and Kelly 1962; McCarthy 1960), these market research technologies were still considered usable. Based on these textbooks we thus argue that there did not exist a fundamental opposition between the power/knowledge of adaptation and convergence, unlike what is sometimes claimed. Rather, adaptation and convergence-based technologies could be used complementarily. Such a mix ensured that the focal organization produced products that the market wanted and needed while simultaneously stimulating demand for these products. Again this clearly shows that there was no paradigm shift between marketing management and earlier approaches.

Targeting as a managerial technology

When the markets have been segmented, companies are advised by the managerial rationality that marketing management discourse prescribes to choose one or several segments to operate on. This is what targeting is all about (see Kotler and Keller 2006; McCarthy 1960). According to Kotler and Keller (2006: 263), 'the firm must look at two factors [when they evaluate market segments]: the segment's overall attractiveness and the company's objective and resources'. This resembles McCarthy's view, when he argues that target decisions should be made 'in the light of the company's capacities and objectives' (1964: 26). Several technologies for choosing the segments to target are suggested. Kotler and Keller (2006) for example differentiate between a 'single-segment concentration', 'selective specialization' (i.e. choosing several segments with little or no synergy but all 'equally attractive'), 'product specialization' (i.e. selling one product to several segments), 'market specialization' (i.e. selling several products to one segment) and 'full market coverage'. McCarthy (1960) suggests the 'market grid' as an overall targeting technology. The market grid, a spreadsheet, is constructed by placing the segmentation variables, for example 'size'/'type' and 'income'/'age', on the X and Y axis of the grid. In this way the segmentation is visualized which can inform targeting decisions.

In Chapter 5 we introduced the taxonomy as a form of heuristic disciplinary technology. Disciplinary technologies frame and order reality in particular ways and facilitate production of knowledge in line with their inherent rationality. According to Townley (1994: 32, emphasis added) taxonomies creates 'a *grid*, a configuration of knowledge, which may be placed over a domain'. Segmentation and targeting technologies in combination constitute a powerful taxonomy and can thus be analysed as forms of disciplinary power. Segmentation is designed to generate knowledge about reality. Since the inherent rationality of segmentation technologies is contingent upon the marketing concept and the customer-oriented type of management it prescribes, segmentation is more specifically designed to generate knowledge about the consumers constituting the market for a company's products or product groups. Marketing segmentation produces a 'truthful' description about the market situation – the market thus becomes objectively known, objectified. In this way, segmentation provides the raw data needed for making targeting decisions. But segmentation also frames targeting decisions in a fundamental way. The information generated through segmentation technologies is about the consumers. Therefore, targeting decisions will always have their basis in the customers and thus always facilitate and further customer-oriented management.

Targeting technologies, such as the marketing grid, facilitate the ordering and framing of reality. Initially, they are used to structure the market in particular segments based on variables such as age and income. Targeting technologies thus visualize and create images of the market, which provides an overview of the possibilities at hand. Then they are used to analyse and inform discussions regarding what segments the product(s) of a particular company is/are most suitable for. According to the literature, which we believe is close to the targeting practices that are utilized in companies, the outcomes of these analyses and discussions should be strategic targeting decisions such as a 'single segmentation design' or 'full market coverage' (see earlier). The literature also prescribes that the choices should be contingent upon overall objectives and resources, but targeting decisions can of course also stimulate transformation of overall objectives and the actions that these strategic changes may lead to might in turn also affect the resources – for example, stronger financial position because of better market position. Nevertheless, targeting decisions will frame managerial actions about many aspects of organizing. Let us take the example of a company that produces perfume, and which traditionally has concentrated on a single segment constituted by well-off customers willing to pay handsomely for luxury perfumes; let us imagine that, after segmentation and targeting activities, a 'full market coverage' is opted for. Such a change of strategy may imply product development of new perfumes that are cheaper to make, an increase of production capacity, changes in marketing communication activities and recruitment of new staff. If after some time the company chooses to move back to the 'single segment-concentration' strategy, it may need to discharge staff and concentrate its marketing activities to the segment targeted in order not to loose profitability, etc. Thus, targeting technologies, such as the marketing grid, enable comparisons between actuality and possibility, which is a central trait of disciplinary power. Current targeting decisions can be compared to potential and, from a managerial perspective, better targeting decisions. By operating on the raw data that segmentation technologies have provided, and informed by overall company objectives, targeting technologies produce norms for what markets to target, display existing gaps between current targeting decisions and the norm and suggest strategies for closing the gap between the two through changing targeting decisions. This is similar to how Foucault (1977) argued that examinations, that is, the technology of the self that he associated with disciplinary power, work. Taxonomies and examinations facilitate management of people from 'the outside in' (see Chapter 3 and Covaleski et al. 1998; Townley 1994), as our analysis of targeting and segmentation shows.

However, it is important to note that there is at least one fundamental difference between the taxonomies associated with the commodity, functional and institutional schools analysed in Chapter 5 as forms of disciplinary power on the one hand, and segmentation and targeting on the other. The latter is more clearly and closely knitted to the ethics of customer orientation. It is thus possible to argue that, through the disciplinary power promoted by segmentation and targeting technologies, marketing has become characterized by governmentality and promotes pastoral power, which always relies on an ethic (Foucault 2000b). We will return to this issue after our analysis of the marketing mix.

The marketing mix as a managerial technology

Based on target decisions the marketing management literature recommends companies to use the technology of the marketing mix in order to develop a strategy for each targeted segment. According to Neil Borden (1964) the technology of the marketing mix was developed at Harvard by himself and his colleagues. Through the gathering of marketing cases and through research from the end of the 1920s, it became evident that for some industries, it was impossible to distinguish common marketing expense figures and marketing functions. Rather, the combination of marketing expenses and functions differed widely between and within organizations in these industries. It was concluded that these differences could be explained by reference to what sector of the market the firm had targeted. Marketing managers simply believed that different marketing communication technologies were appropriate for different segments, which also explained the variance in cost.

Based on these insights, scholars at Harvard rearticulated the subject position of marketing managers referring to them as 'mixers of ingredients' (Borden 1964). This led them to coin the concept of the marketing mix. The major task for the researchers in this endeavour was to describe and distinguish between 'the market forces that cause managements to produce a variety of mixes' (Borden 1964: 4). This resulted in several different 'lists' of 'elements' that could explain variances in the mix of marketing activities and which thus could be used by managers as guidelines for marketing mix decisions. Borden (1964) suggests a list including twelve elements. The most influential list, which soon got a hegemonic position among marketing mix articulations, is McCarthy's four Ps, which have almost gained a holy status in managerial marketing discourse (McCarthy 1960). McCarthy summarizes the practical implication of the process of 'mixing' that he recommends as follows:

> after the target customers are analysed and selected, we develop a *Product* which we feel will satisfy the target customers. Then we find a way (*Place*) to reach our target customers. *Promotion* tells the target customers about the availability of the product which has been designed for them. Then the *Price* is set in light of expected customer reaction to the total offering.
>
> (McCarthy 1960: 40, emphasis in original)

McCarthy (1960: 40) draws attention to the fact that the customer is not part of the marketing mix but argues that 'according to the marketing concept' the customer should be the focal point of all marketing activities. Understanding the customer is seen by McCarthy as the crucial factor for accomplishing a 'good' marketing mix. In order to emphasize this point he presents a figure that resembles a dartboard with the four Ps centred around a C that stand for the Customer. Marketing mix technologies, such as the four Ps illustrated through this 'dartboard', function as taxonomies in a way reminiscent of targeting technologies such as the marketing grid referred to in the previous section. Taxonomies exert disciplinary power through framing people's thoughts and actions. In the case of the marketing mix and the four Ps, the managers' thoughts and actions are targeted, in particular the substance of the strategies for each targeted segment. Accordingly the four Ps frame decisions concerning: 1) what products to produce and offer to the market; 2) how they should be priced; 3) where they should be sold (place); and 4) how they should be promoted. Thus, the four Ps make targeting decisions operational. In addition, the four Ps and other marketing mixes enable comparisons between actual and potential marketing mixes as well as comparisons between several potential mixes. As all disciplinary technologies, the four Ps thus produce norms for appropriate marketing mixes, reveal gaps between these norms and previous marketing mix decisions and suggest strategies for turning the potentiality that is prescribed into actuality. Indeed, the four Ps inherently constitute a norm for marketing mix decisions. As was the case for segmentation and targeting technologies, the disciplinary power of the four Ps is framed by the ethic of customer orientation, which confirms that marketing could be seen as a form of governmentality. We will return to this question in the next sub-section.

The technology of the marketing mix in general and the four Ps in particular also suggest possibilities of control and government of organizations through the promotion of certain subject positions. According to McCarthy (1960), the four Ps should frame the behaviours of the managers – marketing managers in particular. The latter should use the four Ps to determine a marketing strategy for each targeted segment; they are thus given the subject position of 'mixers of ingredients' (Borden 1964). Much like bartenders, they are expected to pour the ingredients of a drink (the four Ps) into a drink mixer, shake it and serve the drink (the marketing strategy). The strategies that are generated through this process should in turn be used for setting more specific objectives, such as product requirements and what marketing communication activities should be pursued. In addition to affecting the managers, the four Ps also turn the salespeople into objects of – and subjects to – their managerialism. The rationale for targeting salespeople is that their interactions with the customers are central to promotion. McCarthy (1960) suggests that sellers should be controlled through recruitment, training, compensation and motivation, which together form a powerful technology for the control of employees through turning their workplace subjectivity into an object of control (see Covaleski et al. 1998; Bergström and Knights 2006; Rose 1999; Townley 1993, 1994). Through recruitment, salespeople with the right attitudes, experiences, education, etc., and thus the right identity, are hired. The training that follows elaborates on and refines certain aspects of this subjectivity. McCarthy suggests the well-known 'AIDA' as one technology for training and thus, according to our theoretical framework, controlling the salespeople through formation of their workplace subjectivity. AIDA advises the salesperson on how to get the customers' 'Attention' and 'Interest', which aims to foster a 'Desire' for the product by the customer leading to 'Action' and the conclusion of the deal. McCarthy also describes the 'helping to buy approach', meaning that the salesman should not only tell the customers about the good aspects of the product but also about its shortcomings. The rationale behind this is, according to McCarthy (1964: 672), that '[modern salespeople] have found that long-term relationships with satisfied customers are maintained easier when customers are helped to buy rather than sold'. The salesperson that behaves in accordance with the training is compensated in monetary terms but also through non-monetary encouragements such as promises of promotion. This makes the salesperson motivated and happy and indicates that s/he is following the 'right way', that is, the ethic of customer orientation, which contributes to reproducing the workplace subjectivity of the 'proper' salesperson. This reproduction of the desirable subjectivity is not achieved through means of sovereign power but rather through advocating a constant kindness vis-à-vis the salesperson. The salesperson is not treated as someone who should be oppressed but rather as a resource to care for – as well as exploit and make use of. This approach to management operates through a constant kindness contingent on a certain ethic – in this case the ethic of customer orientation – which is a typical trait of pastoral power as described in Chapter 3.

The salespeople and the managers, the marketing managers in particular, are the only personnel groups who are explicitly targeted by the power/knowledge of McCarthy's (1960) and other early (see Kotler 1967) articulations of the marketing mix. The production line workers should obviously produce the products that marketing mix decisions lead up to and the employees in distribution should deliver the products to the destinations that the marketing mix analysis has concluded. But as we interpret McCarthy (1960), these types of employees do not need to understand why they should do as they are told in order to function 'properly' – or, with Foucauldian lens, they do not need to be controlled by the power/knowledge of the concept of the marketing mix. When providing an example of good practice, McCarthy (1964) quoted a booklet distributed to production employees in a large industrial organization, stating what these employees need to know about the customer. In this booklet, it is made clear that the company's objective is to fill the wants of the customers with a profit, that the customers expect value when buying and that customers who have good opinions about the company will be very valuable for the company. This supports our earlier interpretation that marketing management scholars in general and McCarthy in particular believed that the personnel outside marketing and selling did not need to be affected by the governmental rationality of the concept of marketing mix – and thus the marketing concept – deeply.

Towards pastoral power?

In our previous analysis of the texts of the pioneers of marketing management discourse we have argued that the marketing concept was established as the nodal point of managerial marketing discourse, which turned marketing into a managerial discourse dominated by the ethic of customer orientation. The particular customer-centred managerialism characterizing marketing management discourse thus governmentalized managerial marketing discourse deeper than was previously the case. In our analysis we have also argued that these pioneering marketing management texts turned the manager into a pastor and accordingly that it seemed as though managerial marketing discourse was transformed from a disciplinary project to a pastoral project with the advent of marketing management. But we have also pointed out that we need to examine whether the technologies associated with the marketing concept fostered pastoral power before proposing a more definitive interpretation concerning this issue.

Through our analysis of the three central technologies – segmentation, targeting and the marketing mix – of marketing management discourse we have shown that the ethic of customer orientation permeates these technologies. Thus, it can be argued that with the advent of marketing management, marketing was turned into an ethical discourse. This is a criterion that we have established, based on our conceptual analysis in Chapter 3, as needing to be fulfilled for marketing management discourse to be classified as a form of pastoral power. Our analysis has also shown that the marketing mix, and the four Ps in particular, prescribes management and control of salespeople through benevolence rather than oppression. The salespeople are treated as a resource, as something to exploit, which is also a central trait of pastoral power (see Chapter 3 and Covaleski et al. 1998; Foucault 2000a, 2000c, 2000d).

However, the most important feature of pastoral technologies is that they facilitate and support confessions. Confessions are needed for the manager as 'pastor' to know the innermost thoughts of his sheep and thus who they really are. The pastor needs this information in order to lead a flock of workers on the right path to salvation. The employees themselves also need to avow and confess this information to themselves if they should be able to govern themselves in line with the ethic that structures the pastoral type of government. After our analysis of the technologies most central to the marketing concept, we must conclude that they do not facilitate and foster confessions. Accordingly, they do not foster government and management from 'the inside out', which is so very central to pastoral power. Rather, the technologies associated with the marketing concept foster disciplinary power and thus management from 'the outside in' (see Chapter 3 and Covaleski et al. 1998; Foucault 1977, 1985a, 2000a, 2000c, 2000d). They thus work as examinations turning humans into the object of knowledge, reveal gaps between the person's present state and the norm which enable management and intervention that fosters a movement towards the norm. By closing gaps between the actual self and the ideal self, the person becomes subjectified, subjected to disciplinary power (Foucault 1977).

In addition, we argue that the premier technologies associated with the marketing concept are primarily designed to gain knowledge about the market rather than to structure organizations. As intra-organizational control technologies they target very few types of subject positions, most notably the salespeople and the (marketing) managers. Even for this type of employee the control prescribed is quite limited compared with later developments within the boundaries of service marketing, to be described in Chapter 7. For example, segmentation, targeting and the marketing mix did not seek to regulate people's emotions and norms in very detailed ways. Even though the technologies associated with the marketing concept are disciplinary technologies with potential intra-organizational effects, they primarily target the management of people through framing formal organizational (social) structures,[6] particularly policies regarding what products to offer to the market. The technologies most closely associated with the marketing concept are thus primarily focused on governing products rather than people. They aim to identify segments in the market that share certain characteristics (age, gender, income, etc.), to decide which of these segments to operate on and to generate information about what kinds of products the consumers constituting the segment want, where and when they want them and what type of marketing communication is most effective in manipulating their needs and accordingly their consumer behaviour. The technologies associated with the marketing concept thus serve two major aims: they define from a marketing perspective the relationship that the organization should have with the market and internally they give input to formulating customer-oriented policies regarding production, marketing communication and distribution. Thus, from an intra-organizational perspective, which interests us here, they primarily give impetus to making formal organizational structures and products more customer oriented.

However, formal structures and actions of the personnel are, as we now are very well aware, often loosely coupled. This knowledge started to surface in the 1940s in the works of Barnard (1938) and Merton (1957) and in works of students of the latter (Gouldner 1954 and Selznick 1949). But with the notable exception of Alderson (1957), whose more nuanced discussion of the marketing concept influenced later scholars very little, this knowledge was not taken up by those who formulated the marketing concept. Our conclusion is thus that the technologies associated with the marketing concept were not designed in order – and do not have the power – to change 'the mindset' of the bulk of the personnel. Even if formal structures simultaneously control employees and are informed by the managerialism of marketing management, the power/knowledge of the technologies associated with the marketing concept does not really target the mentality of most workers. For example, these technologies were never designed to affect the attitudes and norms of the personnel at the production department. The marketing management rationality only assumes that the production personnel produces the products in accordance with formal requirements, and customer orientation does not (directly) play a part there. Even the personnel within the marketing department are not really directly targeted by the technologies of the marketing concept. They are obliged to use these technologies for gaining knowledge about the consumers constituting the market but are not encouraged to change their norms, values, emotions and regulated set of behaviors according to the customer's demands. We thus argue that the power/knowledge of the marketing concept and its associated technologies support employees within the marketing department in their endeavours to know the customer, thereby framing them as 'customer-knowing subjects'. The heritage from rational organization theory, and, in particular, Taylorism and its emphasis on management through formal structures, is thus still evident in managerial marketing discourse as articulated by marketing management. It must indeed be noted that the marketing concept was launched at a time when the Fordist mode of production, emphasizing large batch, standardized goods production, still dominated the economy in the USA (Harvey 1990), which most probably framed articulations of managerial marketing.

We thus conclude that the governmental rationality of the marketing concept and the role that marketing management ascribes to managers and salespeople indicates a move towards pastoral power. On the other hand, the confessional technologies needed to support such a move do not exist within marketing management discourse. The governmental technologies that were promoted foster customer-oriented formal structures and products rather than a deeper customer orientation of people.

Broadening the marketing concept

During the 1960s, marketing management thus established itself firmly at the centre of marketing discourse. But hegemonic discourse is always contingent and can always be opened up. In marketing, this became apparent at the end of the 1960s. At the time the nodal point of managerial marketing discourse, the marketing concept, was problematized from inside the quarters of marketing. This problematization was probably fuelled by the external critique levelled against marketing practices in the 1950s and 1960s (see e.g. Desmond 1998; Morgan 2003). But the governmental rationality of the marketing concept was not redirected or changed as a result of this problematization. Rather, marketing was articulated to include more subject positions, types of organizations and societal sectors.

Making marketing social

The centre of this problematization was the idea of 'broadening the marketing concept', associated with the work of Philip Kotler and his colleagues around 1970 (Kotler and Levy 1969; Kotler and Zaltman 1971; Kotler 1972). The broadening of the marketing concept argument is closely related to 'social marketing' (Kotler and Zaltman 1971) and 'the generic concept of marketing' (Kotler 1972). The central idea was that the managerial rationality of the marketing concept is not only applicable to business organizations but also transferable to non-business organizations (Kotler and Levy 1969). When Kotler launched his 'generic marketing concept' in 1972 he argued that 'marketing is a relevant subject for all organizations in their relations with all their publics, not only customers' (Kotler 1972: 47). Compared to articulations of the marketing concept, articulations of the generic concept of marketing rested on a more abstract understanding of marketing in general and the relationship between organizations and their environments in particular, thus following in the footsteps of the open systems approach in organization theory which gained increasing influence in the 1960s (Scott 2003) – even though this is not explicitly acknowledged by Kotler. If one compares the power/knowledge that the generic marketing concept prescribes with the one that the marketing concept prescribes, one may say that economic life has gone from being thought of as 'customers buying products from private business' to 'stakeholders *exchanging values* with *organizations*'.

The most fundamental shift is from 'buying' to 'exchange'. From the early 1970s, the latter is seen, together with its discursive cousin 'transaction', as the central theoretical concept in marketing (see Bagozzi 1975; Hunt 1976). However, from the viewpoint of the managerialism inherent to marketing and particularly its governmentalization of marketing discourse, it is more important that 'product' is substituted with 'value'. According to this latter rationality, organizations are recommended to emphasize the basic customer needs being served by their offerings, thus keeping a more open mind regarding what their target markets could be. This is considered as particularly important for non-business organizations since they often do not sell products but offer services: if it is the value of these services that is marketed rather than the services as such, non-business organizations may extend their 'customer basis' and change how they view their own offerings. The 'what' of exchange is thus broadened. But this is also the case with the 'who' of exchange. Exchange does not only take place between private businesses and customers but between stakeholders and organizations (Hunt 1976). Kotler (1972) distinguishes between three different types and nine sub-categories of stakeholders: 'input publics' (supporters, employees, suppliers), 'output publics' (agents, customers) and 'sanctioning publics' (governments, competitors, special publics, general public). With the managerial rationality of the generic marketing concept, marketing management becomes applicable to an array of exchanges not previously targeted by marketing; for instance, a church providing 'divine service' to church attendances, a primary school providing education to students, or a research fund providing researchers with scholarships. The domain of marketing is thus considerably expanded and the definition of marketing is expressed in a more abstract way. This is also the case with the marketing concept:

> The core concern for marketing is that of producing *desired responses in free individuals* by the judicious creation and offering of values. The marketer is attempting to get value from the market through offering value to it. The marketer's problem is to create attractive values. Value is completely subjective and exists in the eyes of the beholding market. Marketers must understand the market in order to be effective in creating value. This is the essential meaning of the marketing concept.
>
> (Kotler 1972: 50, emphasis added)

The idea of broadening the marketing concept was criticised by Luck (1969) who was concerned with whether marketing would loose it distinctiveness and analytical sharpness if expanded to include public organizations. According to Luck (1969), marketing should focus on studying market transactions. Ferber (1970) and Lavidge (1970) were not reluctant to the general idea of expanding the scope of marketing, but raised concerns and brought to the surface potential moral implications about applying the marketing concept to non-business organizations: they argued that it is not only important to consider what can be sold but also to consider what should be sold. According to them, marketing needed to take on a 'social responsibility': 'As it matures, as it broadens in function and scope, marketing will become increasingly relevant during the 1970s to the fulfilment of man. And as the impact of marketing on society increases, so does the social responsibility of marketing people' (Lavidge 1970).

As we have argued previously, it was in the interest of the academic elite of marketing to align their discipline with the pro-American values in order to further the discipline and their own careers. Therefore the institutional power of the *Journal of Marketing*, whose editorial policy was framed by the power/knowledge of managerialism, was advocated to silence oppositional voices. A prestigious special issue (*Journal of Marketing* 1971) was devoted to the changing role of marketing: it contains the seminal article by Kotler and Zaltman and a number of other articles that all discuss how marketing could effectively be broadened to societal domains that are traditionally, or were hitherto, considered outside the scope of marketing. Hunt argues that the publication of the special issue was a move that made the movement to expand the marketing concept more or less irreversible, and he further presents the ability of marketing to cover new ground as a consensus:

> There is now a consensus among marketers that most nonprofit organizations, such as museums, zoos, and churches, engage in numerous activities (pricing, promoting, and so forth) that are very similar to the marketing activities of their profit-oriented cousins. There is also consensus that the marketing procedures that have been developed for profit-oriented organizations are equally applicable to nonprofit concerns. These are the two major, substantive issues involved in the debate over the nature (broadening the concept) of marketing. On these two issues there now exists substantial agreement.
>
> (1976: 23–4)

But one might ask: does the problematization provided by the 'marketing broaden-ing' literature rearticulate the basic customer-oriented managerialism central to marketing management? Not really. The governmental rationality prescribing that organizations should adapt themselves to external demands is still the rule even though this rationality, as an effect of the broadening debate, adds to the govern-mentalization of marketing discourse. One might in fact maintain that the broadened marketing concept is after all quite limited, at least in terms of governmental rationality. It certainly extends the applicability of marketing, but its underlying managerial rationality remains more or less unchanged. One might in fact claim that the broadening of the marketing concept turns every stakeholder into customers but the subject position of the customer is not rearticulated. Furthermore, it is still only the 'what' of the offering that is targeted – the values delivered by organizations – and not 'how' the offering is made – that is how value is delivered by the personnel. The latter became central in service marketing discourse (Grönroos 1982), as will be discussed in Chapter 7.

However, the broadening literature supports our earlier interpretation that marketing discourse in the marketing management era is moving towards promoting governmentality and pastoral power. The Kotler quote (page 108) is exemplary of this change. Government as understood in the governmentality literature presupposes a free individual whose freedom is structured by an ethic. Freedom thus becomes instrumental in achieving the goals inherent to the ethic defining it (Rose 1999). Kotler gets very close to this scheme of government (see particularly the emphasized text). However, as we have argued previously, the basic technologies of marketing management discourse do not *per se* foster this type of power.

The governmentality of marketing management discourse

As argued in Chapter 5, marketing was a rather diverse discipline during its early years. The present chapter, however, has displayed a consolidation of marketing discourse led by problematizations articulated within the boundaries of marketing management discourse in general and the governmental rationality prescribed by the marketing concept in particular. Even though such problematizions were formulated quite early in the history of marketing throught, they gained momentum towards the end of the 1950s and led to a turning point in marketing discourse. We have argued that the marketing concept was established as the nodal point in marketing and that the technologies of market segmentation, targeting and the marketing mix were recommended to perform the managerialism inherent to it. In this section we will summarize and elaborate on our analysis of this turning point by particularly drawing on Dean's analytical scheme (Dean 1995, 1999). We thus analyse the governmental rationality of marketing management and the marketing concept by asking the following four questions: 1) what is being governed; 2) how is government achieved; 3) who do we become; and 4) why are we governed in this way.

What is being governed (ontology)?

Since the pioneers of marketing management perceived those articulations of marketing discourse that preceded marketing management as anti-managerial and descriptive, they did not primarily problematize marketing. They rather problematized alternative managerial discourses. With the introduction of the marketing concept, the central aim for managers, according to its governmental rationality, was to produce products adapted to the needs of their target markets. Compared to other 'management concepts' such as the production and the selling concepts, the marketing concept changes the perspective from focusing on the organization's capacity to the customer's needs. In line with the marketing concept, rather than producing products that suit the manufacturing process and selling them by means of massive promotional efforts, the organization should now produce what customers want and adapt its production facilities to suit these needs (Kotler 2003; Levitt 1960; Webster 1992). This is the argument that is put forward by the architects of the marketing concept and that have been very accepted in mainstream marketing discourse.

But what kind of categories of personnel are made objects of this governmental rationality? The managers, not only (though mainly) marketing managers, are targeted by the managerialism of marketing management. According to Alderson (1957), managers are first and foremost 'marketing men' from now on. One of the most profound effects of marketing management is certainly that marketing is articulated as a strategic management issue. The salespeople are also an important object of the managerial rationality of marketing management since they need to understand the importance of selling to the 'new' segmented customer. This new customer is, if we believe marketing management discourse, in a real need of the products and services of the firm and this can of course be important to take into account when selling to the customer, all the more so since this makes selling ethically correct and thus legitimizes the activity of the salespeople. However, as we have argued, the bulk of the personnel of organizations are still not a direct target of the governmental rationality of the marketing concept. Of course they need to be indirectly affected by marketing, through the strategic decision making based on market research of what the customers need and want for example, but they are not required to take the needs and wants of the market into account when constructing their subjectivities. Even the personnel within the marketing department are hardly affected by the managerial rationality of marketing management. Even though it can be argued that marketing management discourse invents the subject position of the modern marketer, involved in market research, segmentation, targeting and marketing mix decisions, and skilled in statistics and survey research, the subject position of the marketer is not turned into the prime object of these control technologies.

How is government achieved (ascetics)?

Within marketing management, segmentation, targeting and the concept of the marketing mix were the central disciplinary technologies promoted by marketing discourse. Technologies presuppose human behaviour in accordance with the rationality of the discourse they are embedded in and contribute to regulate human behaviour by making humans objects of – and subjects to – governmental discourse. But technologies are usually not explicitly defined as these types of behaviour-regulating devices by their advocators, and this is very much the case for the premier technologies of marketing management. Segmentation exhorts people to engage in researching the market and, based on the discovered wants and needs of the customers, to divide it into segments. These wants and needs are considered as 'true' knowledge and are intended to serve as the basis for marketing mix decisions in organizations. Used over and over again, these technologies will establish certain norms that will guide the organization and its relationship to the market in the future. We see these three interrelated technologies as designed to frame and control the strategic decision-making concerning what should be produced, for whom, and when. But it is also evident that they are premised on the assumption that the level of interaction between most employees and customers is, and should be, limited and indirect – they draw a clear line between the object of knowledge in market research (potential costumers) and the subject carrying out the market research. The primary aim is to know the customer.

Who do we become (deontology)?

According to our interpretation of the pioneers of marketing management, the governmental rationality of a fully implemented marketing concept would re-frame the organizational members' worldviews. In our reading, this can be translated as though the power/knowledge of the marketing concept brings about a new type of subjectivity that is distinct from those brought about by other managerial discourses such as 'the production concept' or 'the selling concept' for the bulk of the employees. We have argued that the managers, and marketing managers in particular, are given the role of the pastor and the subject position of the salesperson is also targeted. However, compared to subsequent developments in marketing – for example, service marketing – we would argue that the stipulated change of mindset is limited and that it targets few subject positions. The reason for this is that the premier technologies associated with the marketing concept are primarily used in order to gather information about the customers, and to, in turn, take decisions regarding which markets to focus on and which products to manufacture. In doing so, they introduce a demarcation between organizations and their customers, a demarcation that will be dismantled in service marketing, as we will see. Within the latter, the personnel are conceived of as an important part of the offering (Grönroos 2000), which is not the case in marketing management. The envisioned customer-oriented subject in marketing management knows virtually everything about the segmented markets and targeted customers. The underlying managerial rationality of marketing management discourse is that this power/knowledge should frame the strategic decision-making: what to produce, when to produce it, and how. But this does not require the bulk of the employees to adapt and reconstruct their subjectivities according to customer demands. Adopting such a position can even be an impediment to objective and rational decision-making. In marketing management, the customer orientation and its managerialism are primarily about knowing the customer. Marketing management produces the 'customer-knowing' subject, that is, the modern marketer (cf. Miller and Rose 1997).

Why are we governed in this way (teleology)?

The teleological implications of the governmental rationality of marketing management are never discussed explicitly by those who problematized earlier approaches to marketing and re-directed marketing discourse. Underlying and implicit in marketing management, however, there is a central teleological argument that we shall outline and deconstruct here. This argument is founded on the managerial rationality holding that organizations should adapt their products and services to the needs of the customers rather than finding customers for existing products or convincing customers that they need the products of the focal firm. According to our previous analysis, a differentiation between two types of power/knowledge has been made, expressed by the notions of 'adaptation' and 'convergence' (see Wind 1978). The former is believed to inform the governmental rationality of marketing management and the latter the governmental rationality of those articulations of marketing that preceded marketing management.

The ethical implication of this distinction is that, according to the pioneers of marketing mangement, those articulations of marketing discourse that preceded their works were mainly aiming to manipulate and twist the needs and wants of the customers. Marketing management, on the other hand, is put in a much better light since, according to these same advocators, it aims to contribute to satisfying the 'genuine' needs and wants of the customer. The alleged ethical foundation of marketing management is thus that it makes possible the fulfilment of people's needs and wants, which supposedly empowers them and helps them to realize their freedom. This alleged difference between marketing management and earlier articulations of marketing is spelled out quite clearly by Kotler and Zaltman (1971: 5), even though they somewhat incorrectly write about it in social not ethical terms: 'in social terms, it is held that this marketing philosophy [customer orientation] restores consumer sovereignty in the determination of the society's product mix and the use of national resources'. A similar articulation of this distinction is also implicitly set up by Levitt who argues that a selling approach to the market 'focuses on the needs of the seller, marketing on the needs of the buyer' (Levitt 1960: 50).

We will deconstruct this argument through four lines of reasoning. First, if we for one moment accept the idea that marketing 'restores consumer sovereignty' and that marketing management discourse could be distinguished from earlier articulations of marketing discourse based on the distinction between adaptation and convergence, this still leaves marketing management with serious problems, which we can discuss in a language of ethical relativity and responsibility. If organizations always should fulfil the needs and wants of customers, the effect is that no categorical ethical rule applies to what products and services should be offered to the market. Marketing management implies that someone other than the organizations operating on the market, the customers themselves or the state perhaps, should take responsibility for the ethical problems that marketing-orientated organizations give rise to. This form of 'responsibilization' of others is a typical trait of neoliberal discourse (O'Malley et al. 1997). Ethics is here reduced to a market variable, as Harvey (2005) shows in his analysis of neoliberalism. Some examples of where the rationality of this general argument leads us when applied to some markets are given here:

- If the customers want cigarettes, they should have cigarettes (someone else will take care of the consequences, such as cancer and other health issues).
- If a government wants to start a war in a little repressed Asian country, for example Vietnam or Iraq, let us give them the right weapon (someone else will take care of the consequences – the list would be too long).

- If the customers want to use motor vehicles, we will give them fuel (someone else will take care of the green house effect).

According to the distinction that marketing management sets up between marketing management and previous articulations of marketing, marketing thus stimulates organizations to abandon their ethical responsibility. A critique towards our line of reasoning might be that convergence-based articulations of marketing are just as unethical as adaptation-based articulations since the former does not give organizations any ethical guidelines or prerogatives either. This is true. On the other hand, in the convergence-based articulations, the guiding principle for what products and services should be developed, marketed and sold is located inside the boundaries of the focal organization. Within marketing management this principle is placed outside the organization – decisions regarding what to offer the market are made contingent upon customer needs and wants. Through marketing management discourse organizations are very directly (even though tacitly) recommended to abandon their ethical responsibility. Keeping this problematic within the organizations does not make organizations ethical, but certainly gives them the possibility to take responsibility for their decisions.

Second, it is very questionable whether market offerings in marketing management discourse are based upon genuine needs and wants of customers, which is central to a reasoning informed by the power/knowledge of adaptation. As we have argued previously, we contest the idea of paradigm shifts in marketing, which the articulation of marketing management as restoring customer sovereignty is based upon. If this argument should hold sway, marketing management discourse would have to be incommensurable, or at least would need to strongly contest convergence relationships, with the market. But this is not the case. Already from its early days, marketing management was fused with convergence-based articulations of marketing (see Alderson 1957; Howard 1957; Kotler 1967; Lazer and Kelly 1962; McCarthy 1960). That this is still the case becomes obvious when reading current marketing management textbooks. They do not only include practices that should be associated with marketing management discourse, emphasizing the adaptation of organizations to customers needs and wants, but also include practices that should be associated with convergence. Examples of the latter includes mass marketing communication, including advertising, public relations and sales promotion as well as market research practices (see Brassington and Pettitt 2000; Jobber 2004; Kotler and Keller 2006). As Marion (2006: 254), in his analysis of marketing management discourse, argues: 'marketers are paid to seek for new opportunities, to create markets and develop market shares, to create revenues from new customers buying products or services that they yesterday did not know that they needed and today cannot live without'.

In fact, we would argue that marketing management combines the power/knowledge of adaptation and convergence. Marketing discourse under marketing management thus recommends that organizations should affect the needs and wants of the customers while simultaneously making these customers needs and wants the governmental principle for organizations. When adaptation and convergence approaches to the market are combined in this way, segmented and targeted markets are made objects of advertising, public relations and other types of convergence approaches to market communication, which reinforces the power/knowledge of market communication and most likely also its effectiveness by binding customers more tightly to the focal organization. As Brownlie and Saren (1991: 41) note, the marketing concept 'is not about satisfying consumer needs alone – it must also satisfy company needs'. This way of influencing targeted markets also makes the needs and wants of the customers more in line with the range of needs and wants that the organization's established line of products and services already fulfil or the needs and wants that future products and services will fulfil. Our conclusion is thus that marketing management contributes to manipulate the needs and wants of customers in a more elaborated and perfected way than articulations of marketing based on the power/knowledge of convergence only. It is thus deceptive to portray marketing management as fulfilling genuine needs and wants of the customer, since these needs and wants are never meant to be genuine in the first place, according to the real – although concealed under the rhetoric of restoring customer sovereignty and adaptation to the needs of the customer – governmental rationality of marketing management.

Third, the portrayal of the articulation of marketing discourse that preceded marketing management as solely convergence orientated is as such arbitrary and misleading. As we have shown in Chapter 5, this period of marketing thought was not only orientated towards influencing the market through marketing communication but also towards managing organizations in line with customers demands. Marketing management scholars such as Philip Kotler and Theodore Levitt do not only hide the true discursive nature of marketing management but also reinvent the content of previous research in order to make the ethic of marketing management look fairer (Marion 1993). Accordingly, it would be more correct to describe both the early period articulations and marketing management as promoting both a convergence and an adaptation type of power/knowledge to marketing problems. But it would also be correct to argue that the manipulative effect of combining convergence and adaptation rationality grew stronger and became more elaborated through the development and refining of technologies such as the marketing mix and market segmentation in marketing management discourse.

Fourth, the adaptation rhetoric of marketing management also simplifies and conceals some central management implications of marketing management. These are often put in a very bright light: marketing is either believed to coexist with other managerial practices (Alderson 1957) or, more often, claimed to drive other managerial practices out of competition (Keith 1960; Levitt 1960). But whether marketing in practice dominates or coexists with alternative practices, the establishment of the new marketing-dominated status quo will most likely be associated with conflict and resistance. Such potential complications, however, are never addressed in marketing management discourse, which operates with a very simplified conceptualization of organizations. For a discipline that promotes managerialism and hands-on solutions to practical problems, marketing management theory sometimes seems very distant from practical issues, which makes its practitioner orientation look laboured and dishonest. With Brownlie and Saren (1997), we would claim that the alleged practical orientation is above all used to legitimate marketing as an academic discipline in general and its specific research project in particular. Marketing management discourse in our view is a product of neoliberal governmentality and shaped by the prerogative of economic progress, which is reflected in the rhetoric of practical orientation.

7 Elaborating the power/ knowledge of managerial marketing

In this chapter, we discuss the changes in marketing discourse after the establishment of the marketing concept and its related managerial techniques during the marketing management era. During the last decades of the twentieth century, the marketing knowledge base expanded rapidly, and marketing developed into a complex totality of power/knowledge. Within this totality, we will focus on the governmentalization of marketing and the subject positions fostered by it. We will argue that the main problematization of the managerialism of marketing during this period, that offered by service marketing, is based on pastoral power. In service marketing, managerial marketing is thus turned into a form of governmentality.

The chapter begins with a brief introduction to the intra-disciplinary debate about the scientific status of marketing, which was quite intense from the mid-1970s to the mid-1980s. The scientific claims made by marketing scholars are in themselves examples of how marketing discourse is increasingly invested with power/ knowledge, but the debate is also interesting as it can be seen as an attempt to problematize marketing discourse in a conceptually elaborated way. These ambitions prevail in the somewhat peripheral – albeit lively – field of critical marketing (see Chapter 2), but mainstream marketing discourse quite early reconciled the scientific ambitions with the managerialism established during the marketing management era. This tendency is particularly evident in the problematization of marketing discourse offered by service marketing that we now turn our attention to. By articulating certain central moments of marketing in a more elaborated way, service marketing has at least partly rearranged managerial marketing discourse. However, we will show that service marketing, as well as marketing in general, despite claims of the opposite, has remained true to the governmental rationality of marketing management, the marketing concept and the customer-oriented ethic it promotes. In particular, we will show how the promise of pastoral power that marketing management discourse failed to fulfil came to flourish in service marketing. We will illustrate this move by discussing both the power/knowledge of service marketing as well as some important technologies characteristic of the discursive practice associated with this power/knowledge. After a comment on what signifies the discursive development of the period, we will conclude the chapter by summarizing the governmental rationality of service marketing using Dean's framework as in Chapters 5 and 6.

Scientific aspirations . . .

During the marketing management era, marketing had established itself as a growing and promising discipline. In the late 1970s, there was no longer a need to argue for the existence of marketing as a managerial sub-discipline within business schools, nor as a functional department in companies. Marketing had found a place of residence even in many public organizations, following the introduction of the broadened marketing concept. However, there were other clouds emerging on the discursive horizon. In particular, prominent marketing scholars raised concerns regarding the scientific status of marketing discourse (Anderson 1983; Arndt 1983; Hunt 1976, 1983). The expansion of the scope of marketing and the identification of exchange as the empirical focus of study provided an important point of departure for this problematization (see the discussion about the broadening of the marketing concept in Chapter 6), but equally important was the introduction of rigorous thinking methodology ('metatheory') from the philosophy of science (Arndt 1985; cf. Hunt 1976, 1983; Zaltman et al. 1973, 1982).

A driving force behind these efforts was a common concern amongst marketing scholars that marketing had developed into an applied discipline primarily devoted to improving management practice and research methodology (Arndt 1985), at the expense of more fundamental theoretical development. As Anderson (1983) noted, concerns about the scientific status of marketing have been raised ever since Alderson's and Bartels's days (Alderson and Cox 1948; Bartels 1951), and can even be traced back to the 'salesmanship as craft or science – debate' accounted for in Chapter 5. However, while earlier contributions were made in isolation and largely passed uncommented, there was a significant increase in the temperature of the debate from the mid-1970s onwards, as opposing opinions about the present state of affairs within the discipline were not only described and formalized (as before) but also criticised.

Some scholars, most notably Shelby Hunt (1976, 1983, 1994), have vigorously argued for a scientific ideal based on positivism, realism and the gradual accumulation of knowledge into a coherent 'theory' of marketing in line with the all-embracing ambitions to broaden the marketing concept discussed in Chapter 6. Others have tried to introduce notions of competing paradigms, cultural situatedness, and critical relativism (Arndt 1985; Anderson 1983, 1986). Later on, marketing scholars such as Brown (1995, 1998), Brownlie et al. (1999), Brownlie and Saren (1997) and Holbrook (1993) have complemented the discussion with ideas from postmodernism and critical theory.

As our focus in this book is on the inherent managerial governmental rationality of academic marketing discourse, rather than its nature, merits and shortcomings as an academic discipline and scientific theory, the details of the arguments and positions in this debate are of less importance. In fact, the Foucauldian perspective on knowledge is remarkably open-minded when it comes to epistemology: any formation of knowledge is capable of exerting power and forming hegemony, no matter whether it is scientific, applied or even derived from discourse analysis. That scientific(/positivistic) knowledge does hold a privileged position in contemporary society, and hence is easily invested with discursive power, is another matter.

However, the 'scientific' debate also highlights some interesting features seen from our perspective. In particular, it signifies an ambition to institutionalize more deeply the power/knowledge of managerial marketing discourse. In addition, it exposes the tension between marketing 'practice' and marketing 'theory' that we touched upon in Chapter 2. While some authors, albeit with very different views on science – and in particular on good science – see a problem with marketing continuing to be an applied and 'unproblematizing' (in a metatheoretical sense) discipline (cf. Arndt 1985; Brown 1998; Hunt 1991, 1994), most marketers, both in academia and in industry, seem not to grant much importance to these short-comings.

Consequently, and despite the engagement and debate enthusiasm of the 'paradigm warriors' (Burrell 1999), the attempts to turn marketing discourse into a fully fledged social science (whether logical realist, critical relativist, interpretative or even postmodern) seems not to have been any more successful than Alderson's ambitions of the 1950s. However, looking at the contemporary state of affairs in academic marketing research, it is clear that the positivistic logical empiricism (and later realism) promoted for example by Shelby Hunt does hold the discipline in a firm grip when it comes to ideals for how the discursive knowledge should be produced and framed. Although the epistemological principles of knowledge accumulation and falsification usually ascribed to such approaches are not always adhered to (and sometimes even openly contested, cf. Gummesson 1991b), most mainstream marketing of our third era are firmly rooted in a positivistic ontology and epistemology where there is an external, independent marketing reality 'out there' to investigate and theorize about, using 'proper' qualitative and quantitative methods. This is expressed in a widespread concern with identifying new empirical phenomena – usually defined as managerial problems to be dealt with – and developing ever refined methods for investigating these in order to formulate scientifically legitimized solutions for the practitioners to adopt, and eventually come up with a 'grand theory' of marketing. Our discussion of service marketing later in this chapter will provide a clear example of how this typically unfolds.

... and disciplinary fragmentation

In parallel to the debate about the nature and scientific status of academic marketing, the demand for managerially relevant knowledge has nurtured the emergence and growth of several marketing sub-fields such as advertising, branding, business-to-business marketing, international marketing, marketing strategy, etc., sub-fields that have become recognized as important areas of marketing. However, most of these sub-fields have merely been elaborations of aspects of marketing that have been present for a long time (e.g. advertising), but have now turned into fields of deepened expertise within the general discourse. In terms of our discourse theoretical framework, they express elements turned into moments, articulated within the general managerial marketing discourse. In particular, they provide technologies for consolidating the marketing concept as a manifest aspect of organizational life. The governmental rationality of the marketing concept has thus become more and more embedded in marketing's practices and technologies, and consequently it has been more and more taken for granted. This means that the questioning of truth and rearrangement of central discursive elements associated with problematizations and turning points is not very prominent in these developments.

Despite an occasionally rather critical tone towards previous versions of marketing within some of these sub-fields, we thus cannot classify these new formulations of marketing as problematizations in a discourse analytical sense. The basic rationality, as articulated in marketing management, is seldom, if ever, challenged. As Brown (1998, 2004) and Brownlie and Saren (1997) argue, the academic field of marketing has long favoured a rhetorical style where any new idea can be presented as a revolutionary 'paradigm shift' vis-à-vis previous research, which is exemplified by the discussion in Chapter 6 on how the marketing concept was introduced in contrast with alleged previous 'management concepts'. However, the sometimes rather harsh formulations seldom contain any substantial rearticulation of the central moments of marketing and their internal relations, especially the marketing concept as nodal point of marketing discourse. In other words, the underlying ideas of marketing management are not questioned. The new sub-fields are thus not to be regarded as turning points, but as articulations and attempts at closure involving elements that were hitherto neglected by marketing as well as competing discourses.

Instead, the metaphor of discursive depth (Townley 1998) introduced in Chapter 3 comes to mind, as marketing is getting 'thicker' and 'denser'. Through the sub-fields, marketing, guided by the marketing concept as its main nodal point, is getting more and more comprehensive within its field of discursivity, turning more and more elements into moments. The managerial marketing discourse is hereby gradually expanded, but rather through discursive elaborations on what is already articulated by marketing than by appropriating floating signifiers mobilized by other discourses. At the same time, the emergence of specialized sub-fields has enabled the spread of marketing to new societal sectors into which the basic concept of market exchanges is not easily transferred. For example, cities and countries can use specific techniques to market themselves and develop strong 'brands' (Kotler et al. 1991), without necessarily adopting the entire marketing management apparatus.

However, among these sub-fields, service marketing stands out for two reasons. First, it provides an articulated and elaborated critique of marketing management that at least attempts to reach beyond the mere rhetoric of 'paradigm shifts'. It can thus be conceived of as a problematization of marketing management discourse, seeking to question the prevailing governmental rationality of marketing beyond a purely rhetorical level. Second, although originating out of practical experiences in a specific empirical sector of the economy, service marketing has gradually expanded its domain and, more than any other sub-discipline, contributed to the development and furthering of the managerial ideals of marketing. The problematization offered by service marketing is hereby at least potentially a hegemonic intervention, attempting to open up and close marketing discourse in accordance with the particular rationality of service marketing (cf. Laclau and Mouffe 1985; Laclau 1990). Service marketing thus also signifies an attempt to governmentalize marketing discourse, at least managerial marketing discourse.

Marketing as problematized by service marketing

Over the years, marketing management and its customer-oriented managerialism have occasionally been criticized by authors who found it less relevant for service organizations (e.g. Regan 1963; Rathmell 1966). Initially the problems were seen as being mainly about sensible application: services were yet another element to be articulated as a discursive moment of marketing discourse, albeit carefully. Rathmell for example complained that for marketers in service firms:

> definitions, classifications, data, and concepts are lacking, noncomparable, or unreal from a marketing perspective. Moreover as one attempts to integrate marketing terms, concepts, and practices with firms, institutions, and professions having their own traditions, customs, and practices which are quite foreign to conventional marketing (and much older), the linkage appears awkward and even improper.
>
> (1974: vii)

Rathmell attempted to overcome this perceived gap between general marketing and the idiosyncrasies of service firm practice by adapting and translating the theories and concepts of the former into the context of the latter, that is, by turning the elements of services into moments of marketing. However, others were less optimistic about the state and applicability of marketing, eventually problematizing marketing discourse itself:

> Could marketing itself be 'myopic' in having failed to create relevant paradigms for the service sector? Many marketing professionals who transfer to the service area find their work fundamentally 'different', but have a difficult time articulating how and why their priorities and concepts have changed.
>
> (Shostack 1977: 73)

Shostack based her problematization of marketing discourse on her professional experience as a bank manager (and we thus have an obvious example of the intricate relation between marketing 'theory' and marketing 'practice' touched upon earlier in this chapter). Basically, she claimed that, in its contemporary marketing management articulation, marketing had not much to offer to the practical work in her industry. She ascribed this shortcoming to the inability of marketing to recognize several features distinguishing services from goods. As a consequence of these characteristics, marketing had not been able to offer guidance, terminology or practical rules relevant to services. Marketing had (again) become 'myopic' as Levitt (1960; see also Chapter 6) had famously argued nearly twenty years earlier, and a fundamental 'paradigmatic' reorientation was called for.

Entitling her seminal 1977 *Journal of Marketing* article 'Breaking free from product marketing', Shostack argued that marketing had become too focused on how to market consumer goods and that the foundational spirit of the marketing concept had been lost. In terms of our discourse theoretical framework, Shostack opened up marketing discourse by questioning the articulation of its most central nodal point. As it turned out, Shostack's more radical approach was the one that gained discursive acceptance and the 1977 article is nowadays often referred to as the starting point of service marketing as a distinct sub-field within marketing discourse (see historical reviews by Berry and Parasuraman 1993; Brown et al. 1994; Fisk et al. 1993). Hence, there is empirical support for considering her problematization as initiating a turning point of marketing discourse, and thus worthy of further analysis.

The fundamental argument in Shostack's article is that services are not 'just like products except for intangibility', that is, they are not just a somewhat different sub-category of goods. Instead, the intangibility is perceived as a fundamental ontological characteristic, with such far-reaching epistemological consequences that a different kind of marketing is warranted. In particular, Shostack argued, the intangibility of services makes it necessary to consider 'the marketed entity' in a different, immaterial way. What the customer gets from a service transaction is not a physical object but an experience rendered by various material and immaterial elements which together form the marketed entity. Sometimes these elements are grouped in a way that makes it relevant to conceive of them as a product (e.g. a car). In other situations the elements are grouped to form a service (e.g. public transport). Goods and services are thus viewed as positions on a continuum, positions that require different kinds of marketing strategies.

In other words, Shostack problematized 'the product' as articulated as a moment in marketing management discourse. As we have argued in Chapter 6, the governmental rationality of marketing management and the marketing concept in particular, at least as articulated by the pioneers of marketing management (Alderson 1957; Keith 1960; Levitt 1960; McKitterick 1957), was product orientated despite claims to the contrary. Within marketing management, the product was discursively fixed as a physical as well as mental mediator between the customer and the operations of the company, linking but also separating production and consumption. Further, as one of McCarthy's (1960; see also Chapter 6) famous four Ps, the product was clearly articulated by marketing as an important component of the discursive technologies at the marketer's disposal. Further, adapting product features was also a central strategy for developing market targeting strategies. In fact, designing, producing, delivering and not least describing *products* in accordance with specified customer needs were crucial aspects of the managerial technologies by which marketing management discourse promotes management, that is, attempts to exert discursive control and order the social and discursive ontology. Thus, problematizing the nature of the product as Shostack did opened up and rearticulated a moment central to the nodal point of marketing management discourse: the marketing concept.

The underlying rationality was not new though. As discussed in Chapter 6, Philip Kotler had published a paper in the *Journal of Marketing* a few years earlier (1972), claiming that the provision of 'value' – in general, customer-perceived terms – was the ultimate goal and *raison d'être* of marketing. Kotler's 'values' were tied to the notion of exchange though, and thus also to distinct and separable organizational outcomes or results. Conceptually the 'values' were thus only partially separated from the idea of a 'product'. In contrast, Shostack 'broke free' not only from product marketing but also, and as it turned out more importantly, from the product itself, claiming the superiority of the customer's experience in a more profound way than her predecessors.

This 'breaking free' from the product might be analysed against the background of more general changes in management practices during the 1970s. At this point in time, Harvey (1990) locates a movement in the mode of production from Fordism towards what he labels 'flexible accumulation'. The latter 'rests on flexibility with respect to labour processes, labour markets, products and patterns of consumption' and 'is marked by a direct confrontation with the rigidities of Fordism' (Harvey 1990: 147). In particular, Harvey (1990: 156) argues that 'shifts on the consumption side, coupled with changes in production, information gathering and financing, seem to underly a remarkable proportionate surge in service employment since the early 1970s'. Based on the work of Harvey (1990) we can argue that there has been kinship between service marketing and flexible accumulation in a similar vein as we argued for kinship between marketing management and Fordism/Taylorism in Chapter 6. Accordingly, we contend that the problematization of managerial marketing offered by Shostack, Rathmell, and others who provided the foundation for service marketing discourse was framed by the ideal of flexible production (Piore and Sabel 1984), even though this is not explicitly acknowledged by the pioneers of service marketing.

Shostack's explicit reference to Levitt's 'Marketing myopia' article is also worth mentioning when arguing for a link between marketing management and service marketing, which some service marketing scholars contest very explicitly (for example Grönroos 2007). One of the fundamental ideas underlying Levitt's critique of marketing was that companies need to pay attention to what customers are buying – solutions to their problems – rather than to the products that are currently produced and sold by the company. Shostack's discussion of 'marketed entities' as the experience of tangible and intangible elements is strikingly similar. However, marketing as articulated by Shostack was centred around the direct management of the customer experience itself, rather than around the marketing of objectified products; the power/knowledge of managerial marketing discourse could thus evolve into new forms. The problematization thus elicited a turning point of discourse, rather than a complete 'break' or a 'paradigm shift'.

The introduction of service marketing was thus dependent in a fundamental way on the customer orientation that marketing management had articulated and manifested. This is seldom acknowledged by service marketing scholars who usually position service marketing as being in sharp contrast with marketing management. One important reason for this is that service marketing scholars have been preoccupied with institutionalizing and legitimizing their own discipline (see Berry and Parasuraman 1993; Brown et al. 1994; Grönroos 1994). Some service marketing scholars, several of them found in the so-called 'Nordic school of service marketing' (see for example Grönroos 2000; Grönroos and Gummesson 1985; Gummesson 2002), have, as we see it from our discourse theoretical perspective, been involved in a 'discursive war' aimed at giving service marketing a position as the hegemonic managerial marketing discourse. The prime 'enemy' has been marketing management, which in line with Shostack's (1977) terminology is believed to be lacking approaches for managing service firms. But this 'war' has really been fought in a Don Quichottesque way since the 'enemy' has never really fought back: maybe the marketing management elite (Phillip Kotler, Theodore Levitt, or Shelby Hunt just to name a few) have never really felt the 'threat' or maybe they have not understood what the 'fight' was about in the first place since the goal of promoting customer orientation has been shared by service marketing and marketing management scholars.

For it is indeed the case that service marketing discourse is founded on the same customer orientation so very central to the governmental rationality of the marketing concept. A reason for the neglect of this historical heritage may be that the marketing concept was deeply institutionalized in marketing discourse when service marketing was established and accordingly that customer orientation was perceived as the final goal given by nature. But it must not be forgotten that marketing management scholars fought hard to position the customer orientation prescribed by the marketing concept at the centre of managerial marketing discourse. The critical position vis-à-vis marketing management in service marketing discourse must be seen as what Marion (2006; see also Brown 2004; Hackley 2003) in his analysis of marketing has called the 'rhetoric of a project': service marketing scholars depreciate the discourse of marketing management despite the commonalities that their work shares with it in order to legitimize and make a space for pursuing their own agenda (and of course their own research careers and articles).

The power/knowledge of service marketing

Shostack and her followers established services as something qualitatively different from goods. However, the term 'service' was in itself something of a floating signifier as it was a rather abstract and vague concept with few natural implications for marketing. In other words, from the outset, services had no obvious differential position within marketing discourse. However, as the initial problematization was elaborated on, several central articulations of marketing discourse were reformulated and a distinct regime of power/knowledge particular to service marketing was established.

This regime of power/knowledge is based on taxonomic articulations defining services as the antithesis of the physical good, and by implication, of the old way of conceptualizing 'the product'. What exactly is fundamentally different between goods and services was a topic of extensive debate for several years. However, the following characteristics, originally proposed by Zeithaml et al. (1985) are often mentioned in the literature (see for example Edgett and Parkinson 1993; Fisk et al. 1993; Grönroos 1984, 2000; Lovelock 1991) as a comprehensive synthesis and may be considered as a discursive closure of this moment (cf. Laclau and Mouffe 1985). Later on we will show that this closure may have been rather temporary, but for the time being we will use it to advance the argumentation of this chapter:

- Services are *intangible* and abstract in a physical, but also often mental, sense;
- Services are *inseparable*, that is, produced and consumed simultaneously, with the consumer present and often an active participant in the production process;
- Services are *perishable*, making them unable to store;
- Services are *heterogeneous*, their features vary from occasion to occasion.

What makes service marketing so interesting for our analysis of managerial marketing discourse is the fact that these characteristics have claimed effects on the nature of work in service organizations, which paves the way for a sophisticated rearticulation of the power/knowledge of managerial marketing. By articulating the 'nature' of services in a particular way, service marketing elicits a mentality of government within organizations that elaborates and furthers the power/knowledge of marketing discourse considerably. In fact, as the problematizations offered by service marketing not only open the prevailing marketing discourse but also manage to close it by naturalizing its claims, we would argue that the managerial consequences of the service characteristics constitute a hegemonic intervention.

Dealing with intangibility: the customer experience

The intangibility of services places the customer experience at the centre of the power/knowledge of managerial marketing. As already mentioned, this is not a new idea within marketing. For example, Levitt (1960) was concerned that companies were getting too focused on their products at the expense of the customers who were supposed to buy them and find them useful. As quoted in Chapter 6, he argued that firms should view themselves as 'providing customer-creating value satis-factions' rather than mere 'products'. In a classic quote he exemplified this with customers not buying 'quarter inch drills but quarter inch holes' (Levitt 1969: 343). However, for Levitt the 'provision' was mediated by a physical product (drills), but in the case of services, the value is provided directly through the 'production', that is, the undertakings of the service company. The customer experience then *is* the 'product', the actual outcome of the operations and the entity that is to be marketed (see Grönroos 1978, 1982, 1984).

One important consequence of articulating services as intangible is that the governmental rationality of service marketing fosters service companies to apply the marketing concept in Levitt's 'non-myopic' way, focusing on customer experiences and processes of value creation rather than on any physical product. The key to success then lies in understanding the customer's value creation process

– and indeed in understanding it if necessary better than the customer – and how the company can contribute to it. This places high demands on the employees in terms of customer interest, insights and responsiveness and thus turns them into objects of the power/knowledge of managerial marketing. One important technology for achieving this is the concept of customer satisfaction (and the closely related notion of perceived service quality discussed later in this chapter) which has been readily adopted by service marketing. As a measurable construct directly linked to both organizational performance and the customer experience, customer satisfaction offers a conceptual shortcut that provides the organization with a discursive object of knowledge to focus orientation towards. Further, the intangible nature of services and the following focus on customer experiences also rearticulates the customer's subject position in the market relation. The intangibility is believed to make services difficult for the customers to evaluate in an objective way. In the absence of a physical product, the customer experience has to be based on various cues and proxies that are believed to indicate the quality of a service offering.

The employees of service firms are one such important 'cue' that will be discussed at length later. However, tangibles, such as buildings, equipment, uniforms, etc. can also provide important cues. Physical aspects are thus re-entered into the definition of the immaterial service-product, but, they are now defined as facilitators for the service experience, facilitators that might also play a role as marketing tools as they influence the customer experience beyond their functional role. Services are thus articulated as immaterial even when it comes to their material aspects: what counts is the customer experience, not any objective or company-defined criteria. Bitner (1992) elaborates on this idea by introducing the notion of 'servicescapes', the physical settings in which the service takes place, and how they are integrated in the service as perceived by the customer (and hence also by the customer-oriented company). Physical places are thereby redefined in immaterial terms, and turned into services themselves. As will be argued later in this chapter, this 'immaterialization' and de-essentialization is exemplary of the power/knowledge of service marketing, and is crucial for the elaboration of this sub-field into a general marketing logic.

Inseparability and perishability: the importance of employee conduct

The simultaneous production and consumption of many services is another important characteristic that rearticulates the nodal point of marketing discourse. The fact that services cannot be stored may seem mainly a practical problem from a logistics point of view, but it also brings together the fields of operations management and marketing since the lack of product storage is compensated for by 'storages' of customers, either in queues and waiting lists or indirectly, through differentiated pricing and various demand management systems. However, from our perspective, the most significant effect of the simultaneousness of service is not that marketing is used for managing demand to match supply, that is, that marketing becomes management, but that operations become articulated and co-opted by marketing.

The simultaneous production and consumption of services implies that the customer is present during the production process, which hence becomes an integrated part of the customer's service experience. The outcome of the service is thus paired with the experiences during the production/delivery process. How something is done is then equally important as the outcome when estimating service quality. By articulating customer-perceived service quality as a function of both *what* the customer gets from the service (technical quality) and *how* this result is delivered (functional quality), Grönroos (1982, 1984, 2000) explicitly includes organizational aspects, and in particular employee conduct, into the customer experience, and hence turns the employees into objects of the power/knowledge of service marketing.

The articulation of organizational issues as aspects of the customer experience, and consequently also of service marketing, is also evident in the works on perceived service quality by American professors Leonard Berry, A. Parasuraman and Valerie Zeithaml. In a series of studies, they developed a list of service quality attributes that were eventually reduced to five quality dimensions claimed to explain variances in customer-perceived service quality (see Parasuraman et al. 1985, 1988, 1994):

- *Reliability*: the ability of the personnel to perform the promised service dependably and accurately;
- *Responsiveness*: the personnel's willingness to help the customers and to provide prompt service;
- *Empathy*: the provision of caring, individualized attention to customers given by the personnel;
- *Assurance*: the knowledge and courtesy of employees, and their ability to inspire trust and confidence;
- *Tangibles*: the physical facilities equipment associated with the service, and the appearance of personnel.

The dimensions formed the basis for a service quality measurement instrument developed by the scholars, 'Servqual', which came to occupy a dominant position in service marketing research broadly defined from the 1980s onwards (see Schneider and White 2004). Without disregarding the occasionally rather severe objections that have been raised against the instrument as such as well as its theoretical foundations (Buttle 1996; Cronin and Taylor 1994; Teas 1993), the dimensions are in themselves telling as an illustration of how the notion of 'services' is articulated by service marketing. In particular, it is illuminating to notice what a central position is ascribed to the customer's subjective experience.

Delivering a high-quality service experience – that is, a 'product' that is able to meet the needs and wants of the customer (if we rephrase this in terms of the marketing concept) – is not a matter of developing and manufacturing an exchangeable object with the right features and promote it with the right combination of the marketing mix, as it was under the rationality promoted by the power/ knowledge of marketing management. Instead, the behaviour and attitudes of the service 'production' staff is articulated as crucial for ensuring the 'right' customer experience. *Being* right stands out as equally important as *doing* the right things.

Researchers within the aforementioned Nordic school discussed early on the interactive aspect of marketing (Grönroos 1982; Gummesson 1977). Grönroos (1982) articulated the concept of 'interactive marketing' referring to the part of the production process that takes place simultaneously with the consumption, and which hence becomes part of the service experience. He argues that the service company needs to consider the impact that its operations have during this phase as being an equally important part of its marketing strategy as that of the traditional marketing activities, in particular the management of the marketing mix. Grönroos is heavily influenced by Rathmell (1974), who noted the interactive nature of services but interestingly enough articulated this as a unique aspect of service production that marketing needed to take into consideration, rather than as an additional, novel form of marketing. The incorporation of the interactive aspects of services into marketing by Grönroos, which has become an accepted articulation within service marketing, is thus not a natural, unavoidable consequence of the characteristics of services. Instead it can be interpreted as a successful discursive move by the marketing discipline to articulate and appropriate yet another aspect of the organizational field of discursivity.

The heterogeneity of services and the control of the front-line process

To take advantage of the marketing opportunities that follow from the interactive aspect of service production/consumption is only the beginning. Elaborating on the simultaneous and interactive nature ascribed to services, service marketing has been able to articulate operational aspects of service production in an even more profound way. Through articulating the power/knowledge of services as a customer experience, and through launching managerial technologies such as interactive marketing, the notions of activities and processes have come to occupy central positions in service marketing discourse. In particular, the direct interaction between the service company staff and customers is seen as critical for the success of the service, as manifested in the expression 'the moment of truth' (Normann 1984). This idea was popularized by Carlzon (1987) who argued that, in the customer's mind, the entire organization and its customer offering only exist during the moments of truth, that is, the direct interactions between the customer and an employee. The front-line staff is thus articulated as both the company itself and its 'product', that is, its customer offering. By viewing the service as a series of such 'moments of truths' taking place at the interface between the company and the customer (cf. Normann 1984; Shostack 1977, 1984, 1987), organizational work processes, resources and arrangements, as well as the subject position of the service worker, are directly subjugated to the customer experience, and hence to the governmental rationality of service marketing.

The interest in processes is well in line with other managerial ideas that were popular during the 1980s and 1990s such as BPR (business process re-engineering) and TQM (total quality management). Within service marketing, however, managerialism is legitimized with reference to customer perceptions and experiences of the services, rather than by arguments of quality and efficiency which dominate in mainstream managerial discourse (Clegg et al. 2006). The process orientation of service marketing and its associated subject positions was thus promoted and legitimized through a customer-focused ethic: activities and processes should be designed to provide the customer with the best possible experience.

As service processes are mainly carried out by humans, it comes as no big surprise that controlling the service employees has become a main concern in service marketing. However, the subject position of the front-line employee seems to be a floating signifier in modern managerial discourse, as it is frequently articulated from other discursive positions as well as from service marketing. From a quality management point of view as well as from a traditional cost control perspective, ensuring that the service process (i.e. the chain of activities that make up the service) is carried out in conformance with company standards emerges as a vital concern. In particular, and in line with Taylorism (Taylor 1911), there is a strong incentive for reducing the heterogeneity of service performance through standardization (Levitt 1972) and conformance to pre-specified formal rules and routines. This articulation is frequently contested by service marketers: they argue that on the contrary, front-line employees should be encouraged and empowered to be flexible and responsible in order to be able to meet varying customer needs (Grönroos 2000; Schneider and Bowen 1995; Schneider and White 2004).

Service marketing thus offers the front-line service worker a kind of 'freedom', but a very conditional one, mediated as it is through the power/knowledge of service marketing and the ethics of customer orientation. The service worker as empowered subject is supposed to be guided by a 'genuine' interest in serving the customer, while also looking after the interest of the company. The very freedom of the service worker is thus subjugated to the aims of marketing as it is defined by and within marketing's discursive logic. This implies a governmental regime of a pastoral character, capable of managing free people and their freedom through their freedom (see Foucault 2000b, 2000c; Rose 1999; and our discussion in Chapter 3), ensuring that their freedom is really directed towards the goals of marketing discourse and the neoliberal values it is structured by. As will be evident from our following analysis, the technologies associated with service marketing facilitate this type of control.

The experiential and interactive nature of services makes them inherently heterogeneous, and the only way to deal with this in an efficient yet customer-oriented way is to allow for discretion and initiative in the front-line. Only a fully empowered human being can cope with the idiosyncrasies of customer-focused services, and only an independent human being can engage in a fully interactive service process. When the service encounter – that is, the interface between customers and company staff (Norman 1984) – and its importance for the customer experience are articulated in this way, it is natural that the front-line staff is subjugated through the prerogatives of service marketing discourse. This implies a subject position oriented towards the nodal point of marketing (i.e. the marketing concept and its customer interest) rather than those of other managerial discourses, such as operations or quality management. The exact organization of work may still be a matter of operational planning, but it is certainly also a concern for service marketing which thus is extended to include a more decisive managerial role within the firm.

To sum up, the articulation of service marketing shows a distinctive shift in the governmental rationality of marketing. The shift is based on a problematization of the nature of the 'product' of services, and, by implication, of the market relations in service settings. The problematization rearticulates several central moments of marketing discourse, including the nodal point of marketing management, the marketing concept. The basic idea of the marketing concept is still retained, but when articulated through the power/knowledge of service marketing it attains a more elaborated form. Within marketing management, the product constituted the natural link, but also a natural intermediary, between the customer and the company. With a service perspective, the linking product disappears and company activities are directly related to customer perceptions. This means that where marketing was previously providing input to the organization about *what* to produce, service marketing is now also concerned with *how* things are done in the organization. This makes ground for a governmental rationality emphasizing pastoral power. Pleasing the customer provides the way to salvation for the subject position of the service worker, and stands out as the main ethical principle of the governmentality of service marketing. However, in order to fulfil the desire to please the customer, the service marketing subject needs information about the customer to act on. There is also a need for managerial technologies that make sure that employees will act as envisioned. In other words, service marketing must be performed, not only articulated.

The managerial technologies of service marketing

In Chapter 5, we have argued that the power/knowledge of early managerial marketing discourse mostly focused on, and was most deeply elaborated in terms of, controlling and managing the subject positions of the sales managers and the salespeople. In particular, we showed how the emerging discipline adopted ideas and principles from the managerial movement that was dominant at the time, that is, scientific management. Within marketing management discourse, the manager-ialism of marketing was gradually refined, extended and articulated as a general neoliberal ethic in which customer orientation held a central position. However, we have noted that the managerial technologies associated with the marketing concept (segmentation, targeting and the marketing mix) were not fully capable of exerting the pastoral power latent in the marketing concept since the technologies primarily relied on shaping formal structures and adapting them to the environmental demands as perceived by marketing. They did not foster confessions in accordance with the ethic of customer orientation and thus did not foster subjec-tification from 'the inside out', central to the operation of pastoral power (Covaleski et al. 1998; Foucault 2000b, 2000c). Now, with service marketing, marketing's managerial rationality is redefined. The discussion above indicates a discursively formed claim for marketing to control what is happening in almost every part of the organization. This makes formal structures and technologies that enable the organization to adapt to the environment – and indeed the somewhat 'immature' human technologies of marketing management – insufficient as governmental devices of control. Further, the power/knowledge of service marketing explicitly promotes a governmental rationality founded on pastoral power, which targets the mindsets of the employees, since employee attitudes and behaviour are believed to have a direct impact on the customer experience. This shift in emphasis is paired with a corresponding development of new managerial technologies.

Customer satisfaction

As pointed out in previous chapters, from the outset marketing has included an explicit interest in understanding the customer. From our discussion in Chapter 3, it should be apparent that the knowledge that is generated as a result of this interest is performative rather than descriptive, and that it plays a crucial role for the managerialism of marketing as well as for reproducing the market economy. As discussed in Chapter 5, the marketing pioneers searched to identify and describe their markets in terms of customer characteristics that enabled the abstract market to become comprehensible from a company point of view. The scientific management ideals of the time required first-hand data about the market, the demand and sales operations. National and industry statistics provided the necessary input that were analysed using tables and descriptive summary measures, in addition to econometric technologies from economics. Getting insight into the true nature of the customer became even more important within marketing management discourse: the technologies of segmentation, targeting and the marketing mix all require such knowledge. This required new kinds of data though, and the sub-fields of market research and consumer behaviour were established. Advanced statistical methods, survey sampling and survey construction methods were introduced. Qualitative methods were also developed, such as focus groups and participant observation technologies.

However, the knowledge producing and the structuring technologies developed within marketing management discourse resulted in a managerialism that was still rather fragmented and unformalized. As argued in Chapter 6, although pastoral power is inherent in the marketing concept itself, it does not permeate the technologies of marketing management to any greater extent. Further, the customer envisioned by marketing management is someone 'out there', an autonomous knowledge object who could be investigated and 'orientated towards' in accordance with the governmental rationality of the marketing concept. The envisioned marketing subject is governed by her/his knowledge of the customer, but the subject position itself is not articulated by this knowledge.

Developments within the field of applied psychology during the 1960s and 1970s, in particular within attitudinal research, provided means for articulating the power/knowledge of marketing discourse in a more elaborated way by introducing even more objective, scientific and rigorous modes of customer knowledge. One of the most central managerial inventions emerging from these 'imports' is the concept of customer satisfaction. Based on established research on attitudes and attitude formation within psychology (e.g. Fishbein and Ajzen 1975), customer satisfaction is usually defined as an attitudinal construct built up from the customer's expectations and the perceived performance of the product/service under study (Oliver 1977, 1996; Parasuraman et al. 1985).

The concept of customer satisfaction systematically links the customer experience to company operations on a general level as well as when it comes to specific products/services. It can thus be used to exert disciplinary power as it provides an examination technology for measuring the adherence to the marketing concept. In practice the working subject is made an object of satisfaction measurement through surveys delivered to the customers of a particular firm. Asking the customers about how they perceive the level of satisfaction delivered by the personnel and what level of satisfaction they ideally would want to perceive – in accordance with the expectancy-disconfirmation paradigm for satisfaction measurement dominating satisfaction research (see Oliver 1977, 1996) – provides information about the current state of customer satisfaction and derives norms for the ideal state of satisfaction. In this way satisfaction measurement reveal gaps between potentiality and actuality. By analysing the survey data in greater detail, it is possible to obtain knowledge about what particular factors – and thus aspects of human behaviour – are failing: suggestions for closing the gap between actuality and the norm are given. Satisfaction measurement thus facilitates management from 'the outside in', a typical trait of disciplinary power (see Chapter 3 and Covaleski et al. 1998; Foucault 1977). High satisfaction is the result of a successful alignment of the organization to the needs and wants of the customer. Customer satisfaction can hence easily be incorporated in the customer orientation fostered by the governmental rationality of the marketing concept, since it provides a seemingly scientific and thereby legitimated measure of how well the marketing concept is implemented.

In the service marketing literature it is argued that the notion of customer satisfaction is pivotal for understanding the customer, for example in terms of buying behaviour and loyalty, and hence for the future profitability of the company (Anderson et al. 1997; Berry 1999; Heskett et al. 1997; see also the closely related concept of perceived service quality as discussed for example by Parasuraman et al. 1985). The observation that loyalty sometimes does *not* follow from satisfaction is interpreted not as an evidence against the relevance of customer satisfaction but as an indication of customers not being satisfied with being satisfied but searching even more satisfaction; for example, delight (Jones and Sasser 1995; Schneider and Bowen 1995). The customer satisfaction measures objectify and articulate customer experiences in accordance with the power/knowledge of service marketing and provide feedback to the organizational members regarding to what degree the needs and wants of customers have actually been met. In line with the logic of disciplinary power, the satisfaction measures thus influence the subject position of the service worker from 'the outside in', by providing discursive 'facts' for the subjects to integrate into the governmental rationality provided by the marketing concept.

However, in our view, customer satisfaction surveys are not only, not even primarily, disciplinary technologies; they can also be seen as pastoral technologies. Following the articulation of the nature of services in service marketing discourse, customer satisfaction is directly linked to organizational performance, including impressions made by the staff. These latter links are fundamental for the govern-mentality of service marketing: measures of customer satisfaction provide feedback for the members of the service organization – managers and workers – about how they are perceived by the customers as subjects, and hence about the appropriateness of their behaviours and attitudes. This is not only a form of examination as argued above. The measures of how satisfied customers are with the service experience also provide a basis for the employees to analyse and evaluate themselves in light of the subject positions that are made available to them by service marketing, that is, as part-time marketers for instance, and also enable managers to gain knowledge about the 'true' nature of their employees. In satisfaction measurement, the inner-most thoughts of the working subject are thus directly targeted, which was not the case with the technologies associated with the marketing concept analysed in Chapter 6. Satisfaction measurement gives the manager the role of the pastor – it is up to the managers to interpret what implications the results of satisfaction measurement have for achieving salvation through proper customer orientation. There is also a confessional opportunity associated with the customers' evaluations: employees can draw on them to articulate whether they have adhered to the ethics of customer orientation and managers can use them to govern their flock of sheep. In accordance with the inherent rationality of pastoral power, avowals provide both employees and managers with indications on whether they are on the road to salvation – that is, whether they satisfy the customer and thus whether they con-tribute to the commercial success promised by marketing discourse. The subject, with or without the guidance provided by the pastor, is inclined to correct her/his way of thinking and acting if needed, not primarily because of any coercive pressure but because of the power/knowledge inherent in service marketing in general and the customer satisfaction imperative in particular. This process will also make the working subject 'happy' and fulfilled, since the road to salvation is always full of rewards – both monetary and other types. Accordingly, customer satisfaction measurement devices are typical pastoral governmental technologies that facilitate confessions, avowals and reflexive behaviour framed by a particular ethic, that of customer orientation, and thus make government from 'the inside out' possible.

Satisfaction surveys and measurements thus play a crucial role in the pastoral power of service marketing (cf. du Gay 1996). Basing the pastoral type of control in the judgements of the customer is of course fully in line with the general governmental rationality of managerial marketing: who else could be a better judge than the customer, especially if the verdict is captured in such a scientific way? Satisfaction measurement thus not only turns managers into pastors, it also turns the customer into God. Ideally, the entire organization is subjugated to fulfilling customer's 'commandments'. As du Gay and Salaman (1992) have argued, the customer is the superior organizational imperative, expressed through the satis-faction scores. This form of pastoral power is, as discussed in Chapter 3, typical of advanced liberal societies, and is common in several articulations of modern management thinking (Clegg et al. 2006; Miller and Rose 1990, 1997; Rose 1996), but service marketing provides a particularly comprehensive instance of it because of the deliberate discursive promotion of the customer as 'king' – or God.

Part-time marketers, internal customers and gaps in the customer orientation

The service characteristics paired with customer satisfaction theory and the resulting combination of disciplinary/examination-based and pastoral/confession-based power provide a system of power/knowledge that informs several managerial technologies and subject positions associated with service marketing. One of the most illuminating examples is the idea that front-line employees should consider themselves as 'part-time marketers' (Gummesson 1991a). This is a logical consequence of the definition of interactive marketing as understood by Grönroos (1982, 1984): if every interaction between the company and its customers is part of marketing, then it follows naturally that those who are involved in these interactions are also marketers – albeit not exclusively. Part-time marketers embrace the (service) marketing discourse with its key signifiers of customer focus and customer value, and let these insights guide their behaviour in the interactions with the customer. They are thus aware of the impact of front-line activities on customer satisfaction and of the importance of the 'moment of truth'. Hence, not only are the part-time marketers doing their operational job, they are also conscious of the impression they make while doing it. Further, they are constantly involved in interactive market research, as they observe the customers and learn to understand their needs and consumption processes.

Exactly what part-time marketers are supposed to do and how this differs from their regular jobs is not very clearly defined in the literature. Embracing the ideas of the marketing concept and customer orientation in general (often in terms of accepting a 'service culture' as will be discussed later) is a basic requirement, which is believed to result in a general positive attitude towards the customer as well as an internalized willingness to make sure that the external promises made by the marketing department are kept (Grönroos 2000). This kind of expected behaviour based on reflexive self-management relates well to the concept of pastoral power, and our discussion in Chapter 3 where we have argued that the management of free people and their freedom through and by their freedom is characteristic of governmentality in advanced liberal societies. Here the 'free' front-line employees are explicitly targeted and urged to 'freely' comply with the governmental rationality of marketing, since they are defined as marketers themselves.

The subject position of the part-time marketer is offered to all employees who can possibly influence customer relationships and revenues (Gummesson 1991a; Grönroos 2006) by contributing to the customer experience. A considerable share of the company staff then becomes part of marketing, whether they are formally employed within the marketing department or not. The concept of part-time marketers is thus quite ingenious as it manages to resolve the potential conflict between marketing and operational functions (associated with alternative managerial discourses) that could have been nurtured if marketing had tried to expand at the expense of other discourses. Marketing is rearticulated as a cross-functional dimension rather than as a replacement of other functions, and potential conflicts between competing interests are suppressed and transferred to the individual level – where the role as part-time marketer is to be combined with other 'part-time jobs'. The individual employee's professional identity is thus in a sense a floating signifier that is open to various discursive articulations, but in practice, the inter-discursive contradictions emerge as conflicting demands on the individual employee rather than as competing articulations of subjectivity.

However, the governmental rationality of service marketing does not stop at governing the parts of the organization that have a direct impact on the customer's perception of the service by subjugating front-line employees to marketing through turning them into part-time marketers; service marketing extends its scope still further into the organization. This is done by a discursive move in which the organizational embeddedness of the customer interactions is elaborated on. If what counts is the customer experience, then any organizational activity that can possibly influence this experience directly or indirectly becomes the target of discursive control. Any such decision made or activity carried out, or any attitude expressed should be informed by an ambition to contribute to the customer experience.

> To manage service quality a customer consciousness has to permeate all business functions. An interest in customers must be extended to everyone – and every system and physical resources as well – who has a direct *or indirect* impact on the customer's perception of quality.
>
> (Grönroos 2006: 322, emphasis added)

The governmental rationality of service marketing discourse is hereby not only expanded to include the immediate service delivering capabilities of the organization, but also supporting back office activities and managerial work are subjugated to it. Service marketing thus governmentalizes marketing discourse further by articulating the dependence of the interactive marketing activities on other organizational functions. One popular way of articulating these dependences, albeit not only in service marketing, is to define them as internal customer relationships, thereby using the dynamics of the market or rather those of marketing and market orientation to coordinate the organization (Gummesson 1991a; Gremler et al. 1994; Grönroos 2000). By making the front-line employees customers to the back office, the entire organization can be subjugated to the external customer experience as the latter is translated into 'internal customer' demands. The governmentality of marketing is hereby permeated throughout the entire discursive ordering of the organization, as organizational subject positions are rearticulated as customers and (customer-oriented) suppliers, that is, as exactly the same subjectivities that marketing discourse is designed to govern.

The Gap model (Parasuraman et al. 1985, see Figure 7.1 below) is another central articulation of this rationality, although it does not explicitly deal with inter-departmental relations but with the organizational hierarchy. In the model, any shortcomings in the customer experience are attributed to various internal failures (gaps) to translate the customers' needs into a deliverable service product. That is, the final gap (gap 5) is the accumulated sum of gaps 1–4 which hence can be related to the customer perceived 'service quality determinants' discussed earlier – reliability, responsiveness, empathy, assurance and tangibles (Parasuraman et al. 1985, 1988, 1994). The intra-organizational gaps are thus articulated as a function of several central human qualities.

The five gaps are defined as follows in Parasuraman et al. (1985):

1. The gap between what customers expect from a service and management perception of these expectations.
2. The gap between the management perception of customer expectation and service quality specifications.
3. The gap between service quality specifications and the actual service delivery.
4. The gap between actual service delivery and external communications.
5. The gap between customer perceptions and expectations.

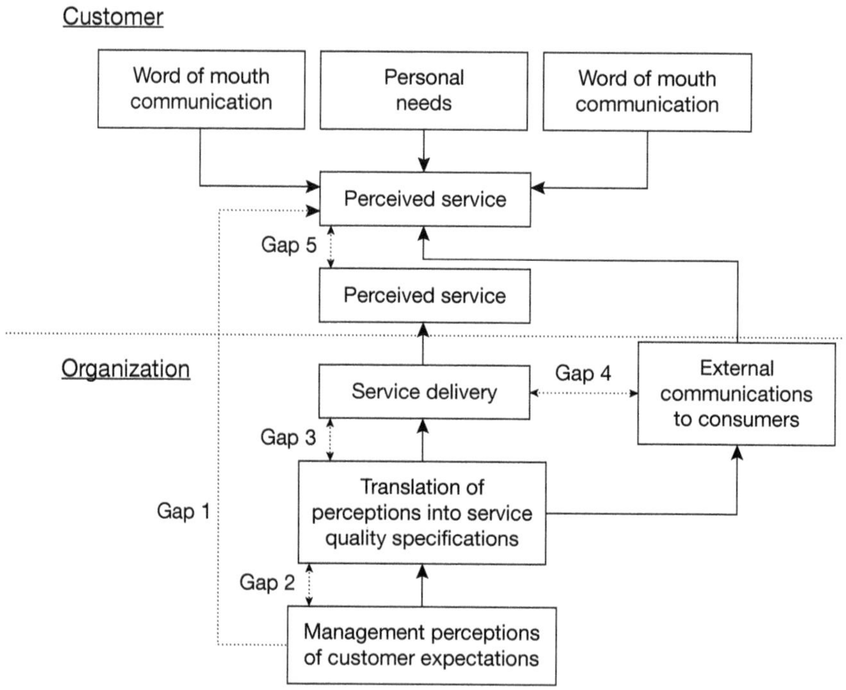

Figure 7.1 The Gap model

Source: Adapted from Parasuraman et al. 1985: 44

This managerial technology schematically shows how the entire organization is linked to the customer's expectation–performance evaluation, and can be seen as an elaboration of the standard customer satisfaction survey which is normally limited to gap 5. By explicitly articulating the internal relations as the sources of failures in meeting the demands of the customer, that is, in living up to the governmental rationality of the marketing concept, and by targeting central human capabilities, the model expresses a confessional logic that is well-suited to foster the pastoral power that we claim is characteristic of the governmentality of service marketing. The Gap model thus helps the service employees, including those in managerial positions, to identify their shortcomings as service marketing subjects, and also offers guidelines on what to do about it – how to close the gaps. The Gap model also supports the pastors, that is, the managers, to detect deviations from the 'right way' to salvation, that is, believing in and acting in accordance with the ethic of customer orientation. Thus, the working subject can be managed from 'the inside out' – a central feature of pastoral power (Covaleski et al. 1998; Foucault 2000a, 2000b) – through self-regulation or more directly guided by the pastor.

The hierarchical structure of the model is of particular interest as it highlights a discursive ambiguity between the rationality of internal customers, which would equal a downward movement in the figure – with internal customers translating the needs of the external customers further up the organizational hierarchy – and a traditional managerial view of the organization – in which management interprets the customers and translates this knowledge into organizational action. In the latter rationality, the internal customers are ascribed a less active role than they are in the former. While many authors argue for the empowerment and superiority of internal customers (e.g. Berry and Parasuraman 1991; Gremler et al. 1994; Gummesson 1991a; Heskett et al. 1997), the logic of the model itself rather articulates the presence of gaps as signs of a lack in management knowledge (gap 1) or in internal leadership, communication and control (gaps 2–4).

The latter approach is closely related to another concept which has received considerable interest also in other marketing areas than service marketing, namely that of internal marketing. Rafiq and Ahmed offer the following definition of internal marketing:

> [Internal marketing is] a planned effort using a marketing-like approach to overcome organizational resistance to change and to align, motivate, and inter-functionally co-ordinate and integrate employees towards the effective implementation of corporate and functional strategies in order to deliver customer satisfaction through a process of creating motivated and customer oriented employees.
>
> (2000: 449)

Here the employees are seen as targets of marketing activities and strategies, designed to accomplish desired results; for example, in times of organizational change, when new products are launched or whenever a particular kind of organizational behaviour is to be changed or reinforced. In fact, according to some authors, the entire worker–employer relationship can be formulated in marketing terms, as a product that is to be sold to the employee (cf. Berry 1981). As an early illustration, Sasser and Arbeit (1976) have argued for a recruitment approach where jobs, as any market-oriented product, are designed to fit employee needs. However, it is clear that the aim of internal marketing is not only to 'sell the product' and attract staff, but is also, and possibly to an even greater extent, a managerial means for influencing the staff already employed. Grönroos (2000), for example, formulates two managerial aims of internal marketing: to manage attitudes and to manage communications. Marketing is then turned into a deliberate and explicit tool for organizational control: perhaps even more deliberate than is the case for external marketing as management is often believed to be able to exert a considerable amount of influence over the employees in comparison to external customers. Interestingly, the governmental rationality of the marketing concept is strikingly lacking in the operational articulations of internal marketing: the marketing strategy promoted is more in line with the elusive selling concept and the convergence type of power/knowledge discussed in Chapter 6 (cf. Varey and Lewis 1999). This is, for example, evident in the earlier quote where the 'customer' is supposed to be 'aligned' and 'motivated', and even 'created' to fit the demands of customer orientation, quite in opposition to the imperative of embracing customer needs and wants that is urged for in the discursive rhetoric referring to external customers.

As a technology for shaping the 'conduct of conduct', internal marketing can promote various kinds of government. It can, for example, be used to establish norms enabling the operation of disciplinary power, but it can also articulate and promote the desired value system that should guide the 'free', self-regulating individuals subjected to pastoral power. However, it is interesting to note that the articulation itself does not draw on the adaptation rhetoric so dominant in other formulations of marketing.

Service culture: win–win in the organization

The technologies previously discussed have in common that they promote certain values and attitudes in the organization. A common way of articulating this 'soft' side of the managerialism of service marketing is through the notion of service climate or culture. The service culture, which is supposed to encompass the entire organization, is characterized by a constant strive to deliver superior customer value (Edvardsson and Enquist 2002; Schneider and Bowen 1995; Schneider and White 2004).

> To become customer focused, the firm must really change the way it thinks and behaves, such that the customer is always in the center of the value creation and delivery. The firm must have in place the appropriate people with the appropriate attitude. When the goals, structures, processes, and rewards are also in place, the culture and climate should follow for the firm to become customer focused . . . Value creating and delivering processes may be designed

so that firms can become customer focused. But if the culture does not provide the climate, the firm cannot become customer focused.

(John 2003: 201)

The exact nature of this culture is seldom made very explicit in the service marketing literature. Grönroos describes it as 'a culture where an appreciation for good service exists, and where giving good service to internal as well as ultimate, external customers is considered by everyone a natural way of life and one of the most important values' (Grönroos 2000: 360). Although expressing a rather functionalistic 'variable perspective' (Smircich 1983) on culture, which is more in line with managerial conceptualizations in the popular press and the consultancy literature (cf. Deal and Kennedy 1982; Peters and Waterman 1982) than with cultural studies in organization studies or anthropology for instance, this is a significant 'development' from how organizations were conceptualized in earlier versions of marketing. We are no longer talking about how the marketing function can contribute to the business missions and long-term goals; instead, marketing expresses an ambition to dominate the entire organization, defining its missions and goals in terms of the marketing concept.

The governmentality fostered by a proper service culture reduces the need for other means of control, which might seem to be a strike of luck since the articulation of the nature of services makes many means of control (such as detailed work descriptions and the disciplinary power associated with professions) difficult to exercise anyway.[1] By making the creation of customer value something that the organizational participants really want, not just something that they are paid to provide, it is possible to allow for a far-reaching empowerment which makes it possible for employees to respond to various customer needs, thereby turning the general heterogeneity of services into a competitive advantage instead of a problem of government. If properly achieved, the service culture will create a situation where all participants in the organization strive for the same goal, the creation of customer value. This common strive is what provides the basis for coordination of activities in the organization and is what ultimately holds it together. This does not mean that there are no other interests prevailing in the service organization. However, those other interests – in profits, job satisfaction or whatever – are believed to be best pursued within and coordinated through the frame of customer orientation. The service culture thus works as a means of achieving win–win situations, situations where differing goals are reached simultaneously, without infringing on each other.

The service culture is not only a tool for organizational coordination and implementation of a customer focused strategy. The ideal is to foster employees who act as internal entrepreneurs, continuously searching for new ways of creating customer value (cf. du Gay and Salaman 1992; Rose 1996, 1999). Hence they must be enterprising and knowledgeable about the customers' situation as well as about the organization and its various capacities. They must also have the ability to develop ideas into profitable business deals, and hence balance the financial interest against those of the customer. In short, service employees are supposed to have internalised the values of the service culture and hence of service marketing, and thus act as an integrated yet autonomous part of the organization.

The role of the manager in the creation of the service culture is to function as a pastor, which means to guide, facilitate and support – some would say manipulate – rather than to give orders or advocate direct control (cf. Foucault 2000b, 2000c). Management is also responsible for developing and fostering the culture, which is hence conceived of as a tool under managerial control (cf. Smircich 1983). Ideally the organization is turned into a basically self-regulating system where the prevailing culture makes it natural for the autonomous, competent, committed, responsible, self-managed and service-minded employees to constantly seek to satisfy the customer's needs which provide the all-dominating organizational imperative.

It should be noted that the culture envisioned is one of harmony and mutual interests. Service marketing builds on a twofold win–win assumption, where the 'winners' should be the customer and the organization on the one hand, and everyone within the organization on the other. The former assumption follows from the marketing concept: if the organization exists to satisfy its customers' needs, there is no ground (nor room) for conflict between the buyers and the sellers, as both parties are devoted to maximizing customer value. The opposing interests of supply and demand constituting the driving force behind the market model in economics are thus replaced with an idealized win–win relationship. As was the case with the customer orientation in marketing management, the mutuality is heavily biased, as it is the company who defines and articulates the customer's needs and values through the power/knowledge of market research technologies and technical expertise. For example, the not-too-unlikely situation of different opinions about how to define the value, and in particular how 'value' should be 'valued' in monetary terms, is not discursively articulated within service marketing, and thus excluded from the discursive scene.

Regarding the latter assumption, that is, the internal win–win situation, the service culture is effectively suppressing potential conflicts within the organization by providing a common focus and a unified rationality for all organizational members. This suppression of conflicts includes not only functional groups but also any structural conflicts between workers and management/owners. Any interest that is not compliant with the managerialism of service marketing remains unarticulated, or is rearticulated in win–win terms. Employees striving for personal growth and emancipation soon find that the only means for achieving these are through serving the customer (cf. the previous discussion about pastoral power and avowals in connection with customer satisfaction measurements, in this chapter). If success-fully implemented, the service culture will ensure a workplace situation where conflict is absent and everybody is a winner simply because everybody's interests are defined in line with the governmental rationality of service marketing. In service marketing discourse, government is thus achieved through making the working subject happy and fulfilled in a particular qualified way. Managing people in this way rather than oppressing their happiness is, as we have noted several times, a central trait of pastoral power.

In summary, the analysis in this section has shown how service marketing is gradually governmentalizing the discursive understanding of organizations as well as the management of organizations inherent to managerial marketing discourse deeper and deeper through offering subject positions such as part-time marketers and internal customers. By introducing sophisticated governmental technologies (such as customer satisfaction measures, the Gap model and cultural engineering) that are directly targeting employee thinking as well as behaviour, service marketing stands out as a fully developed managerial discourse. As a member of a service organization one is required to not only comply and act as a marketer in the full sense of the word, but one is also required to feel and think like one. Emerging from a turning point in marketing discourse where the rationality of marketing management, and the marketing concept in particular, was purified and refined rather than abandoned despite the rhetoric of radical breaks and paradigm shifts, service marketing has significantly contributed to the development of the marketing discipline. In the next section, we will show how service marketing is currently growing still further, into a hegemonic intervention of managerial marketing discourse, as the sub-field, somewhat ironically, is breaking free from services.

From empirical sub-field to hegemonic managerial rationality

Although its original articulations were based on what were believed to be idio-syncrasies of service, service marketing has evolved from an industry- and function-based sub-field into an aspiring general management discourse, supposedly applicable to any kind of organization and reaching far beyond the traditional functional area of marketing. The arguments for this all-encompassing ambition are closely related to the ideals of market orientation and its focus on the customer as the prime strategic imperative of modern organizations:

> Once the [customer-] focus becomes a given, then the firm will find itself in the mode of serving its customers while ensuring a reasonable profit. The realization is that you cannot achieve a sustainable competitive advantage to command sustainable profits unless you are customer focused. Serving the customer contrasts with the notion of marketing a product. It is more than providing a solution for the customer. It is about *serving* the customer. The firm looks at the customer's need in the broadest possible context, going beyond the scope of the core product that satisfies the core need in a particular consumption activity. The service oriented firm is one that focuses on serving the customer, regardless of whether its core product is a physical goods or an intangible.
>
> (John 2003: 9)

By expanding the articulation of the product into that of serving (not service), and by emphasizing that the task of identifying and developing the solution are perhaps the most important aspects of the customer offering, John here turns virtually every organization into a customer-oriented service company, providing holes, not drills. In fact, Levitt (1972) himself claimed that 'everybody is in services', and many – albeit mainly service marketers – have followed his line of argument ever since: Gummesson, for example, argues that 'Customers do not buy goods or services: they buy offerings which render services which create value' (1995: 250).

Such an articulation dissolves the good-service dichotomy and brings forward the customer experience centred rationality of service marketing not as an empirically contingent replacement when a physical product is missing, but as the core of all marketing. This is reminiscent of the 'immaterialization' of physical objects, which was already evident in Shostack's 'breaking free' article, but it is now extended beyond supporting and facilitating resources in services to encompass goods as well. As a consequence, service marketing has arguably shifted from being a problematization of marketing management and goods marketing (Rathmell 1974; Shostack, 1977) into gradually becoming an (at least aspiring) hegemonic intervention of managerial marketing discourse elaborating on the marketing concept rather than replacing it. It may be that service marketing is not *the* dominant approach in contemporary mainstream marketing, unlike what service marketers sometimes claim. However, its articulations certainly warrant a closer examination, as it is within service marketing that we find the most elaborated articulations of contemporary managerial marketing.

An important step in the quest for establishing the rebellious service perspective as the new core of marketing was the publication of an article by American professors Stephen Vargo and Robert Lusch in the *Journal of Marketing* in 2004, entitled 'Evolving to a new dominant logic of marketing'. In the article, the authors present eight premises that are said to pave the way for a new, service-oriented articulation of marketing, one that is in fact promoting much of the managerial rationality of service marketing as the core of past, present and future mainstream marketing and even management in general:

> Thus, the service-centered dominant logic represents a reoriented philosophy that is applicable to all marketing offerings, including those that involve tangible output (goods) in the process of service provision . . . The foundational premises of the emerging paradigm are 1) skills and knowledge are the fundamental unit of exchange, 2) indirect exchange masks the fundamental units of exchange, 3) goods are distribution mechanisms for service provisions, 4) knowledge is the fundamental source of competitive advantage, 5) all economies are service economies, 6) the customer is always a coproducer, 7) the enterprise can only make value propositions, and 8) a service centered view is inherently customer oriented and relational.
>
> (Vargo and Lusch 2004: 2–3)

Their articulation is interesting from a discourse theoretical view as it fixates the meaning of several central moments and relations between them within marketing discourse. The first premise deals with the unit of exchange and argues that whether the firm offers goods or services, in essence what is exchanged is combinations of skills and knowledge. With reference to Alderson (1957), it is claimed that such a definition captures the true nature of the process of creating utility on the market. The second and third premises subjugate goods under this definition: organizations and monetary resources are nothing but exchange enabling devices, goods are nothing but services embedded in physical things.

The fourth premise is interesting as it turns the strategic capabilities of the firm into an object of the power/knowledge of service marketing. Competitive advantages are believed to stem from a better understanding of the market (in a dynamic, learning sense), and from being able to act on this better understanding. The strategic stance promoted lies close to the marketing concept and is directly related to the formulations within the market-orientation tradition. Naturally, the role of the marketing function – both the marketing department and the interactive part-time marketers – is considered central and becomes a critical part of the core business processes. The fifth premise should come as no surprise after the introduction to this section, and the sixth is also well known from service marketing where the simultaneous production and consumption of the service often involve moments of co-production (Grönroos 2007). Here this view is expanded upon as the focus is shifted towards value creation in the consumption process in general. The value of a good is derived from its use, which makes it natural to view the customer as a co-producer of value even in non-service settings.

This leads us to the seventh premise, where the logical consequence of the consumption-based value definition is made explicit. If value is created during consumption, and only then, all that the company can offer is a proposition for such value creation, whether in the form of a good or a service. This is elevated still further by the last premise where the mutual nature of service-centred value creation is stressed. Value can only be created together with the customer, preferably in long-term relationships where the parties learn from and adapt to each other (Grönroos 2007).

It is easy to argue that the eight principles are not the foundational manifesto of future marketing, as the authors suggest, but on a general level they do capture the spirit of contemporary marketing in a telling way. Many of the ideas promoted have developed independently, not only within service marketing but also within other fields, but it is when they are brought together that their true potential for developing a totalizing managerial marketing discourse becomes evident. What happens is that the customer is put at the core of the strategic process of the firm, not as an important, or even imperative, environmental factor to consider but as an integral part of it. A consequence of such a perspective is that it is necessary to really know one's customer, not only as a counterpart in the market exchange – as is the case within marketing management – but also as a long-term partner or even a spouse (Gummesson 2002). This gives marketing a strategic role within the firm: as experts on customers and customer relations, marketers – and as we have seen, most employees can be defined as such, at least part-time – have control over the ultimate organizational imperative, the Customer.

Service marketing – pastoral power in a neoliberal society

In service marketing, several central moments of marketing discourse are rearticulated, such as the notion of the product and the relation between the subject position of the customer and the working subject – notably, not only salespeople and marketing managers, unlike in previous eras. An important consequence of these rearticulations is that the 'human factor' comes to stand out as a central object of managerial control. According to the power/knowledge articulated through the service characteristics, virtually all organizational members can influence the customer experience, directly or indirectly, and must hence be placed under marketing's discursive control. In order to manage the 'how' of services, and thus the service worker, several measurement and control technologies have been developed which embody the governmental rationality of service marketing. Some of these have been presented in this chapter but there are several others, such as customer relationship management, cognitive maps, empowerment, personnel development discussion, mentoring and coaching. Governmental schemes such as these are often borrowed from other managerial discourses, particularly from Human Resource Management (Schneider and White 2004) and are not usually perceived as control technologies within marketing itself, but we argue that to control the personnel is really their final objective (cf. Townley 1993; 1994).

When it comes to the specific form of power that service marketing promotes, we contend that service marketing discourse is founded on pastoral power and that the disciplinary and sovereign power that it also fosters are recast to serve bio-political aims. Further, we argue that the presence of this particular form of power is at least partially contingent upon certain historical processes. Service marketing mainly developed in the United States (even though there have been some important contributions from other parts of the world as well, especially Northern Europe) during a specific period in time, the 1980s. The politics of this time period can largely be seen as relying on neoliberalism for regulating the economy and neoconservatism for regulating the social, which signifies, in Foucault's terminology, a governmentalization of Western societies in general, and the United States in particular, by those mentalities (see also Harvey 1990, 2005).

The American freedom rhetoric was heavily emphasized throughout this period. This liberal type of freedom is not about letting people do whatever they want. Rather, it is a freedom that is a product of liberal and conservative ethics (Dean 1995, 1999; Rose 1996, 1999). It is thus a governed freedom, a governmentality. As Dean (1999) and Rose (1999) have shown, 'advanced' liberal governmentality fosters productive and 'active' citizens who contribute to economic performance as defined by liberalism. 'Productive' here may mean healthy, socially competent, emotionally stable, intelligent, good-looking and/or all dependent on trade; 'active' refers to individuals who see themselves as 'enterprising selves'. In compensation for being productive and active, workers are paid a salary, which they are expected to use in order to realize their 'freedom' through acts of consumption – they cannot really use it for much else in a market economy. Since the market economy is regulated by liberal economic discourse, consumption is also ordered by liberal values. Citizens are thus governed both by and through their freedom.

This type of freedom has strong traditions in the United States and service marketing was developed at a time when it really was emphasized. In our view, service marketing discourse can be understood as a form of advanced liberal ethic for the service sector, and if we should believe some service marketing scholars, as a management ethos for all organizations. (Service) workers who express the qualities prescribed to them by service marketing discourse (see Parasurman et al. 1985, 1988, for example) and who are thus empathic, reliable, responsive and self-assured, are valued in advanced liberal societies as well as by the organizations of our time. By being and behaving in this way, workers are accepted and rewarded, and they are enabled to pursue the freedom inherent in their subject position which makes them more integrated in society. For these free persons, in liberal societies, are not on the margins: they constitute very much the core of society.

In the service marketing articulation, marketing is thus definitely characterized by governmentality. Rather than being coerced into doing things that they would not want to do, people are governed in line with their *free* will. This is not something that is unique to marketing. This essentialist conceptualization of human beings is shared with other academic disciplines based on modernistic assumptions, for example psychology (Rose 1999), and even with critical approaches that advance emancipatory claims (e.g. Thompson and Ackroyd 1995). But this freedom is really a conditional freedom, which the governmentality approach uncovers. The theory of identity that is underlying modernistic social sciences is historically contingent and a product of Western liberal and conservative values. Within Western societies, institutions – such as schools, hospitals, jails, kindergartens, etc. – where the prime aim is to fabricate this identity that modernistic social sciences take for granted abound.

'Liberal-free' people are thus not free in accordance with any inherent personal characteristics, but programmed, normalized people. Both their freedom and their 'free' subjectivities are products of the social, that is, of discourse, and are thus subjected to a productive form of power (Foucault 1981a). What marketing envisions in its most elaborated managerial articulations (service marketing in particular) is to control these people more thoroughly by embedding them more deeply in society through producing discursive freedom, by means of rhetoric and managerial technologies. This in turn serves the person's internalized personal goals of becoming a free individual by learning to play the citizen game better and thus providing her/himself with the self-esteem and psychological comfort of rightful salvation – as well as more status and money so that s/he can do more things within the boundaries of the regulated society. But this also serves the goals of the organizations and the society at large, which in return will take advantage of hard-working and docile bodies that fulfil the goals of political economy through constantly striving for economic profitability. Service marketing is thus primarily an ethic that fosters management of freedom, through freedom – not the science urged for by the worried marketing academics in the introduction of this chapter.

That service marketing promotes pastoral power does not imply that service marketing does not promote disciplinary and sovereign power as well. However, in service marketing these forms of power have been rearticulated to serve bio-political aims and thus government of the social body. Service marketing promotes examinations, aiming to individuate the service worker through objectification. It thus subjectifies from 'the outside in' as well as from 'the inside out'. But the subjectification through objectification is framed by the rationality of neoliberalism, particularly its freedom rhetoric. It is also possible to see expressions of sovereign power in service marketing. The executives are, for example, the ones granted with the power to change organizations in line with the customer orientation prerogatives. But since these prerogatives are a function of service marketing ethics the sovereign power is also framed by neoliberalism.

The governmentality of service marketing

It is now time to summarize the governmentality of managerial marketing discourse in its late form as expressed through service marketing. Some characteristics have already been indicated; for example, the explicit reliance on cultural control and the disciplinary and pastoral role of customer satisfaction surveys. However, to fully understand how marketing governs its subject(s), we once again turn to the framework outlined by Dean (1995, 1999).

What is being governed (ontology)?

One key notion in service marketing is that services (and to an increasing extent most goods as well) are both processes and outcomes. *How* something is done is considered to be equally important as the end result, from a customer point of view (Grönroos 1982, 1984). The conduct of employees, especially staff with direct customer contact (cf. Normann, 1984 and the earlier discussion of the 'moment of truth' where the face-to-face interactions between front-line employees and customers have been especially emphasized), but also employees in supporting and/or managerial functions, then becomes crucial and emerges as a central target for the managerialism of marketing (Larsson and Bowen 1989; Schneider and Bowen 1995). The subject position outlined by Gummesson (1991a), referred to as 'part-time marketers', as well as the idea of internal customer relationships are two expressions of this 'everybody is a marketer' position. Consequently, it is argued that the entire staff should consider themselves as marketers, with obligations towards both their 'internal' and their 'external' customers. Hence, in this late development of marketing discourse, all organizational members are subjected to the governmental rationality of managerial marketing and the type of control it implies.

In addition to this intra-organizational governmentalization, there is also an inter-organizational governmentalization, as outlined earlier. Originally formulated as a reaction to the perceived shortcomings of traditional marketing, the new approaches now form a general, revitalized and updated marketing discourse, applicable to virtually any organizational situation (Grönroos 2000; Levitt 1972). In fact, the discussion in the present chapter shows that marketing, in its new form, is ready to take the role of an all-encompassing managerial rationality for the entire modern economy (Vargo and Lusch 2004). Virtually any organization can then be governed by service marketing.

The ambitions to broaden the marketing concept introduced in Chapter 6 are thus very much alive, not least due to the elevation of perceived customer values (as opposed to traditional, financial ones). This makes marketing more attractive in sectors where the financial and economic logic of the market is traditionally opposed to. Accordingly, when everybody is in services and everything is said to be a matter of understanding customers and providing value through services, it is argued that service marketing should become the 'dominant marketing logic' (Vargo and Lusch 2004) – in our reading, the hegemonic governmental rationality – not only in commercial companies but also in organizations of all kinds. In comparison to previous formulations of marketing discourse, the 'governed substance' (Dean 1999) being targeted is thereby considerably expanded.

What about the customers then, are they governed by the late marketing discourse? Although beyond the scope of this text, that question is worthy of at least some thought. Somewhat surprisingly, this is a much more difficult question to answer than when the interest is directed inwards in the organization. On the one hand, social scientists have for long been discussing a growing consumer culture with people thinking and behaving to an increasing extent in accordance with the subject position ascribed to them by marketing (e.g. Baudrillard 1970; Featherst one 1991; see also du Gay 1991 and his discussion of enterprise culture). On the other hand, there is also room for a considerable amount of decoupling, since service marketing, despite its customer-centred rhetoric, is mainly a managerial project, targeting organizations and their members. Technologies such as customer satisfaction measurements and the Gap model actually produce their own customers by making them objects of – and subjected to – their performativity. The relation between this discursively produced managerial subject of knowledge and the 'real', empirical customer is not specified. As we see it, there are actually two related discourses operating: one targeting consumers and one (the one we are focusing on in this book) targeting customer-oriented workers. However, as we have an intra-organizational focus in this book, we leave it to future researchers to resolve the matter of the relations between these two discourses.

How is government achieved (ascetics)?

The governmental regime of service marketing is characterized by two seemingly mutually contradictory, yet integrated, control ideals: standardization and flexibility. The interest in the '*how*' of the service manifests itself through the central concern with controlling processes and activities, that is, with what is actually happening during the simultaneous production and consumption of the service. Ensuring that the service process (the chain of activities that make up the service) is carried out in conformity with customer expectations is considered vital (Oliver 1996; Zeithaml et al. 1993) and thus there are strong incentives to reduce the heterogeneity of service performance through standardization (Levitt 1972). This in turn implies a specific kind of employee conduct control. Direct managerial surveillance is often viewed as difficult to exercise and/or deemed inappropriate in service settings, but other managerial control technologies – for example, evaluative customer satisfaction surveys and customer perceived quality measurement methods – are frequently utilized. The argument in service marketing is that these and similar technologies will ensure employee conduct to be characterized by empathy, reliability, trust and responsiveness, which are all believed to be crucial for service excellence (Zeithaml et al. 1985).

The new management technologies and discursive practices of marketing enable the exertion of power at a distance (Foucault 1977, 2000a) and thus a government that transcends the inherent idiosyncrasies of modern enterprise, but only to a limited extent. Too much reliance on standardization is believed to obscure the employees' possibilities to satisfy customer needs (Pine et al. 1995) by hindering flexibility (Zeithaml et al. 1985). Therefore, the control technologies referred to above are not designed to govern employee conduct in detail. They do not, for example, give exact instructions as regards how empathy, trust, etc. should be expressed by the personnel. Rather, they are aimed at establishing normative control and thus a distinct conduct by instilling and promoting managerial values which are believed to shape employees so that they may deal with the service encounter in an 'adequate' way. The direct control is thus relaxed and the subjects are empowered to handle situations discretionally, according to their own (discursively controlled) judgement. As previous critical research has pointed out, this kind of empowerment not only makes people 'freer' but also shapes freedom (Cruikshank 1994).

Fully implemented, the customer orientation of service marketing is meant to become the dominant way of thinking throughout the entire organization, giving rise to a service culture, characterized by a constant striving to deliver 'superior' customer value (Berry 1999; Edvardsson and Enquist 2002; Schneider and Bowen 1995). When the creation of customer value is established as something that the organizational members really think they want to strive for, they will be truly and fundamentally controlled by the power/knowledge of marketing, not by direct surveillance and control, but according to a pastoral scheme. The evolution of marketing into a discourse of pastoral power, which we see as evident in service marketing, presumes a power/knowledge that reveals the inner qualities of the subjects (e.g. the service marketing governed employee) and that conveys an ethic for managing the self from 'the inside out'. Articulating the customer experience as directly contingent on the service-providing organization and its employees provides one important contribution to such a pastoral power/knowledge system. If the self is believed to influence the 'how' of the service, then the customer service experience can serve as an indirect 'confession', if properly structured and articulated, as for example through the Gap model.

Who do we become (deontology)?

The subject position produced by service marketing in particular could be described as the 'customer-determined subject'. Working subjects are supposed to have internalized the service culture which frames their actions, thoughts and feelings in a managerialistic fashion. Hence, they are knowledgeable about the customer's situation as well as about their own role in creating customer satisfaction, and continuously searching for new ways of creating customer value. Accordingly, the 'customer-determined subject' is not a passive but an active self. In order to relate to the discussion about the enterprising self (Dean 1995; du Gay 1991, 1994, 1996, 2004; du Gay and Salaman 1992; Rose 1996, 1999), we would argue that the 'customer-determined subject' regulates her/himself towards the discursive norm. It is, thus, a truly governmentalized self (Foucault 2000a).

Hence, discursively, service marketing is a pastoral project built on the marketing concept, which is retained – despite claims to the contrary. However, in service marketing the customer is articulated as someone to be led or even defined by, not just an external factor that employees need to be knowledgeable about. As mentioned in the previous chapter, the discursive ethic for such a move was present already in the marketing management era, but it was first with service marketing that the managerial technologies necessary for making this happen were introduced. Service marketing thus not only promotes the ambition to establish a govern-mentality with a subject determined by the customer, but also offers the means for it, through the technologies that we have analysed in this chapter.

An important aspect of this governmentalized self is the fact that it is promoted as a novelty. The rhetorical device of contrasting supposedly new insights with the alleged misconceptions of the past is routinely evoked in marketing and is something of a signum of the discourse. As a consequence, one characteristic of the subjectivity that is produced is that it is defined in contrast with the 'marketing men' of the past. This raises an interesting question for the future: will there be additional (rhetorical) 'paradigm shifts', that is, will the new, enlightened marketer and 'the dominant logic' of service marketing be problematized and eventually replaced by a still more 'enlightened' version of marketing, one which would be even more customer oriented? From a modernistic perspective believing in scientific progress as the fundamental aim of an academic discipline like marketing, this may seem like a probable, and even desirable development. If one looks at the intrinsic argumentation within marketing discourse, the answer changes though. How could one possibly become more customer oriented than a fully customer-oriented marketer? Could it be that marketing has come to its final destination, from where there is no further 'breaking free'?

The question could also be posed in terms of our theoretical framework. If hegemony is achieved and most elements are turned into moments – in the case of service marketing, if everybody is in marketing and if marketing is everything – could there be any furthering of marketing as discourse? Or will it stabilize and eventually stagnate, giving room to new, perhaps currently not yet born and more reflexive discourses in the future? The question remains of the debate of the early 1990s about the 'end of history and the last man' (Fukuyama 1992) and the suggested supremacy of the liberal society after the fall of the Eastern block and the communist world order. However, although an articulation seems to be hegemonic when studied from within (or when critically examined from a discourse theoretical point of view), the stability might be more fragile than it appears. Marketing is constantly evolving, unfolding in new directions, transforming the glorious present into condemned past. The customer focus of today is thus likely to be broken free from in the future, in one way or another.

Why are we governed in this way (teleology)?

In this chapter, we have linked the ethics of service marketing to neoliberal values characteristic of the late modern society. We argue that service marketing should be seen as an instance of the general project of governmentalization and the promotion of freedom and the management of free subjects and their freedom through their freedom, that is, as an instance of advanced liberal governmentality (Dean 1999; Rose 1999).

On a more concrete level, the general ethics of marketing discourse, that of consumer sovereignty and company satisfying customer needs, which were discussed in Chapter 6, basically remain, as does our critical deconstruction of it. General teleological arguments for marketing are rare nowadays, as marketing discourse is now solidly positioned as a managerial discipline (cf. the introduction to this chapter). However, it is also interesting to focus on how teleology is defined and handled by discourse itself, that is, how the claims of service marketing are justified and motivated by service marketing.

The operational teleology of service marketing is clearly related to the previous rationales of marketing discourse. There is a strong belief in the necessity of the proposed way of working caused by environmental pressures from contemporary markets and society in general. Accepting the discourse and adopting the customer-oriented way of working, that is, becoming a true marketer, is the only way to survive, whether one works in a competitive firm or a public agency. Rhetorically this logic is evident in the frequent claims – often with reference to practice – that the world has changed, that 'old' marketing has lost its contact with reality, and that a reorientation of the discourse is necessary, a reorientation that either already is taking place or is proposed. This was for example the main message of Shostack's 'Breaking free' article. As we have shown in this chapter, this claim of 'breaking free' is to a large extent rhetorical since service marketing builds, elaborates and is in fact dependent upon previous articulations of marketing, particularly marketing management and the marketing concept.

As usual when the environment is used to legitimize a discursive practice, both the environmental conditions and their exact linkage to the promoted discursive elements seem vague and ambiguous if viewed from outside the discourse. However, it follows from the hegemonic nature of marketing discourse that such a position is not naturally taken. The market, as conceived of within marketing, is indeed demanding to be oriented towards, and the customers, as studied through market surveys etc., require extended, customer-focused solutions delivered with empathy, care and understanding. There is simply no other alternative than to join the marketing revolution.

The functional teleology is enhanced still further by the reconceptualization of value offered by service marketing. When value is defined in terms of customer use and utility, taking interest in the customer's value-creating process, and adapting one's own behaviour to it seems like a natural strategy. Since the new concept of value is both defined and operationalized within marketing discourse itself, this teleology is endogenous to discourse and hence not dependent on any external rationality. This makes it possible to establish a stable hegemony independently of general management discourse and sub-fields such as accounting, operations and finance.

8 Customerism: a critique

A fundamental theme of our analysis in Chapters 5, 6 and 7 has been that marketing prescribes a management of organizations that is centred around the customer. We will open this chapter by recapitulating and explicating this aspect of the analysis. We will use the term *customerism* for signifying the underlying governmental rationality of marketing, present in the different forms of management centred around the customer that marketing discourse has prescribed at different points in time. Then, in the second section, we will articulate in what ways and to what extent this governmental rationality of customerism has governmentalized marketing discourse and what type of power managerial marketing discourse has emphasized at different points in time. We argue that marketing has been rearticulated from primarily promoting a managerialism founded on sovereign and disciplinary power into a managerialism emphasizing pastoral power. The discussion and analysis in the second section attempt to draw together and explicate the analysis of governmentalization and the reorientation of the power base that have been central themes in Chapters 5, 6 and 7. In the third section we elaborate on our critical analysis of customerism by drawing on the notion of 'moral distance' (Bauman 1989). In the last section of the chapter we formulate our explicit critique of marketing discourse. We argue that perceiving marketing discourse as a governmentality and thus conceptualizing marketing as a form of power/knowledge and ethic, and not a science, is as such a form of critique. But this analysis also fuels our more particular critical discussion where we de-legitimize managerial marketing discourse by bringing into light: its relationship to itself; its relationship to marketing practice; and its relationship to economic theory and the market economy.

Representing, inventing and reinventing customerism

Customerism is a form of governmental rationality that, through prescribing certain practices and technologies, aims to establish customer needs and demands as the point of reference for management, organizational behaviour, the design and development of organizational forms and the products and services that organizations offer. Within marketing discourse customerism is signified by concepts such as customer orientation, marketing orientation, market orientation, service dominant logic and the marketing concept (Keith 1960; Kholi and Jaworski 1990; Kotler 1967; Levitt 1960; Vargo and Lusch 2004; Webster 2002), which all are or have been central moments or nodal points of marketing discourse. Since the customeristic governmental rationality is embedded in most articulations of managerial marketing discourse, its meaning is also indirectly expressed through technologies such as the four Ps, the Gap model, or customer satisfaction measurement.

We construct customerism as a governmental rationality that is clearly distinct from – and complementary to – how consumerism has been articulated in academic marketing research. While consumerism is about the turning of citizens into consumers, that is, persons whose personal fulfilment is contingent upon the consumption of goods and services, customerism is about making organizations, their forms and employees conditioned and determined by their customers' needs. A customerized organization allegedly offers customers what they want and delivers its offerings in the way customers want. We contend that the final aim with (power/)knowledge production in managerial marketing has always been to develop practices, concepts and technologies that aim to foster and mould a customeristic attitude in organizations by attributing certain features to the customerized manager/ worker. However, we also argue that customerism has been deepened, elaborated and perfected over time, culminating in the later articulations of marketing, service marketing in particular. The book can thus be seen as an archaeology and genealogy of customerism, since we have illuminated significant developments in marketing discourse leading up to the present discursive order (Foucault 1988).

In Chapters 5, 6 and 7, we have analysed what types of customerized subject positions different articulations of marketing have promoted. Our analysis shows that a customeristic governmental rationality started to be developed already in the early twentieth century, that it was furthered by the Taylor-inspired discourse on 'scientific' selling and established as the central governmental rationality in managerial marketing through the introduction of the marketing concept, that it was elaborated on through the broadening of the marketing concept and that it was further developed and redirected in service marketing. The result of our analysis is interesting for at least two reasons. First, most marketing scholars hold the position that a customeristic managerial rationality was introduced to marketing with the marketing concept around 1960. Our analysis shows that customeristic managerialism has been *represented* in academic marketing already since the second decade of the twentieth century. The discourse analysis presented here thus supports and is supported by some of the previous works in marketing history (Fullerton 1988; Hollander 1986) that have contested mainstream marketing's retrospective accounts. Second, while many mainstream marketing scholars have argued that managerial marketing is characterized by paradigm shifts and ruptures in the governmental rationality of marketing (Grönroos 2007; Keith 1960; Levitt 1960; Vargo and Lusch 2004; Webster 1992) we emphasize continuity between traditions. Even though we acknowledge that turning points, redirections and changes have taken place, we contend that these changes have always been contingent on – and elaborations of – previous articulations of marketing discourse.

In accordance with scholars such as Brownlie and Saren (1997), Hackley (2003) and Marion (2006), we believe that arguing for 'uniqueness' is an often-used rhetorical trick in academic marketing. This rhetoric holds that previous research has been unable to solve the 'pressing problems' that are found in 'practice' and that the present research is able to do so, but that for this to take place a complete rearticulation is needed. Marketing is continuously believed to be in a state of crisis. However, the real effect of this 'crisis argument' has paradoxically not been research that brings a helping hand to 'practice' – marketing researchers often worry about the lack of practical impact of academic marketing research (see Brownlie and Saren 1991; Grönroos 2007; Wind and Robertson 1983). Rather, the effect has been an opening up of spaces and gaps that serve the purposes of individual marketing academics who want to produce more legitimate (i.e. publishable) research in order to further their academic career rather than addressing the 'real' needs of marketing practitioners. It could be posited that rather than elaborating on customerism, managerial articulations of marketing discourse have repeatedly *reinvented* customerism – and the need for it.

The governmentalization and governmentality of marketing discourse

In this section we analyse the governmentalization of managerial marketing discourse by customerism and the type of power that has dominated articulations of marketing at different points in time and we show how marketing has become a form of governmentality. In analyses of governmentalization, the notion of governmentality is not understood as a form of power but rather as mentalities of government and management. Such mentalities are forms of knowing and thus rationalities that give rise to managerial practices and technologies. Customerism is one such form of knowing. The governmentalization of discourse refers to the development and dispersion of governmental mentality in discourse (Foucault 2000a). As argued in the previous section, we see customerism as the governmental rationality characteristic of managerial marketing discourse and it is accordingly on the governmentalization of managerial marketing discourse by customerism that we will focus. We will do this from two perspectives. By analysing the inclusiveness of governmentalization we will focus on the amount of and what types of subject positions articulated by the totality of management discourses customerism targets at different points in time. By analysing the permeation of governmentalization we will focus on to what extent and what dimensions of people's subjectivities customerism has been aimed for at different points in time.

The analysis of the type of power that has been emphasized in different articulations of marketing will be made by drawing on the distinction between sovereign power and power/knowledge and within the latter, the distinction between pastoral power and disciplinary power – which we presented in Chapter 3 and recapitulate briefly here. Central to theories of sovereign power is the idea that power is in the hands of certain people or institutions which can force people to do things against their will (Lukes 1974). Power/knowledge emphasizes that power is not the property of someone or something. Rather, it is embedded in discourse and forms of knowledge. Knowledge thus always presupposes power relations (Foucault 1981a). Power/knowledge empowers and restrains people, which sets it aside from sovereign power, which only constrains. It is also possible to distinguish pastoral power and disciplinary power from each other (see Foucault 1977, 2000a, 2000b, 2000c). The first is a historically contingent form of power depending upon an ethic in order to operate and be effective. Foucault developed the notion of pastoral power through analyses of Christian power practices, contingent as they were (and are) on the Christian ethic and the figure of the pastor who guides and leads his flock of sheep according to this ethic. However, Foucault argues that contemporary regimes of power operate in a similar way. Accordingly, the notion of pastoral power has predominantly been used to analyse the power effects of governmental rationalities such as neoliberalism and neoconservatism (Rose 1999) and their operationalization in governmental regimes such as the 'third way' (Fairclough 1993) and the 'active society' (Dean 1995, 1999). Regimes such as these aim to control people through structuring their freedom: by supporting people to be – and through controlling that they really are – wealthy, healthy, emotionally and psychologically stable and socially competent, it is possible to 'make' people free (Rose 1999). Disciplinary power is not historically and ethically contingent in this way. Rather, it is dependent on the establishment of 'objective' and 'true' norms that are produced by the social sciences, quasi-sciences and forms of expertise. It is a form of micro power that acts on the bodies of those it targets, thereby making the body political. Since disciplinary power normalizes people from 'the outside in' it does not particularly focus on the uniqueness of the human beings it objectifies and subjectifies, but rather on the gap between them and the norm. Disciplinary power aims to close that gap. In pastoral power the uniqueness of the individual is the starting point. In order to shape her/his subjectivity from 'the inside out', the pastor who leads his flock needs to know the innermost thoughts of his sheep. This is indeed also needed if the sheep are going to be able to regulate themselves towards the type of ethic that a particular from of pastoral power is contingent on – and thus towards the mentality it fosters. As we have argued in Chapter 3, governmentality marks the emergence of pastoral power (Foucault 2000b, 2000c). Accordingly, it is not self-evident to treat contemporary managerial discourse as forms of governmentality.

A disciplinary project

As discussed in Chapter 5, in the marketing thought that was articulated before the advent of marketing management, that is, roughly between the 1900s and the 1950s, customerism was definitely present but not dominant. None of the articulations of marketing discourse that were developed during this period clearly dominated. The functional, institutional and commodity schools of thought were all influential but none of them reached a hegemonic position. These schools were not explicitly managerial, at least not in terms of articulating a clear understanding of cus-tomerism. Accordingly they did not provide any detailed discursive practices and technologies for establishing customer needs and demands as the point of reference for the design and development of organizations, and for the products and services they offer to the market in particular. However, this does not imply that these articulations did not promote a certain type of power that fostered managerialism. Rather, as we have argued in Chapter 5, these approaches to marketing can be seen as forms of disciplinary power: the classifications that they prescribe, when legitimated as 'truths' through marketing's status as an academic discipline, frame the managers' worldviews and foster certain examinations which set up norms of appropriate employee behaviour. By comparing these norms with actual behaviour, gaps between actuality and potentiality are revealed. As we have repeatedly discussed, disciplinary power is played out exactly through revealing and recommending the closure of such gaps (Foucault 1977). The alleged descriptive nature of the functional, institutional and commodity schools can thus be interpreted as functioning in accordance with the schemata of disciplinary power.

But as we have shown in Chapter 5, early marketing thought also included a more explicit (and customerist) managerial orientation. Scholars at Harvard very early on articulated marketing as a managerialistic discipline by adopting and translating Taylorism to marketing. This was particularly evident in the discourse on sales management which led up to a re-evaluation of the function of selling, the management of salespeople and the subject position of the salesperson. The introduction of Taylorism into marketing discourse signifies a shift in the power promoted within marketing, and sales management in particular, from sovereign power to disciplinary power. As an effect, the subject position of the sales manager was rearticulated from a subject relying on managing salespeople and securing results through using means of sovereign power such as 'sheer force' and 'brute strength' to relying on 'method' (Hoyt 1929[1912]: 10–11). Managing through method in the context of scientific management means that managers are responsible for producing knowledge about how work tasks are carried out most efficiently – it is not sufficient to rely on rules of thumb or the judgement of the workers (Taylor 1911). As a result, selling, which had been often conceptualized as an 'art' – and/or an ability that some people were born with while others were not – turned into an ability that could be 'scientifically' studied, trained, controlled and developed. Taylorism is a typical exponent of power/knowledge and more particularly disciplinary power (see Clegg et al. 2006): through detailed examinations of work tasks, knowledge is produced that prescribes norms which are used to reveal and minimize gaps between potentiality and actuality (Foucault 1977, 1981a). In addition to being thought of as an ability that could be developed rather than an 'art', selling was at least rhetorically redefined from being considered as an act of persuading customers to buy to an act of giving the customers what they wanted and needed. The subject position of the salesperson was thus redefined from being thought of as an aggressive persuader to being framed by a customeristic mentality. These changes contributed to articulate the subject position of the customer-interested salesperson.

Despite these rearticulations, it is our belief that early on the customerism of marketing was not that inclusive: it mainly targeted the sales managers and the salespeople. It is also doubtful whether the human technologies that were promoted early on fostered a power/knowledge that had the ability to extensively change people's attitudes and behaviours in a customeristic way.

An ethical project

Through the launch and 'broadening' of the marketing concept in the period from the late 1950s to the early 1970s, the ethic of customerism was articulated more forcefully and in a more rhetorically convincing way, which made it diffuse throughout marketing discourse. The marketing concept turned the customer into the reference point for every function of the firm, not only the sales function. The inclusiveness of governmentalization was thus considerably expanded as an effect of crystallizing the marketing concept as the nodal point of managerial marketing discourse. As we have argued in Chapter 6, this rearticulation of the general managerial ethic that is inherent in managerial marketing discourse indicates a move towards a neoliberal form of pastoral power. Indeed, the very central idea of customerism as expressed in the marketing concept is that organizations should produce what the free market 'orders' them to produce. The marketing concept is thus framed by the power/knowledge of the doctrine of the free market and simultaneously reproduces this governmental rationality. However, as we have shown in Chapter 6, the premier technologies that were aimed to further the governmental rationality of the marketing concept – market segmentation, targeting and the marketing mix – were informed by customerism but they were not really designed in such a way as to change organizational members in a customeristic way. Even though the subject positions of the manager – the marketing manager in particular – and the salesperson were targeted by the disciplinary power of these technologies, giving the manager the role of the pastor, they did not promote confessions and avowals, central features of pastoral power, in line with cus-tomeristic ethics. Therefore the subject position of the manager/pastor was given no technologies for gaining knowledge about the innermost thoughts of the working subject, which is a prerequisite if the pastor should be able to guide the salesperson on the road to salvation, that is, towards a fully internalized customerism. The technologies most closely associated with the marketing concept were primarily designed in order to make formal organizational structures customeristic. The legacy from rational organization theory, and particularly Taylorism, which devel-ops the management through formal organizational structures, is evident here. However, formal structures and actions of the personnel are often loosely coupled.

In our reading, marketing management discourse and the articulation of the marketing concept turned marketing as a whole into a definite customeristic and ethical project. However, the technologies of marketing management did not foster confessions informed by customerism. Therefore, marketing management did not turn marketing into a governmentality but it prepared for such a shift, which was to be realized later. The governmentalization of marketing discourse by cus-tomerism during the development of marketing management was expanded in its inclusiveness. Compared to the earlier period, however, minor changes took place in the permeation of governmentalization.

A pastoral project

The elaboration, institutionalization and hegemonization of customeristic ethics in marketing discourse, which was accomplished during marketing management, informed the pastoral project that managerial marketing was turned into in service marketing. As we have argued in Chapter 7, the cardinal idea informing this change was the belief that in a service organization, customer-perceived quality is a function not only of *what* is offered to the market but it is also equally important to consider *how* it is delivered by the employees during the service encounter (Berry 1981; Grönroos 1982, 1983, 1984). This important reconceptualization repositioned the object of the managerialism of marketing from producing rules for informing decisions about product, price, place and promotion to producing productive, appropriate-looking and well-behaving employees. This shift was made possible through the invention and adoption of pastoral technologies such as the Gap model and customer-satisfaction measurement models.

In Chapter 7, we have also contended that service marketing discourse is based in neoliberal values, thus fostering an integration of people in advanced liberal society through fulfilling their dreams and hopes which in themselves are determined by neoliberal values. We have connected these ambitions to a freedom mythology mainly originating from the United States, which we claim is embedded in the managerial technologies promoted by service marketing. By subjugating the service worker to a conditional freedom determined by the imperative of customer orientation, service marketing comes to control its subjects' freedom through their freedom.

Service marketing discourse is not only characterized by the fact that all personnel is turned into objects of the customeristic ethic as in marketing management. Customerism also deeply permeates managerial marketing discourse – all working subjects are reframed as part-time marketers. In order for this reframing to occur, technologies for operating on and controlling the working subjects' regulated set of behaviours are developed. When management is armoured with these technologies, it makes it possible to change the subjectivity of the personnel in accordance with the customerism of marketing, for the first time in the history of marketing thought. Service marketing discourse is thus completely governmentalized by customerism: all the involved subject positions are targeted, and all aspects of subjectivity too.

Marketing and moral distance

Analyzing discourses by showing how they are mentalities of government and thus how they frame the world, as we have done here, is what governmentality analysis is all about. Articulating discourse as forms of governmentalities is also a form of social critique, but it is perhaps not a complete social critique since it does not always clearly advance possibilities of desubjugation and desubjectification – which

Foucault (1997) himself argued should be the ultimate aim of critique. Foucault-inspired forms of critique do not always deliver in terms of this aim, which in our view stems from the fact that Foucauldian, typically decentred types of analysis cannot easily be combined with a clearly articulated positive ethical standpoint. Foucault analyses what effects norms, values and ethics have on people but he does not focus on articulating any principles informing how the society ought to be – he has a relativistic position towards ethics, a position which is also characteristic of most 'post-Foucauldian' research. This position can be seen as both a strength and a weakness: a strength because it does not limit and restrain the analysis; a weakness because it gives the analysis no clear centre and point of reference, which we believe might reduce its potential in delivering a social critique.

We have chosen to follow Foucault and his disciples quite closely throughout these pages. In order to construct the inherent ethical totality of managerial marketing discourse, which we have labelled customerism, we have thus taken our point of departure in the moments constituting marketing discourse. In our analysis thus far, we have not been addressing this ethic from a fixed position outside marketing discourse. Rather, we have tried to uncover what it stands for, its internal contradictions and what subjects and society it envisions. We have thus not chosen to inform our analysis by a positive ethical principle, because we believe that this might have framed and restrained our analysis.

In this section we divert from our decentred analysis. We introduce the notion of *moral distance* in order to explicate and deepen what possible negative consequences the customerism embedded in managerial marketing might lead to. Our analysis of moral distance draws on Bauman's (1989) analysis of how the horrors of the holocaust were made possible. Bauman sees it as related to how it was bureaucratically organized, and develops a broad ethical critique of bureaucracy. In his view, bureaucracy objectifies and makes those consuming the products and services of bureaucratic organizations faceless. This creates a moral distance between organizations and the people consuming their services. As a result, 'once the face of the other has been "effaced", employees are freed from moral responsibility to focus on the technical (purpose centred or procedural) aspects of the "job at hand"' (Desmond 1998: 178). To the bureaucrats of the German Nazi administration, the Jews, the disabled, the Gypsies, and others who were sent to concentration camps were thus not really seen as humans but rather as 'figures' on statistical charts, 'units' or 'packages' that should be delivered from point A to B, or as 'input' and 'output' in a production process. According to Bauman, the great danger with bureaucratic organization is thus that its governmental rationality is applicable to every type of business and that it is blind to the social effects that it may have. The serious problem arises when bureaucratic organizations have human beings as their objects because then they might dehumanize them, which may have devastating consequences, as Bauman's analysis of the bureaucracy surrounding the Nazi concentration camp system clearly shows. 'Large numbers of people can be subjected to an essentially utilitarian calculation concerning the best means available to meet a particular end. People become a set of problems to be solved, objects framed within organizational language in terms of competitive advantage and sales figures' (Jones et al. 2005: 91).

Desmond (1998) has applied Bauman's concept of moral distance to his studies of how marketing objectifies consumers. Desmond argues that the governmental technologies that are central to marketing management discourse such as market segmentation, targeting and the marketing mix – analysed in Chapter 6 in the present book – contribute to create a moral distance between the focal organization and its customers, which makes organizational members perceive the latter as faceless.

> The actual removal of the face in marketing takes place at a number of levels. Principally this involves a denial of the moral capacity of the other . . . However it also takes place in terms of the construction of the target market, the targeting of a particular group by means of mass marketing or segmentation. The key factor here is that the individual in the target group is no longer regarded as a moral agent, but as someone to whom something must be done (i.e. as a target for the marketing mix). This process is indifferent to whether the target is someone who is identified as an object for the purposes of selling insurance, promoting a 'no smoking' campaign, or 'ethnic cleansing' for that matter. The key point is that *someone else* decides that it is in the person's or society's best interest to sell them insurance, or the no smoking campaign, or ethnic cleansing; the person's own moral capacity is silenced.
>
> (Desmond 1998: 183–4, emphasis in original)

The type of 'consumerism' promoted by marketing, though not the main object of study in the present book, is thus exemplary of the moral distance as discussed by Bauman (1989). But as Jones et al. (2005: 90) argue, 'organizational hierarchies produce distance too', which implies that moral distance is not only created between organizations and consumers but also within organizations as an effect of the objectification brought about by managerial discourses.

Our analysis of the customerism inherent in marketing discourse shows that such objectifications of typical subject positions articulated by general management discourse have been present in marketing discourse since the early twentieth century, although it must be admitted that before the development of service marketing, marketing had been more successful in developing practices and technologies for objectifying consumers than in doing the same for organizational members. We contend that service marketing has brought about the managerialism that marketing had been in need of. As we have shown, service marketing discourse targets and objectifies most subject positions associated with general organizational discourse – managers and workers, front-line and back office employees in manu-facturing and service organizations – and most aspects of subjectivity too. In the name of customerism, the technologies of service marketing thus turn employees into numbers, bracket them into parts, provide norms of action, make gaps between norms and actuality visible and recommend means of intervention. Service marketing discourse articulates the working subject as a means to reach the goal of customer satisfaction and thus as the major problem for not reaching this satisfaction. But it also articulates solutions for how the working subject should be in terms of what level of empathy should be expressed, what values should be embraced and what feelings should be concealed. As Jones et al. (2005: 91) put it, 'lurking behind the language of the objectified collective is . . . the division of human beings into functional parts, with specific requirements that go with them . . . If you divide people into sets of competencies, or desires waiting to be fulfilled, then you are less likely to see them as complete persons'. This schema seems to have been fulfilled in service marketing which not only dehumanizes the working subjects through objectifying them and making them faceless, but also promotes particular paths of subjectification by providing working subjects with guiding principles for how they should conduct themselves.

Does service marketing then emancipate the customer, as some have suggested (see the discussion in Desmond 1998)? At first glance this might seem as a reasonable argument since in service marketing the will of the customer should guide the design of organizations and their members: the customer is supposedly given the role of governing organizations. But this is not the only possible interpretation. According to us, customer satisfaction is not really the final goal in service marketing. It is clear that service marketing is a neoliberal discourse, and that as such it aims before all to increase capital accumulation, or, as David Harvey (2005) would argue, to make the rich richer and the poor poorer. The customer is treated as the most important means to achieve profitability and profit; at the same time, the customer is instrumentalized as a means for managing employees. The moral distance between organizations and customers is thus not reduced in service marketing – customers are still objectified and made faceless even though the rhetorics are claiming the contrary.

Towards (reflexive) marketing studies

Mainstream marketing research holds that marketing is a positivistic and functionalistic science able to produce truths about how organizations should be managed (Arndt 1985; Hunt 1976, 1983, 1994). Through our Foucauldian analysis we have problematized and deconstructed this position. Our standpoint is that marketing is an ethic designed to govern people in organizations. Our position is supported by critical scholars outside marketing such as du Gay and Salaman (1992), Fairclough (1993), Hochschild (1983) and Clarke and Newman (1997). The analyses of customerism (although under another label) presented by these scholars have revealed how customerism has governmentalized discourse and societal domains. Even though their analyses have been loosely connected to marketing, their understanding of customerism is similar to ours and their work is thus relevant to our project. Our position is also supported by – and similar to – those of critical marketing scholars such as Brownlie and Saren (1997), Hackley (2003) and Marion (2006) who have all discussed the ideological dimensions of managerial marketing discourse.

We have, however, extended the critical analysis of these latter scholars in several ways and we will spell out the most important extensions here. First, while Brownlie and Saren (1997), Hackley (2003) and Marion (2006) have all focused on marketing management discourse, we have studied academic managerial marketing discourse from the birth of the discipline to the latest articulation of service marketing. Second, this historical approach has enabled us to show that the dominant managerial rationality of marketing, that is, customerism, was present in marketing discourse early on, and also to discuss how customerism emerged, was developed, elaborated and how it has hegemonized managerial marketing discourse. Third, our theoretical position differs somewhat from those of previous critical research focusing on the ideological content of the managerialism of marketing – we have opted for a governmentality approach. Accordingly, previous research deconstructs marketing discourse by showing how it is a distortion of reality and thus assumes that there exists an alternative right way to portray reality.[1] Our governmentality analysis does not suggest that there is one way of articulating marketing discourse that is right since ethics is always contingent. Rather, it deconstructs marketing through explicating and using its own implicit ethics as ammunition; and based on this deconstruction, it shows the internal contradictions inherent to it (see the end of Chapters 5, 6 and 7). In addition, our analysis drawing on the notion of moral distance in the previous section has elaborated on this deconstruction. Thus, our analysis brings impetus to desubjectification and thus desubjugation from marketing discourse. As we have argued in Chapter 1, to us this should be one of the aims of critical research (see also Foucault 1997).

In this last section we will reflect more explicitly on how our analysis has contributed to this critical project, the potential desubjectification from subject positions and how future research can further contribute to this project. In our reflection, we will loosely draw on Marion's (2006) analysis. We contend that: academic marketing legitimizes itself through reference to 'successful' marketing practice (or what is discursively defined as successful practice) while at the same time it legitimizes these practices; and marketing is legitimized by the market economy and theories of economics and vice versa. But we also show in what way the distinction between 'theory' and 'practice' informing this line of reasoning is arbitrary. In addition we will also claim that managerial marketing discourse is legitimizing itself with reference to itself through its constant self-mirroring or self-referentiality – marketing discourse can indeed be thought of as a narcissistic discourse always preoccupied with itself and its own identity as a positivistic discourse. Our analysis in Chapters 5, 6 and 7 focused mostly on this self-referential form of legitimization and we will start this last section by explicating how marketing discourse serves this function. Then we will turn to the first two aspects of legitimization and in relation to them we will articulate most of our suggestions for future research.

Marketing: An unethical ethic

The legitimization of the customeristic rationality inherent in managerial marketing discourse by marketing discourse itself is, as we have shown, an ethical project. But it is not only that: it is also an unethical project in the sense that marketing discourse is articulated inconsistently with its own implicit ethics. Our deconstructions of marketing discourse, in Chapters 5, 6 and 7, have made this evident. In Chapter 5, we have argued that marketing scholars seized the opportunity that the 'Great Depression' gave rise to: they used the Great Depression to further their own agenda by positing marketing as the answer to people's prayers. We have also questioned whether private firms managers, who were singled out as the subjects most suited for implementing the alleged great social progress programme of marketing are really the best people for turning such a seemingly philanthropic agenda into practice. Managers are usually not appointed to serve the common good but rather the interest of those who employ them.

In Chapter 6, we have shown that marketing management discourse was articulated as a reaction to what was alleged to be earlier marketing thought (which we showed was an inaccurate conceptualization). According to the reasoning within marketing management discourse, articulations of early marketing were unethical. The alleged reason behind this was that before marketing management, marketing was believed to be designed for changing the needs of the consumers so that they accorded better with products offered by the focal organization. Manipulating the needs of consumers in this way was believed to be unethical. It was much better to satisfy the 'real' needs of the consumers. Therefore it was argued that organizations should adapt what they offered to the customers' needs rather than manipulating these needs. This argument was, and is, central to the *raison d'être* of the marketing concept. Accordingly, at the heart of marketing management discourse there is the notion that, for the relationship that organizations have with the market to be considered ethically fair, it must be characterized by adaptation to the needs of the market and not by convergence of the needs of the customers to what the organization is offering. As we have shown in Chapter 6, however, marketing management discourse combines adaptation and convergence approaches to the market which enables an even greater manipulation of customers compared to only relying on convergence. The alleged unethical nature of early marketing discourse as reinvented within marketing management discourse can thus be seen as also an integral part of marketing management itself; if anything, when complemented by the customeristic managerial rationality, the unethical nature can be seen as being given impetus.

As Vance Packard (1957) argued, marketing scholars sometimes try to make the theory and practice of marketing look fairer by arguing that consumers do not always know what they want, that their needs are latent, and that therefore marketing communication is needed to guide them in the right direction. Psychoanalysis, which can supposedly cure people from psychological problems such as neuroses through turning unconscious cognition into conscious cognition, is used as a model for this argument. But marketing communication cannot be compared to psychoanalysis, which typically involves a very long period of individual counselling in order to be effective. Marketing communication is thus not primarily aimed at turning latent needs into conscious intentional needs. Rather, it manipulates the needs of the consumers and according to the very ethics advanced within marketing management discourse, it does this in an unethical way.

In Chapter 7, we have shown that service marketing, while ostensibly pretending to disregard previous articulations of managerial marketing discourse – especially from marketing management – has in fact mostly elaborated on the rationale found in the marketing concept, and thus largely owes its existence and articulated identity to marketing management discourse. We have contended that the reasons why service marketing scholars have argued against marketing management have mostly been about wanting to legitimize their own field of research – and maybe furthering their own careers by publishing their own articles in prestigious journals. Mainstream managerial marketing research in general and service marketing research in particular is characterized by the 'rhetoric of uniqueness'. The general argument of this rhetoric is that previous research in marketing has not given a true picture of 'reality' and therefore it has not managed to provide much help to organizations for improving their operations. As Brownlie and Saren (1997) suggest, this alleged existence of a gap between theory and practice does not really stimulate research that aims to close the gap (even though this is the argument within mainstream marketing) but it rather works to open up a space for new research by implying that *this time* contributions to practice and more particularly to the management of organizations will be made. Somewhat provocatively, we contend that the alleged gap thus serves the purpose of the marketing academics who want to produce more legitimate (i.e. publishable) research in order to further their academic careers rather than the 'real' needs of marketing practitioners. Again, we see marketing research as a largely egoistic – and at times perhaps even autistic – enterprise, and not the philanthropic project that it has been claimed to be by its advocates.

In our analysis of service marketing, we have also claimed that since managerialistic articulations have become so hegemonic within marketing discourse, the possibility of reflexivity is almost completely lost. Many service marketing scholars never seem to have been outside the narrow box of service marketing. Their subjectivities seem to be strongly determined by neoliberal discourse, but as they see it they are really doing objective research. The legitimization of their project to a 'reality' outside discourse is thus fundamentally biased and so are their recommendations for changing this 'reality'. To us, it seems as though service marketing scholars have created their own, in-bred 'discursive universe', which has little or no relevance for anything outside it.

This claim that marketing is not only an ethic but that it can also be seen, according to its own standards, as an unethical ethic fuels the critique that we have raised against marketing throughout this book and brings impetus to our delegitimization of academic managerial marketing discourse. It provides good reasons for aiming for desubjectification from marketing: for whom would it be desirable to let oneself be governed by an internally contradictory discourse, which inherently contradicts its own fundamental underlying ethic?

In addition, our analysis of customerism informed by the notion of moral distance in the present chapter emphasizes this critique. Based on this analysis we can argue from a position outside marketing that managerial marketing furthers moral distance and thereby may have highly undesirable consequences. By increasing the distance between those who manage organizations and the working subject and by dividing the working subject into parts that can be acted upon and transformed, managerial marketing in general and service marketing in particular does not treat humans as persons but rather as faceless objects.

Academic marketing vis-à-vis practice and economy

Marketing legitimizes itself through reference to 'successful' marketing practice and the market economy/economics. Even though we have analysed these relationships less rigorously compared to how marketing legitimizes itself with reference to itself, we still have discussed them to some extent.

The relationship between academic marketing discourse and practice is definitely a major topic in marketing research. The marketing concept, for example, suggests and legitimizes customeristic management of organization offerings and service marketing legitimizes certain types of management of employees in order to make them more customeristic in their thoughts, expressed emotions and values. Since we have claimed that managerial academic marketing discourse is an ethic and that it is contingent and relative, we have contributed to the deconstruction of this privileged position given to academic knowledge in marketing discourse. Our argument has particularly been built on showing that marketing represents different articulations of customeristic governmental rationality such as that of the marketing concept, informed as it is by the alleged customer orientation at Pillsbury (Keith 1960) and other American organizations (Levitt 1960; McKitterick 1957) at a particular point in time. Similarly, we have pointed out how the governmentality of service marketing is contingent on neoliberal values. In our view, it is desirable and important that such contingent representations be not considered as objective truths – which they unfortunately tend to be in our Western, increasingly neo-liberal(ized) societies. The practice of marketing as represented and conceptualized by academic discourse has thus informed and fuelled our critical analysis.

On the other hand, we have not written much about how customerism is played out in organizations. The reason for this is that academic marketing discourse lacks accounts of how the discourse of customerism is used in organizations – the scarce research that does exist tends to be managerially biased (see Gebhart et al. 2006). Managerially unbiased qualitative research is a prerequisite for under-standing the organizational manifestations of the type of customerism that mar-keting discourse prescribes, and for critically analysing it. Thus, if we want to understand how marketing is used for controlling and repressing in practical organizational life as well as how such initiatives are resisted, we must, as Brownlie and Saren (1997) and Morgan (2003) have argued, engage in thorough ethnographic and interview-based research. It would be particularly interesting to focus upon how humans are re-imagined and controlled through the application of technologies associated with service marketing, such as the Gap model and relationship market-ing, since these technologies directly target people's subjectivities. What effects do they have? Previous research on customeristic programmes loosely connected to marketing suggests that customerism has influenced organizations deeply (see Clarke and Newman 1997; du Gay and Salaman 1992; Fairclough 1993; Hochschild

1983; Miller and Rose 1997) but the role that marketing has played in this process remains unclear: a clear research agenda emerges from this gap.

That managerial marketing discourse is legitimized by economics and the market economy is undisputed. As we have shown, and as marketing historians have shown previously (Bartels 1976; Cochoy 1998; Jones and Shaw 2002; Sheth et al. 1988), marketing emerged out of economics and marketing needs a market economy in order to operate. However, in previous research – and with the notable exception of Cochoy (1998, 1999) – less emphasis has been put into discussions of how marketing discourse legitimizes and reproduces the market economy. We have touched upon this issue by analysing managerial marketing discourse as an advanced liberal governmental discourse that governs through and by freedom. By making this rationality central to its customeristic governmental agenda and by conceptualizing this as the scientifically proven best way of managing organizations, it can be argued that marketing furthers and legitimizes the broader neoliberal governmental project. Marketing thus should be criticized through a critique of the market economy and economics just as economics and the marketing economy need to be criticized through marketing (cf. Marion 2006). In order to deliver this critique, marketing discourse and economic discourse should be analysed in parallel, which we have not done here.

In conclusion we would argue that it is not very productive to treat marketing as a positivistic science, simply because it is misleading. As we see it, it should be treated as an ethic. Academic marketing needs to be reformulated from prescribing how to do marketing to . . . well, studying marketing. Marketing practice should be the object of study rather than the outcome of study. What is needed is a change of identity and culture in marketing academia and not, as is usually claimed by marketing academics, a change of identity and culture in organizations. Hopefully we have contributed to taking steps towards such a change of perspective.

Notes

1 Introduction

1   We see the notions of service marketing and service management as synonymous. For reasons of convenience, throughout the book we use the label service marketing rather than service management. This is not to say that we think the field should be labelled 'marketing' rather than 'management'; in fact, the relationship between marketing and management is a main theme in the book.

2   If we have opted for a more particular and not general critique of marketing, other perspectives such as feminist and post-colonial perspectives would have been possible point of departures.

3   In this book we will sometimes use the notion of 'marketing research' without the qualifier 'academic' (see, for example, further in this section). 'Marketing research', as we use it, always refers to academic research and should not be mistaken for the notion 'market research', which refers to the activity of gaining knowledge about the market for informing marketing decisions, usually within private companies.

4   As a reaction to the standpoint that words and sentences only describe the world, the philosopher and logician J.L. Austin introduced the notion of performative utterances for signifying utterances that say and do what they say simultaneously (e.g. 'I now declare you man and wife'). Even though discourse analysis shares the basic idea that language not only describes but also performs reality, the notion of performativity is not used to refer to how sentences or individual words do this. Rather, it is used to signify that language systems and discourse regulate what is possible and impossible to think, say and do in the domains they refer to.

2 Critical marketing research

1   Another paper that would qualify in the third category is the one written by the three of us (Skålén et al. 2006) which the present book is inspired by and elaborates on.

3 Power/knowledge, governmentality and government

1   The present text was written before Foucault's 1978 and 1979 lecture series at Collège de France about governmentality were made available in English.

2   As we have argued in the introduction to this chapter, Foucault's work on governmentality was under way when he died in 1984. As a consequence, the relationship between the notion of governmentality and some associated concepts in Foucault's work is slippery. This is the case with the verb 'to governmentalize'. As we interpret Foucault's work on governmentality, the notion of 'governmentalizing' is used to signify how and to what extent 'the art of government' – or simply government as a form of power, as

understood by Foucault – rather than Machiavellianism gradually came to characterize the rule of states (see Foucault 2000a: 220–1 and 2000b: 345). Foucault thus uses the concept to signify how the governmental rationality of government during history spread in institutional and societal domains. In this book we use the verb 'to governmentalize' in a similar way but we want to qualify our usage vis-à-vis Foucault's in two ways: first, we use it to refer to how governmental rationality(ies) is/are spread in discourse (particularly marketing discourse) not institutional domains; and second, we use it to refer to how more particular governmental rationalities than government in general 'governmentalize' (marketing) discourse. We thus use the verb in an active and transitive way (similarly to how 'to hegemonize' can be used), rather than merely referring to passively 'governmentalized' domains.

4 Studying governmental discourse

1   We would like to point out that the 'methodology' and 'theory' distinction that we sometimes use, in this chapter especially, is a bit arbitrary in a discourse analysis such as this: the methodology does not only serve the purpose to structure our analysis but should also be seen as an input for the substantial part of it.
2   In discourse theory the objective is thus equal to the ideological.

5 Founding the power/knowledge of managerial marketing

1   Translated from the French: 'parler d'attelage attire l'attention sur les racines profondément individuelles du processus en cause'.
2   Translated from the French: '[S'atteler, c'est] non seulement adopter une configuration plurielle et solidaire, mais c'est aussi rejoindre ceux qui, avant vous, ont déjà entrepris d'avancer de concert, se raccrocher au convoi, le prendre en route'.

6 Consolidating the power/knowledge of managerial marketing

1   As Marion (1993) shows, Theodore Levitt has been explicit in stating that his aim was to summarize and pedagogically present to a broader audience emerging 'knowledge'.
2   The differences in sheer size and depth between Keith's article and Alderson's *Marketing Behavior and Executive Action* cannot be greater. Keith's article consists of four pages of easily readable text, while Alderson's rather abstract prose is 487 pages long.
3   Keith (1960) also describes a fourth era which he names 'Marketing Control'. When Keith wrote his paper, Pillsbury had not reached this era, which was introduced as a speculation regarding what was going to happen in the future. It has not been referred to extensively by those who draw on Keith within marketing, therefore we do not review it here.
4   A similar distinction has also been made by researchers outside the marketing discipline. Fligstein (1990), for example, differentiates between four 'conceptions of control' – a notion closely related to that of 'governmental rationality' as we use it – where 'the sales and marketing conception of control' is one and the same.
5   Another more particular example of the relationship between McCarthyism and marketing academia is the documented link between the American Marketing Association and Walter Rostow. Rostow, an economist, economic historian and a security affairs adviser to several American administrations (including Kennedy's and Johnson's), is known for his anti-Communist position and his defence of free enterprise economics manifested in one of his most important works: *The Stages of Economic Growth*, subtitled *A Non-Communist Manifesto* (1960). Rostow was invited as guest speaker at meetings held by the American Marketing Association (see Lavidge 1970).
6   Scott distinguishes between formal and informal social structures. 'A *formal* social

structure is one in which the social positions and the relationships among them have been explicitly specified and are defined independently of the personal characteristics and relations of the participants occupying these positions. By contrast, in an *informal* social structure, it is impossible to distinguish between the characteristics of the positions and the prescribed relations and the characteristics and personal relations of the participants' (Scott 2003: 20, emphasis in original).

7 Elaborating the power/knowledge of managerial marketing

1   This of course does not exclude such forms of power and control from being present in service settings. However, they are not based on the power/knowledge of service marketing but on other managerial rationalities that compete in the discursive field of service organizations.

8 Customerism: a critique

1   Marion's research can be seen as a partial deviation from this type of critical theory-inspired ideological analysis since he also adopts an anthropological definition of ideology (Marion 2006).

References

Agnew, H.E. (1941) 'The history of the American Marketing Association', *Journal of Marketing*, 5 (4): 374–9.

Alderson, W. (1957) *Marketing Behavior and Executive Action: A Functionalist Approach to Marketing Theory*, Homewood, IL: Irwin.

Alderson, W. and Cox, R. (1948) 'Towards a Theory of Marketing', *Journal of Marketing*, 13 (2): 137–52.

Alvesson, M. (1994) 'Critical theory and consumer marketing', *Scandinavian Journal of Management*, 10 (3): 291–313.

Alvesson, M. and Deetz, S. (2000) *Doing Critical Management Research*, London: Sage.

Alvesson, M. and Willmott, H. (1992) 'On the idea of emancipation in management and organization studies', *Academy of Management Review*, 17 (3): 432–64.

Alvesson, M. and Willmott, H. (1996) *Making Sense of Management: A Critical Introduction*, London: Sage.

Alvesson, M. and Willmott, H. (2003) 'Introduction', in M. Alvesson and H. Willmott (eds), *Studying Management Critically*, London: Sage.

American Marketing Journal (1934) 'The American Marketing Journal, a journal for the advancement of science in marketing', *American Marketing Journal*, 1 (1).

Anderson, E.W., Fornell, C. and Rust, R.T. (1997) 'Customer satisfaction, productivity, and profitability: differences between goods and services', *Marketing Science*, 16 (2): 129–45.

Anderson, P.F. (1983) 'Marketing, scientific progress, and scientific method', *Journal of Marketing*, 47 (4): 18–31.

Anderson, P.F. (1986) 'On method in consumer research: a critical relativist perspective', *Journal of Consumer Research*, 13 (September): 155–73.

Applebaum, W. (1947) 'The Journal of Marketing: the first ten years', *Journal of Marketing*, 11 (4): 355–63.

Arndt, J. (1983) 'The political economy paradigm: foundation for theory building in marketing', *Journal of Marketing*, 47 (Fall): 44–54.

Arndt, J. (1985) 'On making marketing science more scientific: the role of orientation, paradigms, metaphors and puzzle solving', *Journal of Marketing*, 49 (3): 11–23.

Bachrach, P. and Baratz, M.S. (1962) 'The two faces of power', *American Political Science Review*, 56 (4): 947–52.

Bagozzi, R.P. (1975) 'Marketing as exchange', *Journal of Marketing*, 39 (October): 32–9.

Barnard, C.I. (1938) *The Functions of the Executive*, Cambridge, MA: Harvard University Press.

Bartels, R. (1951) 'Can marketing be a science', *Journal of Marketing*, 15 (3): 319–28.

Bartels, R. (1962) *The Development of Marketing Thought*, Homewood, IL: Irwin.

Bartels, R. (1976) *The History of Marketing Thought*, 2nd edn, Columbus, OH: Grid.

Bartels, R. (1988) *The History of Marketing Thought*, 3rd edn, Columbus, OH: Publishing Horizons.

Barton, B. (1929) 'Introduction', in C.W. Hoyt, *Scientific Sales Management Today*, 2nd edn, New York: The Ronald Press Company.

Baudrillard, J. (1970) *La Société de Consommation*, Paris: Denoël (in French).

Bauman, Z. (1989) *Modernity and the Holocaust*, Cambridge: Polity.

Berger, P.L. and Luckmann, T. (1967) *The Social Construction of Reality: A Treatise in the Sociology of Knowledge*, London: Penguin Books.

Bergström, O. and Knights, D. (2006) 'Organizational discourse and subjectivity, subjectification during processes of recruitment', *Human Relations*, 59 (3): 351–77.

Berry, L.L. (1981) 'The employee as a customer', *Journal of Retail Banking*, 3 (1): 33–40.

Berry, L.L. (1999) *Discovering the Soul of Service: The Nine Drivers of Sustainable Business Success*, New York: The Free Press.

Berry. L.L. and Parasuraman, A. (1991) *Marketing Service: Competing through Quality*, New York: The Free Press.

Berry, L.L. and Parasuraman, A. (1993) 'Building a new academic field: the case of services marketing', *Journal of Retailing*, 69 (1): 13–61.

Bitner, M.J. (1992) 'Service scapes: the impact of physical surroundings on customers and employees', *Journal of Marketing*, 56 (2): 57–71.

Borden, N.H. (1964) 'The concept of the marketing mix', *Journal of Advertising Research*, 4 (2): 2–7.

Borgerson, J. and Schroeder, J. (2002) 'Ethical issues of global marketing: avoiding bad faith in visual representation', *European Journal of Marketing*, 36 (5/6): 570–94.

Borsch, F.J. (1957) 'The marketing philosophy as a way of business life', in *The Marketing Concept: Its Meaning to Management*, Marketing Series No 99, New York: American Management Association.

Bourdieu, P. (1984) *Distinction: A Social Critique of the Judgment of Taste*, London: Routledge.

Brassington, F. and Pettitt, S. (2000) *Principles of Marketing*, Harlow: Financial Times Management.

Brown, H.W. (1914) 'Scientific management in the sales department', *Bulletin of the Taylor Society*, 1 (December): 3–4.

Brown, S. (1995) *Postmodern Marketing*, London: Routledge.

Brown, S. (1998) *Postmodern Marketing Two: Telling Tales*, London: International Thomson Business.

Brown, S. (1999) 'Postmodernism: the end of marketing', in D. Brownlie, M. Saren, R. Wensley and R. Whittington (eds), *Rethinking Marketing: Towards Critical Marketing Accountings*, London: Sage.

Brown, S. (2003) 'Crisis, what crisis? Marketing, Midas, and the Croesus of representation', *Qualitative Marketing Research: An International Journal*, 6 (3): 194–205.

Brown, S. (2004) 'Writing marketing: the clause that refreshes', *Journal of Marketing Management*, 20 (3–4): 321–42.

Brown, S. (2006) *The Marketing Code*, London: CYAN Marshall Cavendish Business.

Brown, S., Fisk, R.P. and Bitner, M.J. (1994) 'The development and emergence of services marketing thought', *International Journal of Service Industry Management*, 5 (1): 21–48.

Brown, S., Kozinets, R.V. and Sherry Jr., J.F. (2003) 'Teaching old brands new tricks: retro branding and the revival of brand meaning', *Journal of Marketing*, 67 (3): 19–33.

Brownlie, D. and Saren, M. (1991) 'The four Ps of the marketing concept: prescriptive, polemical, permanent and problematical', *European Journal of Marketing*, 26 (4): 34–47.

Brownlie, D. and Saren, M. (1995) 'On the commodification of marketing knowledge: opening themes', *Journal of Marketing Management*, 11 (7): 619–27.

Brownlie, D. and Saren, M. (1997) 'Beyl
ce', *International Journal of Research in Marketing*, 14: 147–61.

Brownlie, D., Saren, M., Wensley, R. and Whittington, R. (1999) 'Marketing disequilibrium: on redress and restoration', in D. Brownlie, M. Saren, R. Wensley and R. Whittington (eds), *Rethinking Marketing: Towards Critical Marketing Accountings*, London: Sage.

Burrell, G. (1988) 'Modernism, post-modernism and organizational analysis 2: the contribution of Michel Foucault', *Organization Studies*, 9 (2): 221–36.

Burrell, G. (1999) 'Commentary', in D. Brownlie, M. Saren, R. Wensley and R. Whittington (eds), *Rethinking Marketing: Towards Critical Marketing Accountings*, London: Sage.

Burrell, G. and Morgan, G. (1979) *Sociological Paradigms and Organizational Analysis: Elements of the Sociology of Corporate Life*, Brookfield: Ashgate.

Burton, D. (2001) 'Critical marketing theory: the blueprint?', *European Journal of Marketing*, 35 (5/6): 722–43.

Bussière, D. (2000) 'Evidence of a marketing periodic literature within the American Economic Association: 1895–1936', *Journal of Macromarketing*, 20 (2): 137–43.

Butler, R.S. (1923) *Marketing and Merchandising*, New York: Alexander Hamilton Institute.

Buttle, F. (1996) 'SERVQUAL: review, critique, research agenda', *European Journal of Marketing*, 30 (1): 8–32.

Canfield, B.R. (1940) *Salesmanship Practices and Problems*, New York: McGraw-Hill.

Carlzon, J. (1987) *Moments of Truth*, Cambridge: Ballinger

Cassels, J.M. (1936) 'The significance of early economic thought on marketing', *Journal of Marketing*, 1 (2): 129–33.

Clark, F.E. (1922) *Principles of Marketing*, New York: Macmillan.

Clarke J. and Newman J. (1997) *The Managerial State: Power, Politics and Ideology in the Remaking of Social Welfare*, London: Sage.

Clegg, S.R. (1989) *Frameworks of Power*, London: Sage.

Clegg, S.R., Courpasson, D. and Phillips, N. (2006) *Power and Organizations*, London: Sage.

Clegg, S.R., Pitsis, T.S., Rura-Polley, T. and Marosszeky, M. (2002) 'Governmentality matters: designing an alliance of inter-organizational collaboration for managing projects', *Organization Studies*, 23 (3): 317–37.

Cochoy, F. (1998) 'Another discipline for the market economy: marketing as a performative knowledge and know-how for capitalism', in M. Callon (ed.), *The Laws of the Market*, Oxford: Blackwell.

Cochoy, F. (1999) *Une Histoire du Marketing*, Paris: La découverte (in French).

Cochoy, F. (2002) 'Une petite histoire du client, ou de la progressive normalisation du marché et de l'organisation' ('A short history of "customers", or the gradual standardization of markets and organizations'), *Sociologie du travail*, 44: 357–80 (in French).

Copeland, M.T. (1923) 'Relation of consumers' buying habits to marketing methods', *Harvard Business Review*, 1 (3): 282–9.

Covaleski, M.A., Dirsmith, M.W., Heian, B.H. and Samuel, S. (1998) 'The calculated and the avowed: techniques of discipline and struggles over identity in big six public accounting firms', *Administrative Science Quarterly*, 43 (4): 293–327.

Cowan, S. (1924) 'An example of scientific marketing procedure: a yardstick for measuring the buying public and advertising circulation', *Bulletin of the Taylor Society*, 9 (June): 143–51.

Cronin, J.J. and Taylor, S.A. (1994) 'SERVPERF versus SERVQUAL: reconciling performance-based and perceptions-minus-expectations measurement of service quality', *Journal of Marketing*, 58 (1): 125–31.

Crowell, J.F. (1901) *Report of the Industrial Commission on the Distribution of Farm Products*, Vol. 6, Washington, DC: US Government Printing Office.

Cruikshank, B. (1994) 'The will to empower: technologies of citizenship and the war on poverty', *Socialist Review*, 23 (4): 29–55.

de Selincourt, A. (1962) *The World of Herodotus*, New York: Little, Brown and Company.

Deal, T.E. and Kennedy, A.A. (1982) *Corporate Culture: The Rituals of Corporate Life*, Reading: Addison-Wesley.

Dean, M. (1995) 'Governing the unemployed self in an active society', *Economy and Society*, 24 (4): 559–83.

Dean, M. (1999) *Governmentality: Power and Rule in Modern Society*, London: Sage.

Dennison, H.S. (1920) 'Proceedings of a conference of sales executives', *Bulletin of the Taylor Society*, 5 (October): 200–2.

Desmond, J. (1998) 'Marketing and moral indifference', in M. Parker (ed.), *Ethics & Organizations*, London: Sage.

Dixon, D.F. (1979) 'Prejudice v. marketing? An examination of some historical sources', *Akron Business and Economic Review*, 10: 37–42.

Dixon, D.F. (1999) 'Some late nineteenth-century antecedents of marketing theory', *Journal of Macromarketing*, 19 (2): 115–25.

Douglas, A.W. (1919) *Traveling Salesmanship*, New York: Macmillan.

Drucker, P.F. (1954) *The Practice of Management*, New York: Harper and Row.

Du Gay, P. (1991) 'Enterprise culture and the ideology of excellence', *New Formations*, 13 (1): 45–61.

Du Gay, P. (1994) 'Making up managers: bureaucracy, enterprise and the liberal art of separation', *British Journal of Sociology*, 45 (4): 655–74.

Du Gay, P. (1996) *Consumption and Identity at Work*, London: Sage.

Du Gay, P. (2004) 'Against "Enterprise" (but not against "enterprise", for that would make no sense)', *Organization*, 11 (1): 37–57.

Du Gay, P. and Salaman, G. (1992) 'The cult[ure] of the customer', *Journal of Management Studies*, 29 (5): 615–33.

Eagleton, T. (1991) *Ideology*, London: Verso.

Edenius, M. and Hasselbladh, H. (2002) 'The balanced scorecard as an intellectual technology', *Organizations*, 9 (2): 249–73.

Edgett, S. and Parkinson, S. (1993) 'Marketing for services industries – a review', *The Service Industries Journal*, 13 (3): 19–39.

Edvardsson, B. and Enquist, B. (2002) 'Service culture and service strategy: the IKEA saga', *The Service Industries Journal*, 22 (4): 153–86.

Fairclough, N. (1992) *Discourse and Social Change*, Cambridge: Polity Press.

Fairclough, N. (1993) 'Critical discourse and the marketization of public discourse: the universities', *Discourse and Society*, 4 (1): 133–68.

Fairclough, N. (1995) *Discourse and Social Change*, Cambridge: Polity Press.

Fairclough, N. (2001) *Language and Power*, 2nd edn, London: Pearson Education.

Featherstone, M. (1991) *Consumer Culture and Postmodernism*, London: Sage.

Ferber, R. (1970) 'The expanding role of the marketing in the 1970s', *Journal of Marketing*, 34 (1): 29–30.

Firat, A.F. and Shultz C.J. (1997) 'From segmentation to fragmentation: markets and marketing strategy in the postmodern era', *European Journal of Marketing*, 31 (3/4): 183–207.

Firat, A.F. and Venkatesh, A. (1993) 'Postmodernity: the age of marketing', *International Journal of Research in Marketing*, 10 (3): 227–49.

Fishbein, M. and Ajzen, I. (1975) *Belief, Attitude, Intention and Behavior: An Introduction to Theory and Research*, Reading: Addison-Wesley.

Fisk, R.P., Brown, S.W. and Bitner, M.J. (1993) 'Tracking the evolution of the service marketing literature', *Journal of Retailing*, 69 (1): 61–103.

Fligstein, N. (1990) *The Transformation of Corporate Control*, Cambridge, MA: Harvard University Press.

Foucault, M. (1967) *Madness and Civilization: A History of Insanity in the Age of Reason*, London: Routledge.

Foucault, M. (1970) *The Order of Things: An Archaeology of the Human Sciences*, London: Routledge.

Foucault, M. (1972) *The Archaeology of Knowledge*, London: Routledge.

Foucault, M. (1973) *The Birth of the Clinic: An Archaeology of Medical Perception*, London: Routledge.

Foucault, M. (1977) *Discipline and Punish: The Birth of the Prison*, London: Penguin.

Foucault, M. (1981a) *The Will to Knowledge: The History of Sexuality*, Vol. 1, London: Penguin.

Foucault, M. (1981b) 'The Order of Discourse', in R. Young (ed.), *Untying the Text: A Post-Structuralist Reader*, London: Routledge.

Foucault, M. (1985a) *The Use of Pleasure: The History of Sexuality*, Vol. 2, New York: Vintage Books.

Foucault, M. (1985b) *The Care of the Self: The History of Sexuality*, Vol. 3, London: Penguin.

Foucault, M. (1988) *Politics, Philosophy, Culture: Interviews and Other Writings, 1977–1984*, London: Routledge.

Foucault, M. (1997) *The Politics of Truth*, New York: Semiotext(e).

Foucault, M. (2000a) 'Governmentality', in J.D. Faubion (ed.), *Power: The Essential Works of Foucault*, Vol. 3, New York: The Free Press.

Foucault, M. (2000b) 'The Subject and Power', in J.D. Faubion (ed.), *Power: The Essential Works of Foucault*, Vol. 3, New York: The Free Press.

Foucault, M. (2000c) '"Omnes et Singulatim": toward a critique of political reason', in J.D. Faubion (ed.), *Power: The Essential Works of Foucault*, Vol. 3, New York: The Free Press.

Foucault, M. (2000d) 'The political technology of individuals'. in J.D. Faubion (ed.), *Power: The Essential Works of Foucault*, Vol. 3, New York: The Free Press.

Foucualt, M. (2003) *Abnormal: Lectures at Collège de France 1974–75*, Basingstoke: Palgrave.

Foucault, M. (2006) *Psychiatric Power: Lectures at Collège de France 1973–74*, Basingstoke: Palgrave.

Freeland, W.E. (1920) 'Coordination of sales with scientific production', *Bulletin of the Taylor Society*, 5: 202–7.

Friedman, W.A. (2005) *Birth of a Salesman: The Transformation of Selling in America*, Cambridge, MA: Harvard University Press.

Fukuyama, F. (1992) *The End of History and the Last Man*, London: Hamish-Hamilton.

Fullerton, R.A. (1988) 'How modern is modern marketing: marketing's evolution and the myth of the "production era"', *Journal of Marketing*, 52 (1): 108–25.

Furusten, S. (1999) *Popular Management Books: How They are Made and What They Mean for Organisations*, London: Routledge.

Gay, E.F. (1908) 'The new graduate school of business administration', *Harvard Illustrated Magazine*, 9: 159–61.

Gebhart G.F., Carpenter, G.S. and Sherry Jr., J.F. (2006) 'Creating a market orientation: a longitudinal, multifirm, grounded analysis of cultural transformations', *Journal of Marketing*, 70 (4): 37–55.

Geertz, C. (1973) *The Interpretations of Cultures*, London: Fontana Press.

Gouldner A.W. (1954) *Patterns of Industrial Bureaucracy*, Glencoe, IL: Free Press.

Gremler, D.D., Bitner, M.J. and Evans, K.R. (1994) 'The internal service encounter', *International Journal of Service Industry Management*, 5 (2): 34–56.

Grether, E.T. (1988) 'Macro-micro marketing in perspective', in S. Shapiro and A.H. Walle (eds), *Marketing, A Return to the Broader Dimensions*, Chicago, IL: American Marketing Association.

Grey C. and Willmott H. (eds) (2005) *Critical Management Studies: A Reader*, Oxford: Oxford University Press.

Grönroos, C. (1978) 'A service orientated approach to marketing of services', *European Journal of Marketing*, 12 (8): 588–601

Grönroos, C. (1982) 'An applied service marketing theory', *European Journal of Marketing*, 16 (7): 30–41.

Grönroos, C. (1983) *Strategic Management and Marketing in the Service Sector*, Lund: Studentlitteratur.

Grönroos, C. (1984) 'A service quality model and its marketing implications', *European Journal of Marketing*, 18 (4): 36–44.

Grönroos, C. (1994) 'From scientific management to service management: a management perspective for the age of service competition', *International Journal of Service Industry Management*, 5 (1): 5–20.

Grönroos, C. (2000) *Service Management and Marketing: A Customer Relationship Management Approach*, Chichester: Wiley.

Grönroos, C. (2006) 'Adopting a service logic for marketing', *Marketing Theory*, 6 (3): 317–33.

Grönroos, C. (2007) *In Search of a New Logic for Marketing: Foundations of Contemporary Theory*, Chichester: Wiley.

Grönroos, C. and Gummesson, E. (1985) 'The Nordic school of service marketing – an introduction', in Grönroos, C. and Gummesson, E. (eds) *Service Marketing – Nordic School Perspectives*, Stockholm: Stockholm University.

Gros F. (2005) 'Course context', in M. Foucault, *The Hermeneutics of the Subject: Lectures at the Collège de France 1981–1982*, Basingstoke: Palgrave.

Gummesson, E. (1977) *The Marketing and Purchase of Consultancy Services: A Study of Conditions and Behaviour in Swedish Producer Services Markets*, Doctoral Dissertation, Stockholm: Stockholm University (in Swedish [*Marknadsföring och inköp av konsulttjänster. En studie av egenskaper och beteenden i producenttjänstemarknader*]).

Gummesson, E. (1991a) 'Marketing revisited: the crucial role of the part-time marketer', *European Journal of Marketing*, 25 (2): 60–75.

Gummesson, E. (1991b) *Qualitative Methods in Management Research*, Newbury Park: Sage Publications.

Gummesson, E. (1995) 'Relationship marketing: its role in the service economy' in W.J. Glynn and J.G. Barnes (eds), *Understanding Service Management*, New York: John Wiley.

Gummesson, E. (2002) *Total Relationship Marketing*, Oxford: Butterworth-Heinemann.

Hackley, C. (2003) '"We are all customers now . . ." rhetorical strategy and ideological control in marketing management texts', *Journal Management Studies*, 40 (5): 1326–52.

Hammond, M.B. (1897) *The Cotton Industry: An Essay in Economic History*, Publications of the American Economic Association.

Harvey, D. (1990) *The Condition of Postmodernity*, Cambridge, MA: Blackwell.

Harvey, D. (2005) *A Brief History of Neoliberalism*, Oxford: Oxford University Press.

Hashimoto, I. (1972) 'Rise of management-oriented marketing thought: research on A.W. Shaw's thought', *The Economic Review*, 110 (1/2): 1–22 (in Japanese).

Hasselbladh, H. and Kallinikos, J. (2000) 'The project of rationalization: a critique and reappraisal of neo-institutionalism in organization studies', *Organization Studies*, 21 (4): 697–720.

Heaton, H. (1949) 'The making of an economic historian', *The Journal of Economic History*, 9 (Supplement): 1–18.

Herbst, J. (1965) *The German Historical School in American Scholarship*, New York: Cornell University Press.

Heskett, J.L., Sasser, W.E. and Schlesinger, L.A. (1997) *The Service Profit Chain: How Leading Companies Link Profit and Growth to Loyalty, Satisfaction, and Value*, New York: The Free Press.

Hildebrand, B. (1848) *Die Nationalökonomie der Gegenwart und Zukunft*, Frankfurt: J. Rutten (in German).

Hochschild, A.R. (1983) *The Managed Heart: Commercialization of Human Feeling*, Berkeley, CA: University of California Press.

Hodgson, D. (2002) '"Know your customer": marketing, governmentality and the "new consumer" of financial services', *Management Decision*, 40 (4): 318–28.

Holbrook, M.B. (1993) 'Postmodernism and social theory', *Journal of Macromarketing*, 13 (2): 69–75.

Holbrook, M.B. and Hirschman, E.C. (1993) *The Semiotics of Consumption: Interpreting Symbolic Consumer Behavior in Popular Culture and Works of Art*, Berlin: Mouton De Gruyter.

Hollander, S.C. (1986) 'The marketing concept: A déjà vu', in G. Fisk (ed.), *Marketing Management Technology as a Social Process*, New York: Praeger.

Hollander, S.C., Rassuli, K.M., Jones, D.G.B. and Farlow Dix, L. (2005) 'Periodization in marketing history', *Journal of Macromarketing*, 25 (1): 32–41.

Holt, D.B. (1997) 'Poststructuralist lifestyle analysis: conceptualizing the social patterning of consumption in postmodernity', *Journal of Consumer Research*, 23 (4): 326–50.

Howard, J.A. (1957) *Marketing Management: Analysis and Decision*, Homewood, IL: Richard D. Irwin.

Hoyt, C. (1929[1912]) *Scientific Sales Management Today*. New York: The Ronald Press Company.

Hunt, S.D. (1976) 'The nature and scope of marketing', *Journal of Marketing*, 40 (3): 17–28.

Hunt, S.D. (1983) 'General theories and the fundamental explananda of marketing', *Journal of Marketing*, 47 (4): 9–17.

Hunt, S.D. (1991) *Modern Marketing Theory: Critical Issues in the Philosophy of Science*, Cincinnati, OH: Southwestern.

Hunt, S.D. (1994) 'On rethinking marketing: our discipline, our practice, our methods', *European Journal of Marketing*, 28 (3): 13–25.

Hunt, S.D. and Goolsby, J.L. (1988) 'The rise and fall of the functional approach to marketing: a paradigm displacement perspective', in T. Nevett and R.A. Fullerton (eds), *Historical Perspectives on Marketing: Essays in Honor of Stanley C. Hollander*, Lexington, MA: Lexington Books.

Ivey, P. (1937/1925) *Salesmanship Applied*, New York: A.W. Shaw.

Jacques, R. (1996) *Manufacturing the Employee: Management Knowledge from the 19th to 21st Centuries*, London: Sage.

Jobber, D. (2004) *Principles and Practise of Marketing*, Maidenhead: McGraw-Hill.

John, J. (2003) *Fundamentals of Customer-Focused Management*, Westport, CT: Praeger.

Jones, D.G.B. (1997) 'The machine metaphor in Arch W. Shaw's (1915) *Some Problems in Market Distribution*', *Journal of Macromarketing*, 17 (1): 151–8.

Jones, D.G.B. and Monieson, D.D. (1990) 'Early development of the philosophy of marketing thought', *Journal of Marketing*, 54 (1): 102–13.

Jones, D.G.B. and Shaw, E.H. (2002) 'A history of marketing thought', in B. Weitz and R. Wensley (eds), *Handbook of Marketing*, London: Sage.

Jones, J.G. and Comyns, R.J. (1918) *Salesmanship and Sales Management*, New York: Alexander Hamilton Institute.

Jones, S., ten Bos, R. and Parker, M. (2005) *For Business Ethics*, London: Routledge.

Jones, T.O. and Sasser Jr, W.E. (1995) 'Why Satisfied Customers Defect', *Harvard Business Review*, 73 (6): 88–99.

Journal of Marketing (1971) 'Special issue: marketing's changing social/environmental role', 35 (3).

Keith R.J. (1960) 'The marketing revolution', *Journal of Marketing*, 24 (3): 35–8.

Kelemen, M.L. (2000) 'Too much or too little ambiguity: the language of total quality management', *Journal of Management Studies*, 37 (4): 483–98.

Kelley, W.T. (1956) 'The development of early thought in marketing and promotion', *Journal of Marketing*, 21 (1): 62–76.

Kholi, A.K. and Jaworski B.J. (1990) 'Market orientation: the construct, research propositions and managerial implications', *Journal of Marketing*, 54 (2): 1–18.

Kinley, D. (1894) 'Credit instruments in retail trade', *Publications of the American Economic Association*, 10 (March): 72–8.

Knights, D. and McCabe, D. (1999) 'Are there no limits to authority?: TQM and organizational power', *Organization Studies*, 20 (2): 197–224.

Knights, D. and Sturdy, A. (1997) 'Marketing the soul: from the ideology of consumption to consumer subjectivity', in D. Knights and T. Tinker (eds), *Financial Institutions and Social Transformations: International Studies of a Sector*, London: MacMillan.

Knights, D. and Willmott, H. (1989) 'Power and subjectivity at work: from degradation to subjugation in social relations', *Sociology*, 23 (4): 535–58.

Kotler, P. (1967) *Marketing Management: Analysis, Planning and Control*, London: Prentice-Hall.

Kotler, P. (1972) 'A generic concept of marketing', *Journal of Marketing*, 36 (2): 46–54.

Kotler, P. (2003) *Marketing Management: Analysis, Planning and Control*, 11th edn, Upper Sadle River, NJ: Pearson Prentice Hall.

Kotler, P. and Keller, K.L. (2006) *Marketing Management*, 12th edn, Upper Sadle River, NJ: Pearson Prentice Hall.

Kotler, P. and Levy, S.L. (1969) 'Broadening the concept of marketing', *Journal of Marketing*, 33 (1): 10–15.

Kotler, P. and Zaltman, G. (1971) 'Social marketing: an approach to planned social change', *Journal of Marketing*, 35 (3): 3–12.

Kotler, P., Hedier, D.H. and Rein, I.J. (1991) *Marketing Places: Attracting Investment, Industry and Toursim to Cities, Regions and Nations*, New York: The Free Press.

Kuhn, T.S. (1962) *The Structure of Scientific Revolutions*, Chicago, IL: The University of Chicago Press.

La Londe, B.J. and Morrison, E.J. (1967) 'Marketing management concepts yesterday and today', *Journal of Marketing*, 31 (1): 9–13.

Laclau, E. (1990) *New Reflections on the Revolution of Our Time*, London: Verso.

Laclau, E. (1993) 'Power and representation', in M. Poster (ed.), *Politics, Theory and Contemporary Culture*, New York: Columbia University Press.

Laclau, E. and Mouffe, C. (1985) *Hegemony and Socialist Strategy: Towards a Radical Democratic Politics*, 2nd edn, New York: Verso.

Larsson, R. and Bowen, D.E. (1989) 'Organizations and customers: managing design and coordination of services', *Academy of Management Review*, 14 (2): 213–33.

Lavidge, R.J. (1970) 'The growing responsibilities of marketing', *Journal of Marketing*, 34 (1): 25–8.

Lazer, W. and Kelly, E.J. (1962) *Managerial Marketing: Perspectives and Viewpoints*, 2nd edn, Homewood, IL: Richard D. Irwin.

Levitt, T. (1960) 'Marketing myopia', *Harvard Business Review*, 38 (4): 45–56.

Levitt, T. (1969) *The Marketing Mode: Pathways to Corporate Growth*, New York: McGraw Hill.

Levitt, T. (1972) 'Production-line approach to service', *Harvard Business Review*, 50 (5): 20–31.

Lovelock, C.H. (1991) *Services Marketing*, London: Prentice Hall.

Luck, D.J. (1969) 'Broadening the concept of marketing – too far', *Journal of Marketing*, 33 (3): 53–5.

Lukes, S. (1974) *Power: A Radical View*, London: Macmillan.

Lyon, L.S. (1926) *Salesmen in Marketing Strategy*, New York: Macmillan.

McCarthy, E.J. (1960) *Basic Marketing: A Managerial Approach*, Homewood, IL: Richard D. Irwin.

McCarthy, E.J. (1964) *Basic Marketing: A Managerial Approach*, 2nd edn, Homewood, IL: Richard D. Irwin.

McGarry, E.D. (1950) 'Some functions in marketing reconsidered', in R. Cox and W. Alderson (eds), *Theory in Marketing*, Chicago, IL: Irwin.

McKitterick, J.B. (1957) 'What is the marketing management concept?', in F.M. Bass (ed.), *The Frontiers in Marketing Thought*, Chicago, IL: American Marketing Association.

Marion, G. (1993) 'The marketing management discourse: what's new since the 1960s?', in M.J. Baker (ed.), *Perspectives on Marketing Management*, Vol. 3, Chichester: Wiley.

Marion, G. (2006) 'Marketing ideology and criticism: legitimacy and legitimization', *Marketing Theory*, 6 (2): 245–62.

Maxwell, W. (1913) *Salesmanship*, Boston: Houghton Mifflin.

Mayo, E. (1933) *The Human Problems of an Industrial Civilization*, New York: Macmillan.

Mayo, E. (1945) *The Social Problems of an Industrial Civilization*, Cambridge, MA: Harvard University.

Merton, R.K. (1957) *Social Theory and Social Structure*, 2nd edn, Glencloe, IL: Free Press.

Mick, D.G. and Buhl, C. (1992) 'A meaning-based model of advertising experiences', *Journal of Consumer Research*, 19 (3): 317–38.

Miller P. and Rose, N. (1990) 'Governing economic life', *Economy and Society*, 19 (1): 1–31.

Miller, P. and Rose, N. (1997) 'Mobilizing the consumer: assembling the subject of consumption', *Theory, Culture and Society*, 14 (1): 1–36.

Mitsuzawa, S. (1988) 'The origin of controversy in marketing thought in the early days: Shaw vs. Weld', *Doshisha Business Review*, 40 (3): 62–92 (in Japanese).

Morgan, Ga. (1986) *Images of Organization*, Beverly Hills, CA: Sage.

Morgan, Gl. (1992) 'Marketing discourse and practice: towards a critical analysis', in M. Alvesson and H. Willmott (eds), *Critical Management Studies*, London: Sage.

Morgan, Gl. (2003) 'Marketing and critique: prospects and problems', in M. Alvesson and H. Willmott (eds), *Studying Management Critically*, London: Sage.

Normann, R. (1984) *Service Management: Strategy and Leadership in Service Businesses*, New York: Wiley.

O'Malley, P., Weir, L. and Shearing, C. (1997) 'Governmentality, criticism, politics', *Economy and Society*, 26 (4): 501–17.

Oliver, R.L. (1977) 'Effect of expectation and disconfirmation on post-exposure product evaluations: an alternative interpretation', *Journal of Applied Psychology*, 62 (4): 480–6.

Oliver, R.L. (1996) *Satisfaction: A Behavioral Perspective on the Consumer*, Boston, MA: McGraw Hill.

Packard, V. (1957) *The Hidden Persuaders*, Harmondsworth: Penguin.

Parasuraman, A., Zeithaml, V.A. and Berry, L.L. (1985) 'A conceptual model of service quality and it's implications for future research', *Journal of Marketing*, 49 (4): 253–68.

Parasuraman, A., Zeithaml, V.A. and Berry, L.L. (1988) 'SERVQUAL: a multiple-item scale for measuring consumer perceptions of service quality', *Journal of Retailing*, 64 (1): 12–37.

Parasuraman, A., Zeithaml, V.A. and Berry, L.L. (1994) 'Reassesment of expectations as a comparison standard in measuring service quality: implications for further research', *Journal of Marketing*, 58 (1): 111–24.

Parlin, C. (1912) 'Department store report', Vol. B (October).

Peters, T.J. and Waterman, R.H. (1982) *In Search of Excellence: Lessons from Americas Best-Run Companies*, New York: Harper and Row.

Phillips, L. and Jørgensen, M.W. (2002) *Discourse Analysis as Theory and Method*, London: Sage.

Pierre, J. and Peters, B.G. (2005) *Governing Complex Societies: Trajectories and Scenarios*, Basingstoke: Palgrave.

Pine II, B.J., Peppers, D. and Rogers, M. (1995) 'Do you want to keep your customers forever?', *Harvard Business Review*, 73 (2): 103–14.

Piore, M.J. and Sabel, C.F. (1984) *The Second Industrial Divide: Possibilities for Prosperity*, New York: Basic Books.

Potter, J. and Wheterhell, M. (1987) *Discourse and Social Psychology*, London: Sage.

Quist, J., Skålén, P. and Clegg, S.R. 'The power of quality models: the example of the SIQ model for performance excellence', paper presented at the Annual Meeting of the Academy of Management, Philadelphia, August 2007.

Rafiq, M. and Ahmed, P. (2000) 'Advances in the internal marketing concept: definition, synthesis, and extension', *Journal of Services Marketing*, 14 (6): 449–62.

Rathmell, J.M. (1966) 'What is meant by services?', *Journal of Marketing*, 30 (4): 32–6.

Rathmell, J.M. (1974) *Marketing in the Service Sector*, Cambridge: Winthorp Publishers.

Regan, W.J (1963) 'The service revolution', *Journal of Marketing*, 27 (3): 57–62.

Rhoades, E.L. (1927) *Introductory Readings in Marketing*, New York: A.W. Shaw.

Ricœur, P. (1975) *Lectures on Ideology and Utopia*, Chicago, IL: University of Chicago Press.

Rose, N. (1996) *Inventing Our Selves: Psychology, Power and Personhood*, Cambridge: Cambridge University Press.

Rose, N. (1999) *Powers of Freedom: Reframing Political Thought*, Cambridge: Cambridge University Press.

Rostow, W.W. (1960) *The Stages of Economic Growth: A Non-Communist Manifesto*, Cambridge: Cambridge University Press.

Ryan, F.W. (1935) 'Functional elements in market distribution', *Harvard Business Review*, 13 (2): 205–24.

Sasser, E.W. and Arbeit, S.P. (1976) 'Selling jobs in the service sector', *Business Horizons*, 19 (3): 61–5.

Schneider, B. and Bowen, D.E. (1995) *Winning the Service Game*, Boston, MA: Harvard Business School Press.

Schneider, B. and White, S. (2004) *Service Quality: Research Perspectives*, Thousand Oaks, CA: Sage.

Scott, W.R. (2003) *Organizations: Rational, Natural and Open Systems*, Upper Saddle River, NJ: Pearson Education.

Selznick, P. (1949) *TVA and the Grass Roots*, Berkley, CA: Berkley University Press.

Shaw, A.W. (1912) 'Some problems in market distribution', *Quarterly Journal of Economics*, 26 (4): 703–65.

Shaw, A.W. (1916) *An Approach to Business Problems*, Cambridge, MA: Harvard University Press.

Shaw, A.W. (1951[1915]) *Some Problems in Market Distribution*. Cambridge, MA: Harvard University Press.

Shaw, E. (1994) 'The utility of the four utilities concept', in R.A. Fullerton (ed.), *Research in Marketing: Explorationsin the History of Marketing*, Greenwich: JAI Press.

Shaw, E. (1995) 'The first dialogue on macromarketing', *Journal of Macromarketing*, 15 (1): 7–20.

Sheldon, R. and Arens, E. (1932) *Consumer Engineering: A New Technique for Prosperity*, New York and London: Harper.

Sheth, J. N., Gardner, D.M. and Garrett, D.E. (1988) *Marketing Theory: Evolution and Evaluation*, New York: John Wiley and Sons.

Shostack, G.L. (1977) 'Breaking free from product marketing', *Journal of Marketing*, 41 (2): 73–80.

Shostack, G.L. (1984) 'Designing services that delivers', *Harvard Business Review* 62 (1): 133–9.

Shostack, G.L. (1987) 'Service positioning through structural change', *Journal of Marketing*, 51 (1): 34–43.

Skålén, P. and Fougère, M. (2007) 'Be(com)ing and being normal – not excellent: service management, the Gap-model and disciplinary power', *Journal of Organizational Change Management*, 20 (1): 109–25.

Skålén, P., Fellesson, M. and Fougère, M. (2006) 'The governmentality of marketing discourse', *Scandinavian Journal of Management*, 22 (4): 275–91.

Smart, B. (2002) *Key Sociologists: Michel Foucault*, London: Routledge.

Smircich, L. (1983) 'Concepts of culture and organizational analysis', *Administrative Science Quarterly*, 28 (3): 339–58.

Smith, W.R. (1956) 'Product differentiation and market segmentation as alternative marketing strategies', *Journal of Marketing*, 21 (1): 3–8.

Staelin, R. (2005) 'Eras III and IV my reflections', *Journal of Public Policy and Marketing*, 24 (1): 146–9.

Steiner, R.L. (1976) 'The prejudice against marketing', *Journal of Marketing*, 40 (3): 2–9.

Stern, B. (1989) 'Literary criticism and consumer research: overview and illustrative analysis', *Journal of Consumer Research*, 16 (3): 322–34.

Stern, B. (1991) 'Who talks advertising?: literary theory and narrative "point of view"', *Journal of Advertising*, 20 (3): 9–22.

Stern, B. (1996) 'Deconstructive strategy and consumer research: concepts and illustrative exemplar', *Journal of Consumer Research*, 23 (2): 136–47.

Strasser, S. (1989) *Satisfaction Guaranteed: The Making of the American Mass Market*, New York: Pantheon.

Svensson, P. (2003) *Setting the Marketing Scene: Reality Production in Everyday Marketing Work*, Doctoral Dissertation, Lund: Lund Business Press.

Tadajewski, M. (2006) 'The ordering of marketing theory: the influence of McCarthyism and the Cold War', *Marketing Theory*, 6 (2): 163–99.

Taylor, F.W. (1911) *The Principles of Scientific Management*, New York: Norton.

Teas, K.R. (1993) 'Expectations, performance evaluation, and consumers' perceptions of quality', *Journal of Marketing*, 57 (4): 18–24.

Thompson, P. and Ackroyd, S. (1995) 'All quiet on the workplace front? a critique of recent trends in British industrial sociology', *Sociology*, 29 (4): 615–33.

Tipper, H., Hollingworth, H.L., Hotchkiss, G.R. and Parsons, F.A. (1915) *Advertising: Its Principles and Practices*, New York: Ronald Press.

Townley, B. (1993) 'Foucault, power/knowledge and its relevance for human resource management', *Academy of Management Review*, 18 (3): 518–45.

Townley, B. (1994) *Reframing Human Resource Management: Power, Ethics and the Subject at Work*, London: Sage.

Townley, B. (1998) 'Beyond good and evil: depth and division in the management of human resources', in A. McKinlay and K. Starkey (eds), *Foucault, Management and Organization Theory: From Panopticon to Technologies of Self*, London: Sage.

Usui, K. (2000) 'The interpretation of Arch Wilkinson Shaw's thought by Japanese scholars', *Journal of Macromarketing*, 20 (2): 128–36.

Varey, R.J. and Lewis, B.R. (1999) 'A broadened concept of internal marketing', *European Journal of Marketing*, 33 (9/10): 926–44.

Vargo, S.L. and Lusch, R.F. (2004) 'Evolving to a new dominant logic for marketing', *Journal of Marketing*, 68 (1): 1–17.

Vargo, S.L. and Morgan, F.W. (2005) 'Services in society and academic thought: an historical analysis', *Journal of Macromarketing*, 25 (1): 42–53.

Webster, F.E. (1992) 'The changing role of marketing in the corporation', *Journal of Marketing*, 56 (4): 1–17.

Webster, F.E. (2002) *Market-Driven Management: How to Define, Develop, and Deliver Customer Value*, 2nd edn, Hoboken, NJ: Wiley.

Weld, L.D.H. (1916) *The Marketing of Farm Products*, New York: Macmillan.

Weld, L.D.H. (1917) 'Marketing functions and mercantile organization', *American Economic Review*, 7 (2): 306–18.

Weld, L.D.H. (1941) 'Early experience in teaching courses in marketing', *Journal of Marketing*, 5 (4): 380–1.

White, P. (1927) *Scientific Marketing Management: Its Principles and Methods*, New York: Harper & Bros.

White, P. and Hayward, W.S. (1924) *Marketing Practice*, New York: Doubleday.

Whitehead, H. (1917) *Principles of Salesmanship*, New York: Ronald Press.

Wind, Y. (1978) 'Issues and advances in segmentation research', *Journal of Marketing Research*, 15 (3): 317–37.

Wind, Y. and Robertson, T.S. (1983) 'Marketing strategy: new directions for theory and research', *Journal of Marketing*, 47 (2): 12–25.

Zaltman, G., LeMasters, K. and Heffring, M. (1982) *Theory Construction in Marketing: Some Thoughts on Thinking*, New York: Wiley.

Zaltman, G., Pinson, R.A. and Angelmar, R. (1973) *Metatheory and Consumer Research*, New York: Holt.

Zeithaml, V., Parasuraman, A. and Berry, L.L. (1985) 'Problem and strategies in services marketing', *Journal of Marketing*, 49 (1): 33–46.

Zeithaml, V., Parasuraman, A. and Berry, L.L. (1993) 'The nature and determinants of customer expectations of services', *Journal of the Academy of Marketing Science*, 21 (1): 1–11.

Index

Fundamentals of Marketing

Marilyn A. Stone, Heriot-Watt University, Edinburgh, UK and **John Desmond,** St Andrews University, UK

Fundamentals of Marketing provides a sound appreciation of the fundamentals of the theory and practice of marketing. Using case studies drawn from a cross section of sectors, in particular the banking, hospitality, retail and public service sector this textbook critically evaluates the effectiveness of different marketing strategies and approaches. Exploring the principles of marketing this volume engages the reader, not only in theory but also in practice, using a broad range of real-life case studies such as Coca Cola, Apple, FCUK, Virgin, Amazon.com, Barnes and Noble, Dyno Rod and New Zealand wool.

The text analyzes the marketing mix: product development, pricing, promotion (and communications marketing) and place (channels of distribution). It also emphasizes the role of Marketing Information Systems (MIS) using internal reporting, marketing intelligence and marketing research including the contribution from Marketing Research agencies and reviews the role of technology, e-commerce and the Internet, in supporting successful marketing.

Featuring a support website that provides student and lecturer resources Fundamentals of Marketing conveys the main principles of marketing in a challenging yet accessible manner and provides the reader with insights into the workings of marketing today.

Contents: 1.Marketing: Development and Scope of the Subject 2. Strategic Marketing and the Planning Process 3. Consumer Buyer Behaviour 4. Industrial Buyer Behaviour 5. Marketing Research 6. Segmentation, Targeting and Positioning 7. Branding 8. Product 9. Pricing 10. Promotion 11. Place 12. Virtual Marketing 10. Planning and Implementation

2006: 246x189
Hb: 978-0-415-37096-7: **£85.00**
Pb: 978-0-415-37097-4: **£28.99**

Routledge
Taylor & Francis Group

Routledge books are available from all good bookshops, or may be ordered (by credit card) by calling the following numbers: **USA:** 1-800-634-7064
Canada: 1-877-226-2237
UK / Rest of World: +44 (0) 1264 343071
For more information please contact Gemma Anderson on +44 (0) 20 7017 6192 or e-mail gemma.anderson@tandf.co.uk

2 Park Square
Milton Park
Abingdon
Oxfordshire
OX14 4RN
United Kingdom
www.routledge.com

270 Madison Avenue
New York
NY 10016
USA
www.routledge.com

Marketing: The Basics

Karl Moore and Niketh Pareek, McGill University, Quebec, Canada

Marketing: The Basics is a clear, concise resource for students or practitioners looking to improve their understanding of marketing fundamentals in a global context.

Covering the basic functions of marketing, its role in corporate decision-making and the importance of competitive strategies, this accessible text provides international perspectives on the areas discussed through examples of practice from North America, Asia, Europe and the Middle East.

Relating insights and experiences to real-life marketing contexts in order to provide practically applicable information, key areas explored include: What is marketing?; Marketing as part of the firm's corporate strategy; The marketing mix; STP -segmentation, targeting and positioning; Market research and Culture.

A user-friendly, easy-to-follow guide, Marketing: The Basics is perfect for sixth-form, first-year undergraduate and MBA students, plus those professionals who require an understanding of this important subject in their day-to-day working lives.

Contents: Introduction 1. What Is Marketing Management? 2. Marketing as a Corporate Function 3. Product and Placement 4. Price 5. Promotion 6. People 7. Segmentation, Targeting and Positioning 8. Market Research - Seeking Deep Insight into the Customer's World and Mind 9. Global Marketing. Glossary. Index

2006: 198X129:232pp
Hb: 978-0-415-38080-5: **£55.00**
Pb: 978-0-415-38079-9: **£9.99**

Routledge books are available from all good bookshops, or may be ordered (by credit card) by calling the following numbers: **USA:** 1-800-634-7064
Canada: 1-877-226-2237
UK / Rest of World: +44 (0) 1264 343071
For more information please contact Gemma Anderson on +44 (0) 20 7017 6192 or e-mail gemma.anderson@tandf.co.uk

2 Park Square
Milton Park
Abingdon
Oxfordshire
OX14 4RN
United Kingdom
www.routledge.com

270 Madison Avenue
New York
NY 10016
USA
www.routledge.com